PREFACE

1. Scope

This publication provides doctrine for joint counterair operations and protection against air and missile threats across the range of military operations.

2. Purpose

This publication has been prepared under the direction of the Chairman of the Joint Chiefs of Staff. It sets forth joint doctrine to govern the activities and performance of the Armed Forces of the United States in joint operations and provides the doctrinal basis for interagency coordination and for US military involvement in multinational operations. It provides military guidance for the exercise of authority by combatant commanders and other joint force commanders (JFCs) and prescribes joint doctrine for operations, education, and training. It provides military guidance for use by the Armed Forces in preparing their appropriate plans. It is not the intent of this publication to restrict the authority of the JFC from organizing the force and executing the mission in a manner the JFC deems most appropriate to ensure unity of effort in the accomplishment of the overall objective.

3. Application

a. Joint doctrine established in this publication applies to the Joint Staff, commanders of combatant commands, subordinate unified commands, joint task forces, subordinate components of these commands, and the Services.

b. The guidance in this publication is authoritative; as such, this doctrine will be followed except when, in the judgment of the commander, exceptional circumstances dictate otherwise. If conflicts arise between the contents of this publication and the contents of Service publications, this publication will take precedence unless the Chairman of the Joint Chiefs of Staff, normally in coordination with the other members of the Joint Chiefs of Staff, has provided more current and specific guidance. Commanders of forces operating as part of a multinational (alliance or coalition) military command should follow multinational doctrine and procedures ratified by the United States. For doctrine and procedures not ratified by the United States, commanders should evaluate and follow the multinational command's doctrine and procedures, where applicable and consistent with US law, regulations, and doctrine.

For the Chairman of the Joint Chiefs of Staff:

WILLIAM E. GORTNEY
VADM, USN
Director, Joint Staff

Intentionally Blank

SUMMARY OF CHANGES
REVISION OF JOINT PUBLICATION 3-01
DATED 05 FEBRUARY 2007

- Introduces and defines integrated air and missile defense in countering air and missile threats.

- Adds protection to the definition of counterair.

- Characterizes air and missile threats as air-breathing (aircraft and cruise missiles) and ballistic missiles.

- Provides considerations for operations that cross geographic combatant commander area of responsibility boundaries.

- Discusses the global perspective of ballistic missile defense.

- Defines the term air and missile defense.

- Defines global ballistic missile defense.

- Deletes the definition of theater missile.

- Adds appendix on global ballistic missile defense synchronization.

Intentionally Blank

TABLE OF CONTENTS

EXECUTIVE SUMMARY
COMMANDER'S OVERVIEW

- **Covers the Fundamentals for Countering Air and Missile Threats**

- **Addresses Command and Control Relationships and Responsibilities, including those for the Area Air Defense Commander and the Airspace Control Authority**

- **Describes Counterair Planning and the Airspace Control Plan**

- **Discusses Offensive Counterair Planning and Operations and Offensive Counterair as part of the Joint Air Operations Plan**

- **Explains Defensive Counterair Planning and Operations and the Area Air Defense Plan**

Introduction

The joint force commander (JFC) counters air and missile threats to ensure friendly freedom of action, provide protection, and deny enemy freedom of action.

Counterair integrates offensive and defensive operations to attain and maintain a desired degree of air superiority and protection by neutralizing or destroying enemy aircraft and missiles, both before and after launch. **Integrated air and missile defense (IAMD)** is an evolving approach that uses the counterair framework at the theater level. IAMD emphasizes the integration of offensive counterair (OCA) attack operations, defensive counterair (DCA) operations, and other capabilities as required to create the joint force commander's (JFC's) desired effects. The IAMD approach also encompasses global strike and global missile defense beyond the theater level.

Counterair Framework

The counterair framework is based on integrating offensive and defensive operations against both aircraft and missile threats.

The counterair mission integrates both offensive and defensive operations, by all capable joint force components, and counters the air and missile threat by attaining and maintaining the degree of air superiority and protection desired by the JFC. Generally, **OCA operations** seek to dominate enemy airspace and prevent the launch of threats, while **DCA operations** defeat enemy air and missile threats attempting to penetrate or attack through friendly airspace.

Countering Air and Missile Threat Integration and Synchronization

Although OCA and DCA are considered separate operations, they must facilitate unity of effort through integration and synchronization. Integrating a mixture of capabilities from components bolsters the friendly force potential and likely will frustrate the enemy's ability to defend itself. Synchronization of OCA and DCA operations is vital to avoid duplication of effort and help prevent fratricide.

Air and Missile Threats

Potential adversary air and missile threats continue to grow in numbers and capabilities. Expanded technology and proliferation of missiles, including cruise missiles (CMs), ballistic missiles (BMs), and air-to-surface missiles (ASMs), expand the scope and complexity of protecting friendly forces and vital interests. The detection capabilities, engagement ranges, mobility, and lethality of surface-to-air missile (SAM) systems and fighter aircraft have significantly increased the air and missile defenses (AMDs) of US adversaries. CMs and unmanned aircraft also present elusive targets and are difficult to detect, identify, and engage.

Supporting Homeland Defense

There is no higher priority than the security and defense of the US homeland.

Proliferation of advanced technologies for missiles, guidance systems, and weapons of mass destruction warheads has increased the potential missile threat to the homeland. The Commander, US Northern Command, in concert with missions performed by North American Aerospace Defense Command, and the Commander, US Pacific Command, have specific responsibilities for planning, organizing, and as directed, executing homeland defense operations within their respective areas of responsibility (AORs). Although this publication primarily focuses on countering theater air and missile threats (i.e., those affecting an overseas geographic combatant commander's (GCC's) AOR/a subordinate JFC's joint operations area [JOA]), those forces and capabilities employed by overseas GCCs also may support a layered defense beginning in the forward areas against strategic air and missile threats to the homeland.

Global Ballistic Missile Defense

Strategic planning documents task each GCC with some form of missile defense and the employment of appropriate force should deterrence fail. Commander, United States Strategic Command is responsible for synchronizing planning for global missile defense and coordinating global missile defense operations support. Global ballistic missile defense is the overarching characterization of the cumulative (worldwide) planning and coordination for those defensive capabilities designed to neutralize, destroy, or reduce the effectiveness of enemy BM attacks whether within or across the boundaries of any GCC's AOR.

Command and Control

The growing capabilities of air and missile threats (speed, range, accuracy, stealth, lethality) and their proliferation require joint forces to be responsive, flexible, and integrated to effectively counter those threats.

The JFC normally tailors forces to the specific tasks to enable effective spans of control, responsiveness, tactical flexibility, and protection. Because counterair is a joint mission and can involve all components of the joint force, clear command relationships and properly assigned responsibilities are essential for effective and efficient operations.

Command Relationships

The JFC determines the most appropriate command relationships for the component forces/capabilities made available for counterair.

In operations of limited scope or duration, the JFC may organize and conduct counterair operations using the joint force staff (e.g., the operations directorate of a joint staff). If the JFC designates a joint force air component commander (JFACC), the JFC may designate the JFACC as the supported commander for strategic attack, air interdiction, and airborne intelligence, surveillance, and reconnaissance (among other missions). As a joint mission area, counterair is conducted by all components with the necessary capabilities, with the JFC/JFACC ensuring unity of command (or unity of effort), centralized planning and direction, and decentralized execution. When the JFC organizes the joint force, in addition to a JFACC, the JFC also normally designates an area air defense commander (AADC) (for DCA) and an airspace control authority (ACA) (for joint airspace control). Normally, the JFC designates the JFACC as the AADC and ACA, because the three functions are so integral to one another. If the situation dictates, the JFC may designate an AADC and/or ACA separate from the JFACC.

Support Relationships

For counterair operations, support relationships are particularly useful for forces made available for tasking and those shared for conducting other joint operations. An establishing directive normally is issued to specify the purpose of the support relationship.

JFC

Some of the primary responsibilities of the JFC as they apply to joint counterair include the following:

• Develop and maintain a command and control (C2) system to unify the employment of subordinate forces in carrying out assigned counterair missions

• Designate an AADC and approve an area air defense plan (AADP)

• Designate an ACA and approve the airspace control plan (ACP)

• Establish a theater air and missile warning architecture to share warnings

Component Commanders

The Service component commanders are responsible for making available to the JFACC those counterair forces/capabilities not required for their primary roles and tasks per the apportionment guidance by the JFC. Functional component commands serve to ease the burden on the theater and joint task force staffs, free the JFC to focus more on strategic aspects of the campaign, and provide individual air, land, maritime, and special operations forces (SOF) headquarters for coordination with the other components.

Joint Force Air Component Commander

The JFC will typically designate responsibility for joint air operations to a JFACC. Although not a joint air operation, but a joint operation, counterair normally is an assigned responsibility of the JFACC. Some responsibilities of the JFACC relating to joint counterair operations include the following:

• Develop, coordinate, and integrate joint counterair planning with operations of other components for JFC approval

• Provide information operations strategies to neutralize enemy air and missile threats

• Provide centralized direction for allocating and tasking joint counterair capabilities and forces made available by the JFC

• Perform the duties of the AADC when directed by the JFC

• Perform the duties of the ACA when directed by the JFC

Area Air Defense Commander

The AADC normally is the component commander with the preponderance of AMD capability and the C2 and intelligence capability to plan, coordinate, and execute integrated AMD operations, including real-time battle management. Primary responsibilities of the AADC include the following:

• Develop, integrate, and distribute a JFC-approved joint AADP.

• Develop and execute a detailed plan to disseminate timely air and missile warning and cueing information to components, forces, allies, coalition partners, and civil authorities, as appropriate.

• Develop and implement, in coordination with the component commanders and with JFC approval, identification (ID) and combat identification (CID) procedures and authorities, and engagement procedures.

• Establish appropriate joint, fighter, and missile engagement zones.

Regional and Sector Air Defense Commanders

During complex operations/campaigns conducted in a large JOA/theater of operations, the AADC may recommend and the JFC may approve the division of the operational area into separate air defense regions, each with a regional air defense commander (RADC) who could be delegated responsibilities and decision-making authority for DCA operations within the region. The AADC and RADC, as approved by the JFC, may choose to further divide regions into sectors, each with a sector air defense commander (SADC) with appropriate authority for their responsibilities.

Airspace Control Authority

The ACA coordinates use of airspace through the ACP, including integration with the host nation (HN) airspace control system (ACS), and synchronizes/deconflicts all user requirements using the airspace control order (ACO). The ACA responsibilities for counterair operations include, but are not limited to:

• Link the ACP to the AADP when designating volumes of airspace.

• Develop airspace coordinating measures (ACMs) that support and enhance operations.

• Provide a flexible ACP that can adapt to changing requirements of the tactical situation.

Cross Area of Responsibility Command Relationships Considerations	GCCs are supported commanders for assigned missions in their AORs, and they anticipate the possibility for "cross-AOR" operations based on threats and capabilities. **Coordination authority between GCCs should enable coordination at component and tactical levels supporting unity of effort for cross-AOR ballistic missile defense (BMD).**
Multinational Considerations	Most joint operations are now conducted within a multinational context (i.e., an alliance or coalition). The JFC (who may be the multinational force commander) must evaluate key considerations and differences involved in planning, coordinating, and conducting counterair operations in a multinational environment.
Multinational Command Relationships	In multinational force (MNF) operations, understanding the agreed upon command relationships and the related command authorities is key to developing the desired unity of effort for counterair operations. The JFACC/AADC may expect no more than tactical control over MNF counterair units/capabilities, and very likely, may have simple support relationships based on mission-type orders.
Multinational Organization	Each nation normally establishes a national center or cell as a focal point to ensure effective support and control of its forces, to include counterair forces. Because sharing intelligence and warning information is vital to unity of effort, any issues related to the release of intelligence information and products to MNF partners must be resolved early during planning. Before assigning tasks to MNF units, the JFACC/AADC should ensure that all elements can make meaningful contributions to the overall counterair mission. The AADC should ensure that MNF rules of engagement (ROE), engagement authorities, and procedures are consistent with the combined AADP and the MNF ability to identify friendly forces, in order to prevent gaps and ensure joint air forces are not subject to an increased risk of fratricide and MNF are not restricted from self-defense.
Command and Control Systems and Functions	Joint counterair operations require reliable C2 capabilities that allow the JFC/JFACC/AADC, component commanders, and subordinate forces to integrate and synchronize/deconflict OCA and DCA operations. C2 systems must support OCA operations while at the same time detecting, identifying, and tracking threats in order to warn, cue, and coordinate DCA assets, including providing

accurate warnings of enemy missile launches and impact points.

Requirements, Infrastructure, and Resources

The C2 systems should be capable of rapidly exchanging information, interfacing among components, and displaying a common tactical picture (CTP) to all participating components. The C2 architecture among all levels of command should be survivable, interoperable, flexible, secure, and redundant to the maximum extent possible. The C2 infrastructure should consist of interoperable systems that provide complete coverage for an integrated diverse force spread across a theater/JOA including considerations for any MNF assets. Service components, the joint force special operations component commander, and specialized joint communications elements provide the core of the communications capabilities for C2 for the joint force.

Situational Awareness

A primary objective the staff seeks to attain for the commander and for subordinate commanders is **situational awareness, a prerequisite for commanders to understand and anticipate counterair opportunities and challenges.** In simplest terms, this results in the ability "to see first, understand first, and act first" across the full range of military operations. The combatant commander uses the common operational picture (COP) and CTP for theater situational awareness. A subordinate JFC uses the COP and CTP as graphic depictions of the situation within the theater/JOA.

Battle Management

Battle management entails visualizing where, when, and with which forces to apply capabilities against specific threats.

The dynamics of the counterair mission often require flexibility during decentralized execution that normally takes place at the tactical level. This flexibility accomplished through battle management allows the direct, often real-time monitoring and execution of operations based on the intent and within the scope of the operational-level commander's orders.

Counterair Planning

The integration and synchronization of offensive counterair (OCA) and defensive counterair (DCA), in conjunction with the other joint missions supporting

The JFC develops an operation/campaign plan focused on the enemy centers of gravity (COGs) while ensuring that friendly COGs are protected. Counterair operations strive for the degree of air superiority and protection required by the JFC's course of action (COA) to attain the desired objectives. Counterair requires a combination of OCA and DCA operations based on the JFC's air apportionment *the JFC, are the basis for counterair planning.*

decisions and balanced against the enemy's potential COAs and air and missile threats.

Intelligence Preparation

Counterair planning considerations include accurate joint intelligence preparation of the operational environment (JIPOE) and intelligence preparation of the battlespace (IPB).

Joint Intelligence Preparation of the Operational Environment and Intelligence Preparation of the Battlespace

JIPOE supports counterair planning by identifying adversary air and missile capabilities and their likely employment. JIPOE products are used by JFC and component staffs in preparing their estimates and analysis, selection of friendly COAs, and continuing planning requirements (e.g., development of a viable concept of operations.) **IPB** assists the counterair planner in visualizing the operational environment, assessing adversary air and missile capabilities, and identifying the adversary's probable intent and attack locations. IPB is not simply enumeration of adversary air and missile systems, but must describe how the adversary air and missile forces operate.

Airspace Control Considerations

Airspace control is provided to reduce the risk of friendly fire, enhance air defense operations, and permit greater flexibility of operations.

For counterair, all components of the joint force may potentially share a part of the theater/JOA airspace for offensive/defensive operations. The ACA establishes an ACS that is responsive to the needs of the JFC and integrates when appropriate the ACS with that of the HN. The **ACS** is an arrangement of those organizations, personnel, policies, procedures, and facilities required to perform airspace control functions. The **ACP** establishes the procedures for the ACS in the operational area. The **ACO** is an order that provides the details of the approved requests for ACMs. **ACMs** are employed to facilitate the efficient use of airspace to accomplish missions and simultaneously provide safeguards for friendly forces.

Rules of Engagement (ROE)

The JFACC/AADC should offer ROE recommendations to the JFC in anticipation of the need, or when requested to do so. The ROE are an integral part of the AADP and the ACP. Commanders and their staffs must ensure that the AADP contains specific instructions that implement the ROE.

Identification (ID)

ID is the process of determining the friendly or hostile character of an unknown detected contact and the product (classification) of that process. The **CID** process complements the ID process to support application of weapons resources and other military options. For counterair, CID should be accomplished with near real time (NRT) or better exchange of information between airspace control/air defense units and airspace users to meet the time and accuracy demands of combat operations.

Methods of ID

For the purposes of counterair, the intent of an ID process is to either facilitate airspace control or to support an engagement decision through CID. The objective of CID is to obtain the highest confidence, positive ID possible. Lacking positive ID, the objective is to reach the level of confidence in an ID that can be supported by the ROE for an engagement authority to make a decision. **ID can be accomplished through several recognized methods (e.g., positive ID, procedural ID, auto-ID, formation assessment, or formation tracking).** The JFC approves the procedures used for ID and designates who may be delegated that authority in the AADP and ACP.

ID, Commitment, and Engagement Authorities

The authorities of ID, commitment, and engagement are required for decisions based on established criteria that may be tied to operational capability and are rooted in the ROE.

The AADC will establish the policy for **ID authority**, with JFC approval, and will promulgate it via the AADP, special instructions, and/or an operations task link supplement. **Commit authority** may be used (and delegated) by the AADC as a battle management tool. The air defense echelon with commit authority is permitted to authorize assets to **prepare to engage** an entity (e.g., position a DCA fighter to intercept or direct an air defense artillery unit to track and target). **Commit authority does not imply engagement authority.** The JFC is vested with authority to prosecute engagements within the theater/JOA consistent with ROE currently in effect. **The air defense authority with engagement authority is permitted to authorize engagement of an air or missile threat.** For air defense engagements within the integrated air defense system (IADS), the authority normally is delegated to the AADC who may further delegate the engagement authority to tactical levels (e.g., RADC/SADC).

Multinational Considerations

Special attention must be paid to establishing a workable CID system during MNF operations. A mix of units with dissimilar capabilities and differing electronic systems, fire control doctrine, and training can present the AADC with an extremely difficult air defense situation. Advanced planning may be required to compensate for a "patchwork" of separate MNF CID capabilities, not just for the surface air defense and air control units, but for their aircraft as well.

Asset Protection

The JFC and staff, normally the plans directorate of a joint staff, develops a prioritized **critical asset list (CAL)** for each general phase of an operation with inputs from the components and based on the theater level protection required to support tasks/missions assigned by the JFC. The CAL should include designated assets and areas within the joint security areas (JSAs) of the JOA. **For DCA protection, the joint security coordinator designated by the JFC normally coordinates with the AADC to ensure the JSAs are appropriately covered by the AADP.** The completed CAL is forwarded to AADC, who will allocate available active AMD forces to defend the prioritized assets listed. The product of this effort is the defended asset list (DAL). **The DAL is a list of those assets on the CAL that can be covered by JFC AMD forces and capabilities.**

Enabling Capabilities

Some enabling capabilities to take into account during counterair planning are: special operations; information operations; space operations; intelligence support; intelligence, surveillance, and reconnaissance; and air refueling.

Offensive Counterair Planning and Operations

General

OCA operations normally have a high priority as long as the enemy has the air and missile capability to threaten friendly forces and the JFC does not have the degree of air superiority desired to accomplish the objectives required for the end state. OCA operations reduce the risk of air and missile attacks, allowing friendly forces to focus on their mission objectives. The preferred method of countering air and missile threats is to destroy or disrupt them prior to launch using OCA operations.

OCA Planning

OCA planning begins with JIPOE and IPB and considers the JFC's assessment of the overall air and missile threat, the predicted effectiveness of the defense design, target database, ROE, objectives, priorities, missions, available friendly capabilities, and the weight of effort or force apportionment decision. IPB enhances the commanders' ability to find targets, task attack forces, and assess their effectiveness. OCA planning includes targeting enemy air and missile threats and their C2 and supporting infrastructure. OCA targets should be attacked on the surface prior to launch and as close to their source as possible. However, based on the JFC's priorities and ROE, many mobile targets, especially time-sensitive targets (TSTs), may be sought and attacked wherever and whenever they are found.

OCA Assets

The effectiveness of OCA operations depends on the availability and capabilities of friendly assets. The choice of a particular weapon system or capability may depend upon the situation, target characteristics, desired effects, threats, weather, and available intelligence. Whenever possible and within the ROE, commanders should employ weapon systems that minimize the risk to friendly forces and noncombatants.

Enemy Air Defenses

An enemy integrated air defense system attempts to provide a seamless capability to destroy, disrupt, or neutralize intelligence, surveillance, and reconnaissance and air and missile attacks or other penetrations of their airspace.

An enemy IADS could include detection, C2, and weapon systems integrated to protect those assets critical to achieving their strategic, operational, and tactical objectives. To degrade effectiveness of friendly OCA operations, enemy defensive tactics may include jamming aircraft navigation, communications, target acquisition systems, and precision weapons guidance systems. As a target system or number of target systems, enemy IADSs need to be analyzed in depth to neutralize or avoid their strengths and exploit their weaknesses.

OCA Operations

The preferred counterair employment strategy is to execute OCA operations prior to the launch of air and missile threats and as close to their source as possible. Under decentralized execution, units tasked for OCA operations should have the latitude to plan, coordinate, and execute their operations. OCA operations may be conducted by any component of the joint force with the requisite capability using aircraft, missiles, SOF, surface fires, C2 systems, or ground forces. OCA operations can be preemptive or reactive, and may be planned using deliberate or dynamic targeting. OCA operations include attack operations, suppression of enemy air defenses, fighter escort, and fighter sweep.

Defensive Counterair Planning and Operations

General

Because of their time-sensitive nature, DCA operations require streamlined coordination and decision-making processes.

DCA operations consist of active and passive AMD measures executed through a joint C2 infrastructure. The AADC normally is responsible for developing an IADS by integrating the capabilities of different components with a robust C2 architecture. The AADC uses assigned operation/campaign plan tasks to develop the AADP with the coordination of component commanders, MNF partners, and the JFC's staff.

DCA Planning

The AADP is designed to be a plan of action for DCA operations, and the RADCs/SADCs, if established, may be required or may wish to provide supplements to the AADP to reflect additional guidance or intentions. DCA planning should adhere to the following principles and ideals: centralized planning and direction; decentralized execution; planned responses; effective and efficient communications; layered defense; 360-degree coverage; ID and tracking; alert and warning; and establish modes of control.

DCA Assets

DCA operations employ a mix of weapon, sensor, communications, and C2 systems integrated from all components into an IADS to protect friendly forces, assets, population centers, and interests from air and missile threats.

Integrated Air Defense Systems

An IADS is not a formal system in itself but the aggregate of Service/functional component AMD systems comprising sensors, weapons, C2, communications, intelligence systems, and personnel operating in a theater/JOA under the command of an AADC. However, the IADS typically depends on support and enabling functions from national assets and systems not controlled by the JFC. Because the IADS is normally composed of different components, it requires significant integration and interoperability of communications and tactical data link architectures to generate its expected synergistic effects for the JFC. To ensure counterair situational awareness and enable decision making, plans for an IADS must include the requirement for a reliable, consistent COP/CTP available in all major and supporting C2 facilities.

Enemy Air and Missile Threats

Enemy threats comprise two main elements: air threats, including manned and unmanned aircraft and CM, and BM. GCCs should specifically focus intelligence efforts on potential adversaries and their air and missile threats in their theaters and adjacent areas of interest, and assess the vulnerability to cross-AOR threats from outside an established JOA/theater of operations.

ID and Tracking

Execution of efficient DCA operations requires a continuous surveillance and reporting system capable of NRT production and dissemination of the tracking data necessary for effective decision making. As a track is detected, it is identified and labeled and this information is disseminated as rapidly as possible. The track data provided is sufficiently detailed and timely to allow decision makers to evaluate the track, determine the significance of the threat, and either designate DCA forces for interception or engagement or advise units of the passage of friendly aircraft.

Area Air Defense Planning

Development of the AADP and planning DCA operations involves integrating friendly force capabilities and limitations against adversary vulnerabilities to achieve optimum results in a dynamic tactical environment. Weapon engagement zones (WEZs) are a critical part of DCA planning because they represent part of the current defense posture against the air and missile threats. Defense against BMs, CMs, ASMs, and aircraft each have unique requirements for active air defenses. During planning, multiple options should be developed using various combinations of weapon systems and WEZs allowing the flexibility to defend all critical assets, although there may be resources shortfalls.

Ballistic Missile Defense Planning

GCCs should locate, identify, and assess potential BM threats. To facilitate JFC planning, and specifically missile defense planning, those GCCs should produce target folders for potential missile threats. Target folders should be available for a subordinate JFC to complete and use when necessary, including for TSTs. For the joint force, the commander, Army air and missile defense command (normally the deputy area air defense commander) and commander, task force integrated AMD, and their staffs are acknowledged subject matter experts regarding the BM threat and missile defense. They can support OCA planners to help eliminate the threat and DCA planners to defend against it.

DCA Operations

The AADP reflects the JFC's objectives, priorities, and the specific need for air superiority and protection, and the appropriate component commanders provide the surface-, air-, and sea based forces/capabilities for those DCA operations required to execute that plan.

Passive Air and Missile Defense (AMD)

Commanders at all levels are responsible for planning and executing appropriate passive AMD measures.

Passive AMD provides individual and collective protection for friendly forces and critical assets and is the responsibility of every commander in the joint force. It includes measures, other than active AMD, taken to minimize, mitigate, or recover from the consequences of attack aircraft and missiles. Passive measures do not involve the employment of weapons, but they do improve survivability.

Active AMD

Under the counterair framework, active missile defense is integrated with active air defense as a DCA operation. Generally, the same capabilities used for missile defense are capable of air defense. **The important factors are the enemy missile threat and the conservation of missile defense assets to prevent that unique capability from being exhausted against aircraft when an alternative air defense strategy and tactics could be used against air-breathing threats.** Active BMD involves direct defensive action taken to destroy in flight BM threats. Active missile defense systems are primarily SAM systems and their supporting infrastructure. Although BM launches are detected and warnings are sent to the JFC with the predicted impact point, engagements are only possible once organic missile defense radars detect them.

CONCLUSION

This publication provides doctrine for joint counterair operations and protection against air and missile threats across the range of military operations.

CHAPTER I
INTRODUCTION

> *"If we lose the war in the air, we lose the war and we lose it quickly."*
>
> **Field Marshal Bernard Montgomery**
> **British Army, 1908-1958**

1. General

a. The joint force commander (JFC) counters **air and missile threats** to ensure friendly freedom of action, provide protection, and deny enemy freedom of action. Counterair integrates offensive and defensive operations to attain and maintain a desired degree of air superiority and protection by neutralizing or destroying enemy aircraft and missiles, both before and after launch. Offensive counterair (OCA) typically seeks to dominate enemy airspace and destroy, disrupt, or neutralize enemy aircraft, missiles, launch platforms, and their supporting structures as close to their sources as possible before and after launch. Defensive counterair (DCA) normally attempts to degrade, neutralize, or defeat enemy air and missile attacks attempting to penetrate friendly airspace. Counterair operations may also be conducted to ensure access and freedom of action in international airspace. These operations may use aircraft, surface-to-surface missiles (SSMs), surface-to-air missiles (SAMs), artillery, ground forces, special operations, and electronic attack (EA). US forces must be capable of countering the air and missile threats during all phases.

b. **Integrated Air and Missile Defense (IAMD).** IAMD is an evolving approach that uses the counterair framework at the theater level. IAMD emphasizes the integration of OCA attack operations, DCA operations, and other capabilities as required to create the JFC's desired effects. The geographic combatant commander (GCC) is responsible for IAMD operations within the theater. The IAMD approach also encompasses global strike and global missile defense beyond the theater level. The Secretary of Defense (SecDef) establishes command relationships for global ballistic missile defense (GBMD), global strike, and other cross-area of responsibility (AOR) operations. Commander, United States Strategic Command (CDRUSSTRATCOM) is responsible for synchronizing planning for global missile defense.

Refer to Chapter II, "Command and Control," Section A, "Command Relationships and Responsibilities," for cross-AOR command relationships considerations and Appendix E, "Global Ballistic Missile Defense Synchronization," for further discussion.

c. The counterair mission is inherently a joint and interdependent endeavor. Each component of the joint force contributes capabilities necessary for mission success. In addition, Service capability and force structure development reflect a purposeful reliance on all components to maximize complementary and reinforcing effects while minimizing relative vulnerabilities. Due to the joint and interdependent nature, all components of the joint force normally are tasked to conduct operations in support of the counterair mission. Unity of command (or unity of effort), centralized planning and direction, and decentralized execution are also vital tenets for countering air and missile threats.

(1) **Air Superiority.** Air superiority is that degree of dominance in the air battle of one force over another that permits the conduct of operations by the former and its related land, maritime, and air forces at a given time and place without prohibitive interference by the opposing force's air and missile threats. Historically, air superiority has proven to be a prerequisite to success for an operation/campaign because it prevents enemy air and missile threats from interfering with operations of friendly air, land, maritime, space, and special operations forces, assuring freedom of action and movement. Counterair operations usually begin early in the conduct of a campaign to produce the desired degree of air superiority at the times and places chosen by the JFC.

(a) The degree of control of the air domain may vary from local air superiority to theater air supremacy, depending on the situation and the JFC's concept of operations (CONOPS). In some situations the commander may have limited resources, having only adequate assets to establish air superiority for specific periods of time. However, air superiority may not totally eliminate the air and missile threats.

(b) Joint force requirements for air superiority may be continuous or temporary. JFCs conduct continuous counterair operations to maintain the desired degree of air superiority over the homeland, key US assets, and designated portions of friendly territory. When necessary, JFCs conduct counterair operations to establish and maintain the desired degree of air superiority over friendly territory, in international airspace, and over enemy territory in a manner, time, and place of the JFC's choosing.

(2) **Protection.** Protection focuses on conserving the joint force's fighting potential. One of the key tasks associated with the protection function is providing air and missile defense (AMD). In this regard, the JFC is responsible for protecting US and friendly forces, US vital interests, friendly population centers, logistic sites, other critical assets, and politically sensitive assets of host nations (HNs) during all phases of operations. To adequately protect the force, commanders must employ complementary weapon systems and sensors, including active and passive AMD. These operations not only defend against attack, but also ensure that US forces can strike potential threats prior to their employment against friendly forces.

For additional information regarding homeland defense (HD), see Joint Publication (JP) 3-27, Homeland Defense.

2. Counterair Framework

The counterair mission integrates both offensive and defensive operations, by all capable joint force components, and counters the air and missile threat by attaining and maintaining the degree of air superiority and protection desired by the JFC (see Figure I-1). Counterair operations may use the range of military capabilities to neutralize or destroy enemy aircraft, missiles, and launchers before and after launch. Generally, OCA operations seek to dominate enemy airspace and prevent the launch of threats, while DCA operations defeat enemy air and missile threats attempting to penetrate or attack through friendly airspace. Joint forces must be integrated to exploit the mutually beneficial effects of synchronized offensive and defensive operations to destroy, neutralize, or minimize air and missile threats.

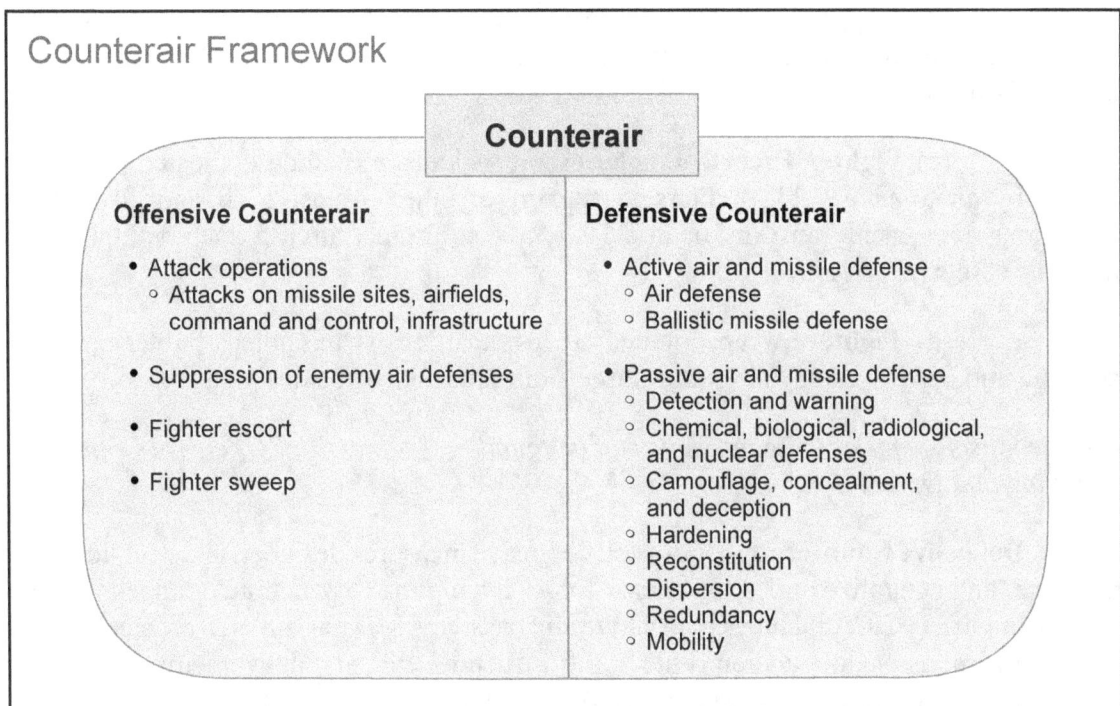

Figure I-1. Counterair Framework

Counterair operations are subject to JFC-approved weapons control procedures and airspace coordinating measures. The counterair framework is based on integrating offensive and defensive operations against both aircraft and missile threats.

a. **Offensive Counterair**

(1) OCA is offensive operations to destroy, disrupt, or neutralize enemy aircraft, missiles, launch platforms, and their supporting structures and systems both before and after launch, and as close to their source as possible. The goal of OCA operations is to prevent the launch of enemy aircraft and missiles by destroying them and their overall supporting infrastructure prior to employment.

(2) OCA operations are the preferred method of countering air and missile threats because they reduce the level of the threat that defensive forces must face. OCA operations generally are conducted at the initiative of friendly forces, and normally are a high priority as long as an enemy has the air and missile capability to threaten friendly forces and regions and conduct aerial surveillance and reconnaissance in friendly airspace. OCA operations also include targeting those assets that directly or indirectly enable enemy airpower, such as petroleum, oils and lubricants, airfield facilities, missile reload and storage facilities, aircraft repair structures, and command and control (C2) facilities. OCA includes the four operations briefly described as follows:

(a) **Attack Operations.** OCA attack operations include targeting enemy air and missile forces on the surface and the infrastructure and systems that contribute to their capabilities. Some Services refer to these as "strike" operations.

(b) **Suppression of Enemy Air Defenses (SEAD).** Activity that neutralizes, destroys, or temporarily degrades surface-based enemy air defenses (AD) by destructive and/or disruptive means.

(c) **Fighter Escort.** Fighter escort includes providing dedicated protection sorties by air-to-air capable fighters in support of other offensive air and air support operations over enemy territory or in a DCA role to protect aircraft such as high value airborne assets (HVAAs).

(d) **Fighter Sweep.** Fighter sweep is an offensive mission by fighter aircraft to seek out and destroy enemy aircraft or targets of opportunity in a designated area.

Detailed discussions of these missions can be found in Chapter IV, "Offensive Counterair Planning and Operations."

b. **Defensive Counterair.** DCA is all defensive measures designed to detect, identify, intercept, and neutralize or destroy enemy forces attempting to penetrate or attack through friendly airspace. DCA includes both active and passive AMD measures to protect friendly forces, critical assets, population centers, infrastructure, etc., and deny enemy freedom of action in friendly airspace. The goal of DCA operations, in concert with OCA operations, is to provide an area from which forces can operate while protected from air and missile threats. DCA operations must be integrated and synchronized with OCA operations and all other joint force operations.

Further discussion of responsibilities for developing weapons control procedures and airspace coordinating measures (ACMs) can be found in Chapter III, "Counterair Planning."

(1) **Active Air and Missile Defense.** Active AMD is direct defensive action taken to destroy, nullify, or reduce the effectiveness of air and missile threats against friendly forces and assets. It includes the use of aircraft, AD weapons, missile defense weapons, electronic warfare (EW), multiple sensors, and other available weapons/capabilities. Ideally, integration of those systems will allow for a defense in depth, with the potential for multiple engagements that increase the probability for success. Air and ballistic missile defenses (BMDs) should be closely integrated to form an essential capability within DCA. While AD is defensive measures designed to destroy attacking aircraft or missiles in the atmosphere, or to nullify or reduce the effectiveness of such attack, BMD is recognized as unique because of the significance of the ballistic missile (BM) threat and the difficulty of the defense. The integration of these elements provides for an integrated air defense system (IADS) that is unique to each JFC and contributes to defense in depth, with the potential for multiple engagements that increase the probability for success.

(2) **Passive Air and Missile Defense.** Passive AMD is all measures, other than active AMD, taken to minimize the effectiveness of hostile air and missile threats against friendly forces and assets. These measures include detection, warning, camouflage, concealment, deception, dispersion, and the use of protective construction. Passive AMD improves survivability by reducing the likelihood of detection and targeting of friendly assets

and thereby minimizing the potential effects of adversary reconnaissance, surveillance, and attack. Passive AMD measures are considered the same for air and BM threats, with one exception: **detection and warning of BM attack is normally provided by supporting assets from outside the theater/joint operations area (JOA) in concert with deployed AMD C2 systems and sensors.**

Further discussion of DCA can be found in Chapter V, "Defensive Counterair Planning and Operations."

3. Countering Air and Missile Threat Integration and Synchronization

a. Although OCA and DCA are considered separate operations, they must facilitate unity of effort through integration and synchronization. Many of the same forces may be required for both OCA and DCA operations; therefore, early, continuous, and close coordination is required. Integrating a mixture of capabilities from components bolsters the friendly force potential and likely will frustrate the enemy's ability to defend itself. Synchronization of OCA and DCA operations is vital to avoid duplication of effort and help prevent fratricide.

b. Countering air and missile threat operations requires integration and synchronization including the actions within and across the following areas:

(1) Integration of OCA elements capable of contributing to attack operations.

(2) Integration of DCA elements includes the integration of active and passive AMD capabilities and measures.

(3) Integration of OCA and DCA.

(4) Focuses on coordination between GCCs.

(5) Balancing the BMD needs at the combatant commander (CCDR) level with the broader global BMD needs, which include HD. GBMD focuses on a collaborative planning process among CCDRs orchestrated/led by a designated commander with coordinating authority.

(6) Participation with and defending our allies is a critical part of IAMD. For this reason, capabilities of US forces and allies must be integrated and leveraged to achieve maximum warfighting potential during all phases of the conflict.

c. Considerations for integrating and synchronizing OCA and DCA include:

(1) Using a single commander with an adequate C2 system to be responsible for both OCA and DCA operations. Typically, this is the joint force air component commander (JFACC), who normally is also the area air defense commander (AADC) and the airspace control authority (ACA).

(2) Establishing and monitoring an interoperable and robust C2 system from the JFC/JFACC through the component commanders and down to the tactical units to facilitate the centralized planning and direction and decentralized execution normally required for counterair. The C2 system should be able to seamlessly flow information and warnings and to control assets from one mission/task to another, based on the daily requirements to support the JFC's operation/campaign. Communications architecture is a critical element for counterair due to the time-sensitivity of some targets. The C2 system must connect sensors to intelligence nodes and decision makers and to operators throughout the operational area.

(3) Ensuring commanders integrate counterair capabilities and optimize the balance between OCA and DCA strengths and vulnerabilities. For example, destruction of BMs prior to their launch provides greater force protection than engaging them in flight. These prelaunch attacks must be planned and synchronized with the overall DCA scheme to maximize the effectiveness of resources.

d. If the adversary is successful in launching BMs against US and multinational forces (MNFs), the joint force relies on the defensive coverage provided by US Navy Aegis cruisers and destroyers and US Army AD systems for missile defense.

e. The GCC's theater counterair effort, and especially the missile defense planning and actions, should be coordinated and synchronized with those of the GCCs in other theaters and the worldwide synchronizing headquarters for missile defense planning, United States Strategic Command (USSTRATCOM), and its subordinate Joint Functional Component Command for Integrated Missile Defense (JFCC-IMD).

f. OCA and DCA operations require sharing many of the same systems (i.e., sensors, weapons, and C2), so integration of the component assets, as well as synchronization of their use, is necessary for unity of effort.

4. Air and Missile Threats

a. Potential adversary air and missile threats continue to grow in numbers and capabilities. Expanded technology and proliferation of missiles, including cruise missiles (CMs), BMs, and air-to-surface missiles (ASMs), expand the scope and complexity of protecting friendly forces and vital interests. The regional threats from short-range ballistic missiles (SRBMs), medium-range ballistic missiles (MRBMs), and intermediate-range ballistic missiles (IRBMs) are clear and present where the US deploys forces and maintains security relationships, and those threats are growing at a rapid pace. The proliferation of weapons of mass destruction (WMD), coupled with a conventional means of delivery (i.e., aircraft, CMs, or BMs), greatly increases potential lethality of any adversary and elevates the importance of maintaining robust counterair capabilities to protect US and friendly forces and areas. The US, while protecting some allies and partners, also works to enable them to defend themselves against the air and missile threats.

b. Other trends also complicate the counterair mission. The detection capabilities, engagement ranges, mobility, and lethality of SAM systems and fighter aircraft have significantly increased the AMDs of US adversaries. CMs and unmanned aircraft (UA) also present elusive targets and are difficult to detect, identify, and engage.

c. Adversaries may employ area denial strategies designed to prevent the protected buildup of US forces. Most "anti-access" strategies today rely in some measure on the threat or employment of advanced aircraft and/or missiles that may be employed alone or in coordinated operations with other area denial capabilities. Targets may include attacks on the infrastructure supporting US power projection capability (e.g., seaports, sea bases, airfields, and communications networks [COMNETs]) or relevant military and political targets. In this environment, adversary use of WMD against US forces, allies, and interests should not be ruled out. Since nations can acquire modern missiles rather cheaply, the number of countries with a small but lethal offensive missile capability will continue to increase.

d. **The JFC also must assess the cross-AOR BM threat from a state/non-state that possesses long-range missiles and may be aligned with the adversary.** See Chapter II, "Command and Control," Paragraph 10, "Cross Area of Responsibility Command Relationships Considerations," for more details regarding cross-AOR operations.

e. Some adversaries may consider military aircraft and missiles to be instruments of political coercion. They may also consider civilian population centers and government, cultural, and religious structures and locations as valid targets. In addition, propaganda value exists in attacking US and MNFs to show their vulnerability, particularly in rear areas.

f. For a given operation/campaign, proper assessment for counterair planning should take into account the possibility that **initial enemy attacks may employ missiles in conjunction with manned and UA** against a variety of targets: air defense artillery (ADA) sites, C2 elements, communications nodes, air facilities, seaports, sea bases, logistic centers, key civilian facilities such as power and water plants, nuclear delivery systems, storage sites, and industrial complexes.

g. Consideration must be given to the potential for irregular forces using civilian aircraft (e.g., hijacked or stolen) to attack friendly forces. Other considerations include the following: intelligence to provide situational awareness of the irregular threat; a security system to prevent illicit use of civilian aircraft; and the proper use of identification (ID), tracking, and combat identification (CID) to engage asymmetric aircraft threats but not accidentally engage innocent civilian aircraft.

For additional details regarding offensive missile threats, see Appendix D, "Threat Missile Systems."

5. Supporting Homeland Defense

a. There is no higher priority than the security and defense of the US homeland. For most CCDRs, a general responsibility from the Unified Command Plan (UCP) is to "detect, deter, and prevent attacks against the United States, its territories and bases, and employ appropriate force to defend the nation should deterrence fail." The homeland is the geographic region that includes the continental United States, Alaska, Hawaii, US territories, and surrounding territorial waters and airspace. The Commander, US Northern Command (CDRUSNORTHCOM), in concert with missions performed by North American Aerospace Defense Command (NORAD), and the Commander, US Pacific Command (CDRUSPACOM), have specific responsibilities for planning, organizing, and as directed, executing HD operations within their respective AORs. Proliferation of advanced technologies for missiles, guidance systems, and WMD warheads has increased the potential missile threat to the homeland. This is significant because the predominant threat is not from a competing superpower, but more likely from the deliberate launch of a BM from a "rogue state," failed state, or terrorist group. Deterrence is not possible against some threats. Although this publication primarily focuses on countering theater air and missile threats (i.e., those affecting an overseas GCC's AOR/a subordinate JFC's JOA), those forces and capabilities employed by overseas GCCs also may support a layered defense beginning in the forward areas against strategic air and missile threats to the homeland.

b. Commander, North American Aerospace Defense Command (CDRNORAD), is tasked to provide aerospace warning for North America that consists of the detection, validation, and warning of an attack against North America, whether by aircraft, missiles, or space vehicles. CDRNORAD is also tasked to provide the aerospace control for North America that includes surveillance and control of Canadian and US airspace, including Puerto Rico and the US Virgin Islands, in coordination with the Federal Aviation Adminstration and Transportation Canada/NAV Canada. To provide integrated tactical warning and attack assessment (ITW/AA) of an aerospace attack on North America, NORAD, as the supported command, will correlate and integrate relevant information. Commander, United States Strategic Command (CDRUSSTRATCOM) supports CDRNORAD by providing the missile warning and space surveillance necessary to fulfill the US commitment to the NORAD agreement. CDRUSSTRATCOM also provides ITW/AA of space or missile attacks on North America to CDRNORAD, should CDRNORAD be unable to accomplish the assessment mission.

c. CDRUSNORTHCOM is the supported commander for HD within that AOR, in concert with missions performed by CDRNORAD, who is the supported commander in accordance with the NORAD Agreement and NORAD Terms of Reference. CDRUSNORTHCOM is responsible for air operations outside the scope of the NORAD agreements along with land and maritime defense within that AOR. CDRUSPACOM is responsible for defense of US homelands within the US Pacific Command (USPACOM) AOR including protection against air and missile threats. However, CDRUSNORTHCOM, as approved by SecDef and in coordination with CDRUSPACOM, has certain homeland BMD responsibilities within the USPACOM AOR to ensure a seamless defense against BMs that target the homeland. CDRUSSTRATCOM aids that seamless defense by globally synchronizing planning and coordinating support for all BMD operations.

d. As assigned in the UCP, CDRUSSTRATCOM aids in the seamless synchronization of planning for homeland BMD and in support of GCCs worldwide. USSTRATCOM provides the warning and attack assessment if a GCC is unable to make that assessment.

e. Both offensive and defensive capabilities are required for deterring or defeating attacks against the homeland, US forces, and protected friends and allies. **A homeland**

BMD strategy should include an offensive capability, because some BM threats cannot be deterred by massive retaliation or BMD. If a strategic threat requires offensive actions/operations to protect the homeland, CDRUSSTRATCOM may provide global strike capabilities in direct coordination with a supported/supporting GCC, as directed by the President. An overseas GCC (or subordinate JFC) may be tasked to support homeland defense by offensive actions against hostile missile threats, or BMD support after the launch of a hostile missile. Because of the time-sensitivity and difficulty of defending against a potential missile threat after launch, GCCs in the forward regions of the world and functional CCDRs should have plans/agreements with appropriate operating procedures for offensive actions/operations supporting defense of the homeland and other friendly nations as may be directed by the President/SecDef.

Refer to JP 3-27, Homeland Defense, *for additional discussion of homeland BMD.*

6. Global Ballistic Missile Defense

The proliferation of WMD and missile technology requires a globally oriented capacity for BMD of the homeland and the overseas theaters. Strategic planning documents task each GCC with some form of missile defense and the employment of appropriate force should deterrence fail. CDRUSSTRATCOM is responsible for synchronizing planning for global missile defense and coordinating global missile defense operations support. GBMD is the overarching characterization of the cumulative (worldwide) planning and coordination for those defensive capabilities designed to neutralize, destroy, or reduce the effectiveness of enemy BM attacks whether within or across the boundaries of any GCC's AOR. GBMD recognizes the phased adaptive approach to BMD tailored to the threats unique to each theater. GCCs should anticipate theater BMD operations, some of which may be cross-AOR BMD. Unless otherwise directed by the President/SecDef, the GCCs of targeted AORs are the supported commanders for BMD planning and operations within their AORs/theaters of operations. Multiple GCCs can potentially conduct BMD operations in their theaters simultaneously. For intratheater BMD, a GCC may control all elements involved but, as the range of threat missiles increases, so does the potential cross-AOR impact. The links from sensors to decision makers to shooters must occur rapidly and reliably, often across traditional geographic and AOR boundaries. For example, a missile launch that crosses AOR boundaries complicates C2 of defensive assets and actions and requires timely planning, coordination, and rehearsal among multiple affected GCCs prior to anticipated execution. Also, GCCs should anticipate planning for some form of support in their AORs for a homeland BMD strategy that includes offensive options against a BM threat should deterrence fail. CCDRs (and their subordinate JFCs as applicable) coordinate their BMD planning and support with CDRUSSTRATCOM (JFCC-IMD).

See Appendix E, "Global Ballistic Missile Defense Synchronization," for additional information about the synchronization of BMD planning and coordination of support for other aspects of BMD.

Intentionally Blank

CHAPTER II
COMMAND AND CONTROL

"Our superiority in precision munitions, stealth, mobility and command, control, communications, and computers proved to be decisive force multipliers."

General H. Norman Schwarzkopf
Commander, US Central Command
1991

1. General

The growing capabilities of air and missile threats (speed, range, accuracy, stealth, lethality) and their proliferation require joint forces to be responsive, flexible, and integrated to effectively counter those threats. The manner in which a JFC organizes forces directly affects their responsiveness and versatility. Based on the situation, the JFC normally tailors forces to the specific tasks to enable effective spans of control, responsiveness, tactical flexibility, and protection. Because counterair is a joint mission and can involve all components of the joint force, clear command relationships and properly assigned responsibilities are essential for effective and efficient operations.

SECTION A. COMMAND RELATIONSHIPS AND RESPONSIBILITIES

2. Command Relationships

a. The JFC organizes forces, establishes command relationships, assigns responsibilities, and promulgates necessary coordinating instructions. The organization should be sufficiently flexible to meet the planned phases of contemplated operations and any subsequent development that may require a change in plans. In operations of limited scope or duration, the JFC may organize and conduct counterair operations using the joint force staff (e.g., the operations directorate of a joint staff [J-3]). If the JFC designates a JFACC, the JFC may designate the JFACC as the supported commander for strategic attack, air interdiction, and airborne intelligence, surveillance, and reconnaissance (ISR) (among other missions). As a joint mission area, counterair is conducted by all components with the necessary capabilities, with the JFC/JFACC ensuring unity of command (or unity of effort), centralized planning and direction, and decentralized execution. The JFC determines the most appropriate command relationships for the component forces/capabilities made available for counterair. Regardless of the command relationship, all counterair forces are subject to the rules of engagement (ROE), airspace control, weapons control measures, and fire control orders established by the JFACC, AADC, and/or ACA as approved by the JFC. Additionally, the AADC will be granted the necessary command authority to deconflict and control engagements and to exercise real-time battle management.

b. JFACCs, as functional component commanders, normally have operational control (OPCON) over only their own Service component forces and tactical control (TACON) or direct support of the other Service/functional component forces/capabilities made available for tasking. For example, air sorties made available for tasking normally are provided under

TACON while surface-based AMD forces are provided in direct support with mission-type orders. Those other component forces typically remain under the OPCON of their Service/functional component commanders. All command relationships (especially support relationships) between the JFACC, AADC, and other joint force component commanders must be clearly established by the JFC.

c. When the JFC organizes the joint force, in addition to a JFACC, the JFC also normally designates an AADC (for DCA) and an ACA (for joint airspace control). Normally, the JFC designates the JFACC as the AADC and ACA, because the three functions are so integral to one another. Those functions are described later in this chapter.

d. If the situation dictates, the JFC may designate an AADC and/or ACA separate from the JFACC. In that case, the JFC must clearly establish the command relationships of the JFC and the JFACC to the AADC and the ACA. The function of the ACA is integral to both the JFACC and AADC, so either may be designated the ACA, if not designated separately by the JFC. When the JFACC, AADC, and ACA are not the same individual, close coordination among all is essential for unity of effort, synchronization/deconfliction of operations, and prevention of fratricide.

See JP 3-30, Command and Control for Joint Air Operations, *for details regarding the JFACC, and JP 3-52,* Joint Airspace Control, *for additional details about the ACA and airspace control.*

3. Support Relationships

SecDef designates support relationships between CCDRs for planning and execution of operations and campaigns. JFCs typically establish support relationships between subordinate commanders for missions and operations when one force is required to aid, protect, complement, or sustain another force. For counterair operations, support relationships are particularly useful for forces made available for tasking and those shared for conducting other joint operations. An establishing directive normally is issued to specify the purpose of the support relationship, and unless limited by that directive, the supported commander will have the authority to exercise general direction of the supporting effort that includes the designation and prioritization of targets or objectives, timing and duration of the supporting action, and other instructions necessary for coordination and efficiency. The supporting commander determines the forces, tactics, methods, procedures, and communications to be employed in providing this support. See JP 1, *Doctrine for the Armed Forces of the United States,* Appendix A, "Establishing Directive (Support Relationship) Considerations," for details normally contained in the establishing directive.

a. **Supported Combatant Commander.** The supported CCDR is designated by SecDef in the appropriate warning/alert order. The supported CCDR may retain direct responsibility for the campaign or operation as a JFC or may designate a subordinate JFC (a commander, joint task force [JTF]) to plan and execute it.

b. **Supporting Combatant Commanders.** In the same warning/alert order that designates the supported CCDR, SecDef designates the supporting CCDRs based on their capabilities. Two typical supporting functional CCDRs are Commander, US Transportation Command, who supports force deployments and movements; and CDRUSSTRATCOM, who is responsible for synchronizing planning and coordinating support for global missile defense operations to minimize operational seams across AOR boundaries, provides missile launch warnings, as well as space and strategic forces/capabilities. For counterair, a good example is BMD against a cross-AOR threat, while another common example is federated intelligence support between CCDRs, as described in JP 2-01, *Joint and National Intelligence Support to Military Operations.*

c. The supported GCC in an overseas theater may concurrently be tasked for a supporting relationship with a functional CCDR or one of the GCCs with a homeland defense responsibility.

Refer to JP 1, Doctrine for the Armed Forces of the United States, *for further information on command relationships and authorities.*

4. Joint Force Commander

a. Primary responsibilities of the JFC as they apply to joint counterair include the following:

(1) Develop and maintain a C2 system to unify the employment of subordinate forces in carrying out assigned counterair missions.

(2) Develop and produce a joint operation plan (OPLAN) or an operation order that includes AMD guidance.

(3) Establish appropriate command relationships for the component commanders.

(4) Define and assign operational areas within which component forces will operate.

(5) Assign tasks, functions, and responsibilities to, and direct coordination among, the subordinate commands to ensure unity of effort in accomplishing joint counterair missions.

(a) Designate an AADC and approve an area air defense plan (AADP) developed by the AADC in conjunction with the joint force components. The AADP also may be synchronized with other BMD planning by direction of the supported CCDR and in coordination with USSTRATCOM.

(b) Designate an ACA and approve the airspace control plan (ACP) developed by the ACA in coordination with the joint force components.

(c) Establish a theater air and missile warning architecture to share warnings with joint force components, allies, interagency entities, and HN agencies, as required by agreements.

(6) Establish, coordinate, and disseminate ROE to all subordinate commanders.

(7) A supported JFC normally designates a space coordinating authority (SCA) to coordinate joint space operations and integrate space capabilities. Based on the complexity and scope of operations, the JFC can either retain SCA or designate a component commander as the SCA.

b. The JFC's staff assists in the decision-making process. The staff's sole function is command support, and its only authority is delegated to it by the JFC. The staff plans, monitors, advises, and coordinates the above listed JFC responsibilities. The JFC has the authority and latitude to organize the staff and assign responsibilities to ensure unity of effort and accomplishment of assigned missions (to include joint counterair operations). The composition of the staff normally reflects the composition of the joint force to ensure those responsible for employing joint forces have thorough knowledge of total force capabilities, needs, and limitations. Normally, each staff division is responsible for a specific area and is required to coordinate its actions, planning, and progress with other concerned divisions and agencies within the command. The primary staff divisions and their responsibilities are discussed in detail in JP 3-33, *Joint Task Force Headquarters*.

5. Component Commanders

a. **Service Components.** The Service component commanders are responsible for making available to the JFACC those counterair forces/capabilities not required for their primary roles and tasks per the apportionment guidance by the JFC. They are responsible for passing warnings of air and missile attacks to their forces and for establishing the means of C2 for the decentralized execution of counterair operations. Some of the Service components are capable of establishing regional/sector AD commands and providing the regional air defense commanders (RADCs)/sector air defense commanders (SADCs). The following are elements of the Service components that support counterair:

(1) **Army.** The commander, Army air and missile defense command (AAMDC), is the Army forces (ARFOR) operational lead for counterair operations who ensures the ARFOR contribution is properly planned, coordinated, integrated, and synchronized. The AAMDC provides a significant focus on countering adversary offensive air and missile capabilities. The commander, AAMDC, is normally designated the theater Army air and missile defense coordinator (TAAMDCOORD) for the theater Army commander or the joint force land component commander (JFLCC), if one is established. As approved by the JFC, the AADC may designate the commander, AAMDC, as a deputy area air defense commander (DAADC) for AMD in support of the AADC for DCA operations. The AAMDC is responsible for balancing the Army counterair assets/capabilities between the Army/JFLCC maneuver units and the theater level requirements established in the JFC approved defended asset list (DAL) and the AADP. The AAMDC ensures that Army theater AMD operations are internally coordinated and properly integrated with the joint force and MNFs. The Army provides C2, sensors, and weapon systems for counterair, but does not provide the capability for regional/sector AD commands within the land component area of operations (AO). Regional/sector AD commands are normally provided by C2 elements

(control and reporting center [CRC], tactical air operations center [TAOC], or an Aegis equipped ship) of the other components.

(2) **Navy.** Navy forces (NAVFOR) contribute to the joint counterair effort by providing sensor, engagement, and C2 capability. In addition to defending maritime forces from air and missile threats, NAVFOR may be employed in support of operations or to defend assets on land. Maritime surface AMD capability is centered on multi-mission capable ships that are employed to meet multiple JFC priorities. To balance competing operational requirements and adjudicate between conflicting demands, the Navy component commander (NCC) retains OPCON and TACON of ships with AMD capability. Navy OCA capability can be employed theater-/JOA-wide, but their DCA capability is normally within the maritime AO. The Navy has an integrated AMD planning and battle management capability, normally performed by a commander, task force integrated air and missile defense (CTF IAMD). CTF IAMD, or a subordinate Navy commander such as an air and missile defense commander (AMDC) may function as a RADC/SADC. Depending on the threat and available forces, the AMDC function may be split between a separate air defense commander (ADC) and BMD commander. For some limited, maritime-centric operations such as an amphibious operation, the NCC may function as the JFACC or AADC.

(3) **Marine Corps.** Marine Corps forces (MARFOR) task organize as a Marine air-ground task force (MAGTF) that remains under the OPCON of the commander, Marine Corps forces (COMMARFOR). The COMMARFOR under a JFC is typically a MAGTF commander who retains OPCON of organic air assets. During joint operations, the MAGTF aviation combat element (ACE) will be in support of MAGTF ground combat element (GCE) to accomplish the MAGTF mission. The MAGTF commander will make sorties available to the JFC, for tasking through the JFACC, for AD, long-range interdiction, and long-range reconnaissance. MAGTF air assets are made available for counterair through the air apportionment process. The MAGTF can provide a joint SADC utilizing its TAOC.

(4) **Air Force.** Counterair is a primary function of the Air Force forces (AFFOR) during joint operations. The AFFOR can make available sensor systems, C2 systems, and weapon systems and is capable of providing one or more RADCs/SADCs throughout the JOA, including within the land component AO. The Air Force operates a number of air and space operations centers worldwide. For joint operations, one of these with suitable joint augmentation is capable of being used as a joint air operations center (JAOC). The commander, Air Force forces (COMAFFOR), maintains centralized control of air operations through the Air Force air and space operations center and the daily air tasking order (ATO). Decentralized execution of the ATO is normally accomplished by subordinate air commanders using elements of the theater air control system (TACS). The CRC may be used as the core element for an AD region/sector and can monitor/direct implementation of airspace control, ID, and weapons control procedures. For a large-scale, extended campaign, the COMAFFOR may provide appropriate elements of the TACS (i.e., CRCs and the Airborne Warning and Control System [AWACS]) in support of joint air operations and counterair operations. If required, several CRCs may be provided to cover various operational areas within the JOA. AWACS may provide an initial TACS capability in the JOA until the CRCs are deployed and operational. The AWACS provides elevated sensors and radios for operational reach and in operations of a limited scope or duration can provide

some of the functions of a CRC such as monitor/control airspace, ID, and weapons control procedures.

(5) The Services support a complex and complementary array of sensor, weapon, C2, and battle management capabilities that are integrated to form the IADS, airspace control system (ACS), and theater air-ground system (TAGS).

For more information on TAGS, see Field Manual (FM) 3-52.2/Naval Tactics, Techniques, and Procedures (NTTP) 3-56.2/Air Force Tactics, Techniques, and Procedures (Instruction) (AFTTP[I]) 3-2.17, Multi-Service Tactics, Techniques, and Procedures for the Theater Air-Ground System (TAGS).

b. **Functional Components.** Functional component commands serve to ease the burden on the theater and JTF staffs, free the JFC to focus more on strategic aspects of the campaign, and provide individual air, land, maritime, and special operations forces (SOF) headquarters for coordination with the other components. The JFC assigns responsibilities to and establishes command relationships among the functional component commanders, to include planning, organizing, coordinating, and executing functional area joint operations based on the JFCs' CONOPS. In addition to the JFACC, functional component commanders can include the JFLCC, joint force maritime component commander (JFMCC), and the joint force special operations component commander (JFSOCC).

(1) **JFLCC.** The JFC normally designates a JFLCC when the land forces comprise two or more component forces (e.g., ARFOR and MARFOR). The JFLCC will provide a better degree of centralized planning and direction for an expansive or complex land operation. The JFLCC, as a single commander for joint land operations, not only enhances synchronization of all land operations, but also provides forces/capabilities in direct support of the counterair mission. While ARFOR and MARFOR maneuver units have organic air defense assets, they have different counterair capabilities. The MARFOR has organic fixed-wing aircraft capable of OCA and DCA operations, limited SAM capability, and armed rotary-wing aircraft capable of limited OCA operations. The ARFOR has armed rotary-wing maneuver units and ground based AD units effective against theater missiles and aircraft, but no fixed-wing AD aircraft. The ARFOR also has the Army Tactical Missile System for a short to medium range offensive capability that could be used in support of OCA.

(a) The MAGTF ACE is sized to support the GCE. The ACE has fixed- and rotary-wing assets and the means to control them. The MAGTF can support both OCA and DCA operations. The MAGTF normally makes aircraft sorties available for counterair tasking under TACON to the JFACC/AADC. The MAGTF commander's AD battle manager is a SADC whose authority is determined by the ACE commander. The MAGTF air control assets while supporting the ACE are normally part of the joint force IADS, and if sized to the mission, can function as a sector AD command.

(b) As discussed previously, the Army component provides an AAMDC that integrates the operational elements of Army active AD, passive AD, attack operations, C2 systems, and intelligence, and synchronizes the Army contributions to counterair operations. Normally, the AAMDC is under OPCON of the JFLCC and in direct support of the AADC.

The AAMDC conducts split-based operations to provide the necessary support and deploys liaison teams to major theater C2 headquarters to ensure Army AMD assets are integrated and synchronized in joint operations. The commander, AAMDC, also commands all Army theater-level AMD forces.

Refer to JP 3-31, Command and Control for Joint Land Operations, *for more detailed information regarding the JFLCC and joint land operations.*

(2) **JFMCC.** The JFMCC is the single commander for joint maritime operations and is normally supported by a maritime operations center (MOC). The JFMCC is responsible for accomplishing the joint sea control mission using multipurpose ships executing multiple missions simultaneously. The JFMCC typically has robust AMD capabilities that can be employed in support of joint counterair. Due to the interrelated nature of air, surface, and subsurface operations, if the JFC establishes a maritime AO, it may include a congruent regional or sector AD command covering the open ocean and littorals, for which the JFMCC should be granted sufficient authorities to conduct operations and defend fleet units, including the authority to engage missile platforms such as submarines, patrol boats, and aircraft, or coastal defense CMs. In the case of maritime air defense regions, the JFMCC may recommend a subordinate maritime commander who possesses planning and battle management capabilities to the AADC for assignment as a RADC/SADC (e.g., CTF IAMD or AMDC).

(3) The JFMCC normally provides aircraft sorties for counterair tasking under TACON of the JFACC/AADC, but retains OPCON/TACON of multipurpose AMD capable ships providing their AMD capabilities in support to the JFACC/AADC.

(4) Task force IAMD is a functionally based Navy organization to which the numbered fleet commander (NFC), who may be the JFMCC, assigns a CTF IAMD with selected planning and execution authorities. CTF IAMD provides a standardized C2 layer between the NFC and subordinate maritime commanders focused on tactical level missions.

Refer to Navy Warfare Publication (NWP) 3-32, Maritime Operations at the Operational Level of War, *and NTTP 3-32.1,* Maritime Operations Center, *for additional discussion of Navy C2 and CTF IAMD.*

(5) **JFSOCC.** The JFSOCC may be the commander, theater special operations command, a subordinate unified command under a GCC. Under a JFC subordinate to the GCC, the JFSOCC may be a designated commander, joint special operations task force (CDRJSOTF). The JFSOCC/CDRJSOTF can provide OCA support through employment of some of their core activities such as direct action, special reconnaissance, unconventional warfare, and information operations (IO), normally in enemy territory. Those core operations and activities represent the collective capabilities of all SOF rather than those of any one unit. Normally, SOF have no capability to support DCA outside of self-defense using small arms or man-portable air defense system (MANPADS). The JFSOCC normally provides a special operations liaison element (SOLE) to the JFACC at the JAOC and a special operations C2 element to the JFLCC, and to the JFMCC, if necessary. The SOLE, in close coordination with all JFSOCC components, coordinates and deconflicts SOF surface

and air operations with the air component including coordination for shared assets and fratricide prevention.

For further details concerning the JFSOCC, refer to JP 3-05, Special Operations.

6. Joint Force Air Component Commander

The JFC will typically designate responsibility for joint air operations to a JFACC. Normally, the JFACC is the Service component commander having the preponderance of air assets and the capability to plan, task, and control joint air operations. The need for a JFACC is based on the JFC's overall mission, CONOPS, missions and tasks assigned to subordinate commanders, forces available, duration and nature of joint air operations desired, and the degree of control required for joint air operations. Although not a joint air operation, but a joint operation, counterair normally is an assigned responsibility of the JFACC. **The functions of the JFACC, AADC, and ACA must be integrated to ensure that joint air operations, OCA, DCA, and airspace control are fully integrated and synchronized.** The responsibilities of the JFACC, AADC, and ACA are interrelated and are normally assigned to one individual, but they may be assigned to two or more individuals when the situation dictates. Based on the situation, if the JFC decides not to assign the JFACC, AADC, or ACA as one individual, then close coordination between all three positions is essential.

a. The JFACCs normally have OPCON over their own Service component forces and TACON or direct support of the other forces/capabilities made available to the JFACC for tasking. The JFACC generally uses centralized direction and planning with decentralized execution for counterair operations. This parallels the JFACC using centralized control with decentralized execution for joint air operations. These are not to be confused with the surface AD control modes of centralized control, when higher echelon AD units direct target assignments over their fire units, and the normal mode of decentralized control, when the higher echelon monitors fire unit actions, making direct target assignments to units only when necessary to ensure proper fire distribution or to prevent engagement of friendly aircraft.

b. The responsibilities of the JFACC normally include, but are not limited to, joint air operations planning, coordinating, allocating, and tasking, based on the JFC's concept of operations and air apportionment decision. **Other responsibilities of the JFACC relating to joint counterair operations include the following:**

(1) Develop, coordinate, and integrate joint counterair planning with operations of other components for JFC approval.

(2) Make an air apportionment recommendation to the JFC, after consulting with other components and supporting commanders, which includes counterair, strategic attack, interdiction, and close air support (CAS).

(3) Provide centralized direction for allocating and tasking joint counterair capabilities and forces made available by the JFC.

(4) Provide IO strategies to neutralize enemy air and missile threats while preserving friendly offensive and defensive capability.

(5) Perform the duties of the AADC when directed by the JFC.

(6) Perform the duties of the ACA when directed by the JFC.

(7) Perform the duties of the SCA when directed by the JFC.

(8) When approved by the GCC and directed by the JFC, coordinate cross-AOR operations with the JFACC/JFC in adjacent AORs.

c. The JFACC plans, directs, and executes counterair operations throughout the theater/JOA in accordance with JFC guidance and priorities, and therefore determines the priority, timing, and effects of counterair fires throughout the theater/JOA. When the JFC designates land/maritime force commanders, they are the supported commanders within their designated AOs, and they synchronize maneuver, fires, and interdiction within their AOs, to include prioritizing targets, effects, and timing of fires. The JFACC has the latitude to plan and execute JFC prioritized missions within a land or maritime AO in coordination with that land or maritime force commander.

(1) Although the JFACC normally has the latitude to plan and execute high-priority counterair operations and to attack targets within the land and maritime AOs, the JFACC must coordinate specific counterair operations with those component commanders to avoid adverse affects and fratricide. If counterair operations would have adverse effects within a component's AO, then the JFACC must adjust the plan, resolve the issue with that component commander, or consult with the JFC for resolution.

(2) The JFC may designate and prioritize certain time-sensitive targets (TSTs) that require immediate action whenever and wherever those TSTs are found. In doing so, the JFC has assessed and approved the higher risk for that priority target. **The JFACC, JFLCC, JFMCC, and JFSOCC must plan, coordinate, and rehearse how the JFACC will engage TSTs within the land and maritime AOs and the joint special operations areas.**

d. A JAOC normally functions as the JFACC's principal operations center. It links with national and theater sensors, intelligence, communications, and component operations centers. The Service component commanders dual-designated as JFACCs will normally use their organic air operations centers to form the cores of their JAOCs. Other component commanders normally will augment the JAOC. The effectiveness of the JAOC also rests on the expertise of component liaisons such as the Army battlefield coordination detachment (BCD), naval and amphibious liaison element (NALE), Marine liaison element (MARLE), the SOLE, and the AAMDC element. These liaison elements enhance coordination between their component commanders and the JFACC. The JFACC may establish one or more joint air component coordination elements (JACCEs) with other commanders' headquarters to better integrate joint air operations with their operations. When established, **the JACCE is a component level liaison that serves as the direct representative of the JFACC.** The component operations centers and liaison elements facilitate the planning, coordination, integration, and deconfliction of all joint counterair operations with other component operations.

e. An IADS normally is established by the JFACC/AADC for DCA with the JAOC leading its operation. The IADS is a robust integration of the Services' AMD capabilities and comprises sensors, weapons, COMNETs, C2 systems, intelligence systems, and personnel. The IADS allows the JFACC/AADC to optimize mutual support with the strengths of the Services' capabilities while "covering" for their limitations.

f. The JFACC establishes a component joint data networks operations officer equivalent (CJE), as does each of the joint force components. The CJEs support the JFC's joint data network (JDN) operations officer (JDNO) who is responsible for the common tactical picture (CTP). The JFC typically designates the JFACC as the designated component commander for the joint multi-tactical data link network (MTN).

Refer to JP 3-30, Command and Control for Joint Air Operations, for more detailed information regarding the JFACC, the JAOC, JACCE, and joint air operations.

Refer to FM 3-01.15/Marine Corps Reference Publication (MCRP) 3-25E/NTTP 3-01.8/AFTTP(I) 3-2.31, Multi-Service Tactics, Techniques, and Procedures for an Integrated Air Defense System, for additional details regarding an IADS.

7. Area Air Defense Commander

a. The JFC designates an AADC with the authority to plan, coordinate, and integrate overall joint force DCA operations. The AADC normally is the component commander with the preponderance of AMD capability and the C2 and intelligence capability to plan, coordinate, and execute integrated AMD operations, including real-time battle management.

b. Normally, for a large operation/campaign, the AADC will establish an IADS through the comprehensive integration of all available component C2 systems and AMD capabilities/assets. In the interest of decentralized execution, the AADC and RADCs/SADCs should be granted the necessary authorities to synchronize/deconflict and control engagements and to exercise battle management. Those authorities may include ID, commitment, emissions control, and engagement, all of which are discussed in Chapter III, "Counterair Planning," paragraph 13, "Identification, Commitment, and Engagement Authorities."

c. The JFC will define the command relationships between the AADC and other joint force component commanders. Components will provide representatives, as appropriate, to the AADC's headquarters to provide both specific weapon systems expertise and broader mission expertise. If the JFACC is the AADC, or they are colocated, those representatives normally are within the same liaison elements provided to the JAOC (BCD, AAMDC, NALE, MARLE, and SOLE). **If the AADC is not located at the JAOC, then appropriate liaison elements will be required from the Service/functional components.**

d. With the support of the component commanders, **the AADC develops, integrates, and distributes a JFC-approved joint AADP.** A critical feature of a joint, integrated plan is a common operational picture (COP) (i.e., a fused and correlated air, ground, and maritime picture) available in all supporting C2 facilities.

(1) The plan also should contain detailed weapons control and engagement procedures for all DCA weapons systems and forces integral to DCA operations.

(2) The plan should be closely integrated with the ACP through the ACA.

(3) The AADP should include IO measures and actions supporting counterair operations.

e. Primary responsibilities of the AADC include the following:

(1) Develop, integrate, and distribute a JFC-approved joint AADP in coordination with Service and functional components.

(2) Develop and execute, in coordination with the intelligence directorate of a joint staff (J-2), J-3, communications system directorate of a joint staff (J-6), and joint force components, a detailed plan to disseminate timely air and missile warning and cueing information to components, forces, allies, coalition partners, and civil authorities, as appropriate. Planning for BMD should include coordination for launch warnings, attack assessments, and other aspects of missile defense, either through the supported GCC or directly with USSTRATCOM, if authorized.

(3) Develop and implement, in coordination with the component commanders and with JFC approval, ID and CID procedures and authorities, and engagement procedures that are appropriate to counterair.

(4) Establish timely and accurate track reporting procedures among participating units to provide a CTP.

(5) Perform the duties of the ACA when directed by the JFC.

(6) For complex operations, the JFC may approve establishment of AD regions/sectors and designation of RADCs/SADCs, as appropriate, to enhance decentralized execution of DCA operations.

(7) Establish appropriate joint, fighter, and missile engagement zones (MEZs) in coordination with the RADCs/SADCs and the ACA.

(8) Appoint DAADCs as required, to advise on how to integrate and synchronize their Service component DCA capabilities/assets for complex DCA plans and operations.

(9) Ensure all support assets, including surface-based and space-based early warning systems, are fully coordinated to support DCA operations.

(10) Make DCA recommendations to the JFC/JFACC after consultation with DCA representatives from the joint force components.

(11) Make OCA attack operations recommendations to the JFC/JFACC to help counter the air and missile threat. The AADC should prioritize those desired effects to be created to support achievement of objectives through OCA.

(12) As approved by the JFC, coordinate with supported/supporting commands for cross-AOR operations (e.g., cross-AOR BMD).

f. **DAADC.** When a significant portion of the DCA capability is contributed by a component other than that of the AADC, a senior officer from that component may be designated by the JFC or AADC as a DAADC. DAADC responsibilities include assisting in AADP development; integrating respective component and multinational AMD into DCA operations; and advising on ROE, ACMs, weapons control measures, air defense warnings (ADW), and respective component AMD operations and capabilities. As the senior Army air defender, the commander, AAMDC, is normally designated as a DAADC and advises the AADC on the best distribution of the Army AMD capabilities between the requirements for the theater level DAL and maneuver forces of the ARFOR/JFLCC. As a DAADC, the commander, AAMDC, will deploy personnel and equipment to the JAOC.

Note: The Army BCD normally deployed to the Air Force air and space operations center or the JAOC is only a liaison element. Although the BCD has an AD section, responsibility to integrate the ARFOR AMDs resides with the senior ADA commander, normally the commander, AAMDC.

8. Regional and Sector Air Defense Commanders

During complex operations/campaigns conducted in a large JOA/theater of operations, the AADC may recommend and the JFC may approve the division of the operational area into separate AD regions, each with a RADC who could be delegated responsibilities and decision-making authority for DCA operations within the region. The AADC and RADC, as approved by the JFC, may choose to further divide regions into sectors, each with a SADC with appropriate authority for their responsibilities. Generally, the regions/sectors are based on geographic size and obstacles/features overland. When RADCs/SADCs are employed in support of BMD operations, regional/sector boundaries are normally assigned on the basis of predicted BM impact points. The open ocean and littorals normally are part of a maritime AO/region and the RADC/SADC may be afloat, so its complete integration with the bordering land-based RADC/SADC and the AADC is essential to prevent a seam in the IADS. **The core of a RADC/SADC is a Service component air control/AD organization with the necessary situational awareness and communications links up to the AADC/JFACC/JFC, down to the tactical units' operation centers, and laterally to other RADCs/SADCs.** A tactical data link (TDL) such as Link 16 enables sharing of the CTP between Service systems and RADCs/SADCs. The COP at the higher echelons, normally a Global Command and Control System (GCCS) environment, includes the Link 16 CTP data.

a. The maritime component (NAVFOR/JFMCC) normally has the open ocean and littorals as a region with a Navy AMDC on an Aegis ship, but the littorals also could be covered by a Navy tactical air control center (TACC) or Marine TAOC. Over land, there may be numerous RADCs/SADCs, normally operated by the AFFOR or the MARFOR. The role of the Army does not require a capability to operate a RADC/SADC.

b. The AADC also may delegate certain planning functions to a RADC/SADC concerning the deployment of air and surface AMD assets. In all cases, the AADC should establish clear guidance concerning the responsibilities and authorities delegated to the RADC/SADC.

c. Each RADC/SADC with a surface-based AD requirement/capability must have that expertise on staff and the requisite C2 links. For a Navy/maritime component, the integration of air-to-air and surface-to-air capabilities is organic to established fleet air defense. The MAGTF also has an integrated organic AD capability. The Air Force must rely on Army augmentation/liaison for surface-to-air expertise. A Navy or Marine Corps RADC/SADC should have that Army expertise as a liaison if they rely on an Army AMD capability within their region/sector. Additionally, if a ground-based RADC/SADC is being supported by a Navy/JFMCC surface-based AMD system (e.g., Aegis-equipped ship), then an equivalent Navy AD specialist should augment or be liaison to that RADC/SADC.

d. Army Air Defense Artillery Fire Control Officer (ADAFCO). The ADAFCO is the single point of contact between Army land-based AMD fire direction centers and the joint/Army controlling authority. An ADAFCO is required in any area/regional/sector air defense command in which an Army AMD capability is employed. The ADAFCO is responsible for coordinating Army AMD for designated assets/areas on the DAL in that area/region/sector and for coordinating and monitoring the tracking and engagement activities of individual Army ADA fire units. The ADAFCO is the Army AMD engagement expert for the AADC/RADC/SADC on what course of action (COA) Army ADA units would likely follow during any situations, especially with degraded communications, and what limitations ROE can have on autonomous Army ADA units, what tactics may be more effective, etc. ADAFCO elements should be part of/liaison to any Service component AMD operations centers that may have control of or support from Army AMD assets. The ADAFCO element should be capable of continuous (24-hour) operations with the AADC/RADC/SADC, and normally is placed under the direct control of the senior air defense officer (SADO), senior weapons director, or mission crew commander. The ADAFCO must have access to dedicated AD communication links (e.g., dedicated AD voice circuit) with Army AD C2 nodes when conducting active AD operations. The ADAFCO also needs a display of the local track data the ADA systems hold and are preparing to engage. Normally, an ADAFCO should not be placed on an airborne warning and control/airborne C2 aircraft that are not designated as a full time SADC directing ground-based AD in conjunction with active air intercepts. Those air control type aircraft normally lack a dedicated seat position and communications for the ADAFCO. However, some operations may require ADAFCO support on those aircraft, so the Army and air component planners must anticipate and properly coordinate for that requirement to ensure effective use of the available ADAFCO assets.

(1) AAMDC ADAFCO. The AAMDC ADAFCO, in conjunction with a Navy liaison for the Aegis, will typically be located with the AADC/JFACC and the SADO at the JAOC, and will be responsible for the coordination and deconfliction of upper-tier (i.e., exo-

atmospheric) BM engagements. Currently, upper-tier engagements of BMs may be executed by Aegis and the Terminal High Altitude Area Defense (THAAD) system, and coordination/deconfliction will normally be accomplished by preplanned tactics, techniques, and procedures. The AAMDC ADAFCO maintains communications with the brigade (BDE) ADAFCOs at the various regional/sector AD commands to share situational awareness. **To accomplish the mission, the AAMDC ADAFCO requires reliable voice and data communications with the Aegis controlling authority, the THAAD battery tactical control officer, and the BDE ADAFCOs.** The AAMDC ADAFCO requires a joint air picture shared with the SADO. Note: For homeland BMD, CDRUSNORTHCOM employs the Ballistic Missile Defense System (BMDS) for exo-atmospheric engagements of BMs.

(2) BDE ADAFCO. The BDE ADAFCO is responsible for lower-tier engagements (i.e., endo-atmospheric) within a particular region or sector. Lower-tier engagements include terminal phase engagements of BMs, ASMs, and air breathing threats (aircraft and CM). The BDE ADAFCOs are normally located with the RADCs/SADCs, and specifically with their mission crew commanders or senior weapons directors. The BDE ADAFCOs are the Army link between Patriot units and the joint controlling agency (e.g., RADC/SADC). The BDE ADAFCO issues all fire control orders to their subordinate units. **The BDE ADAFCO requires voice and data communications with the tactical directors at the battalion's information coordination central and a joint air picture feed from the RADC/SADC or the commander with engagement authority.** Due to the requirement to colocate with a RADC/SADC, BDE ADAFCOs are usually located with a US Air Force CRC, US Navy Aegis, Marine Corps TAOC, or, in very specific circumstances, a US Air Force AWACS. To ensure error free clearing of fires, the ADAFCO should be provided a dedicated position with display of the CTP and supporting voice communications.

9. Airspace Control Authority

a. The JFC designates an ACA who has overall responsibility for establishing and operating the ACS. The ACA also develops policies and procedures for airspace control that are incorporated into an ACP and promulgated throughout the theater/JOA. A key responsibility of the ACA is to provide the flexibility needed within the ACS to meet contingency situations that necessitate rapid employment of forces.

b. The ACA coordinates use of airspace through the ACP, including integration with the HN ACS, and synchronizes/deconflicts all user requirements using the airspace control order (ACO). The ACA must be able to rapidly implement ACMs in the dynamic counterair environment to enhance freedom of action of components while preventing fratricide. The ACP is implemented by the ACO, and all component forces that affect joint air operations are subject to the ACO. However, this control of airspace by the ACA does not imply any type of command authority (OPCON or TACON) over any air asset.

c. The ACA responsibilities for counterair operations include, but are not limited to:

(1) Link the ACP to the AADP when designating volumes of airspace.

(2) Develop ACMs that support and enhance operations.

(3) Provide a flexible ACP that can adapt to changing requirements of the tactical situation.

Refer to JP 3-52, Joint Airspace Control, *for more details concerning the ACA.*

10. Cross Area of Responsibility Command Relationships Considerations

The primary strategic planning documents, *Guidance for Employment of the Force* and *Joint Strategic Capabilities Plan,* discuss "cross-AOR" in campaign planning. GCCs are supported commanders for assigned missions in their AORs, and they anticipate the possibility for "cross-AOR" operations based on threats and capabilities. They must plan accordingly and coordinate with other affected and supporting CCDRs.

a. A significant concern for GCCs is not only long-range BMs that can traverse entire AORs, but also SRBMs, MRBMs, and IRBMs, because they represent the most prevalent threats.

b. When establishing command relationships and C2 for cross-AOR BMD, the following should be considered:

(1) Span of Control. Span of control is based on factors such as the number of subordinates/components, number of activities, range of weapon systems, force capabilities, the size and complexity of the operational area, and the method used to control operations (e.g., centralized or decentralized execution). **Coordination authority between GCCs should enable coordination at component and tactical levels supporting unity of effort for cross-AOR BMD.**

(2) Simplicity. Simplicity is achieved through an unambiguous chain of command, well-defined command relationships, and clear delineation of responsibilities and authorities. **For cross-AOR BMD,** which typically must be executed in a manner of minutes, **simplicity is essential** and enables fully planned and rehearsed actions before execution is actually required.

(3) Unit Integrity. Component forces should remain organized as designed and in the manner accustomed through training, but cross-AOR operations may necessitate unique support relationships, including units supporting forces in other theaters.

(4) Interoperability. **C2 capabilities should be interoperable within the joint force** headquarters, among component commands and other supporting commands, **and between joint forces in support relationships.** Collaborative planning at various levels is an essential aspect of interoperability among joint force components and supported/supporting commands.

c. **Authorities and Battle Management.** Short missile engagement windows place a premium on clearly established authorities. For example, in AORs without active conflicts involving air or missile threats, the GCC may only approve the theater JFACC/AADC for engagement authority of inbound threats within friendly airspace. In an operational area with imminent or ongoing hostilities, the JFC may approve delegation of engagement authority down to a RADC/SADC. The air and missile threats posed by adversaries are normally known, and plans/orders, including ROE, are approved in anticipation of the indications and warnings that would precede a possible hostile launch.

d. Existing plans and orders address a number of known cross-AOR threats. **A primary concern involving cross-AOR fires/operations is the potential difficulty of prioritizing tactical actions of a supporting unit.** Support relationships between GCCs can be clearly established, but responding to conflicting requirements or priorities can create an operational dilemma: How does the unit commander respond to multiple tasks? When may there be conflicting times and locations? This type of situation should be mitigated through exercises and rehearsals.

e. Other essential considerations in cross-AOR BMD are differences in GCCs plans and procedures, command relationships, and battle management procedures. For example, **command relationships and the engagement procedures for homeland BMD are significantly different than those for other regional BMD.** These differences can be overcome through prior planning, training, and rehearsals among the supported and supporting commanders and tasked units. This applies to both the offensive and defensive aspects of a missile defense strategy.

SECTION B. MULTINATIONAL CONSIDERATIONS

11. General

Most joint operations are now conducted within a multinational context (i.e., an alliance or coalition). Each MNF operation is unique, and the international situation, along with the perspectives, motives, and values of each MNF member may vary. The JFC (who may be the multinational force commander [MNFC]) must evaluate key considerations and differences involved in planning, coordinating, and conducting counterair operations in a multinational environment. A major characteristic of operating in the multinational environment is that consensus through compromise is often essential to success. Within designated command authorities and in close coordination with the civilian leadership, the MNFC may have responsibilities to both national and foreign leaders and must be prepared to negotiate with MNF partners when planning and developing ROE, ACMs, weapon control measures, and other appropriate procedures and processes such as CID.

12. Command Relationships

a. The traditional command relationships used by US forces generally may not be possible with all MNF partners because of political necessity. Some MNF partners may accept US command authorities; others may not. In MNF operations, understanding the agreed upon command relationships and the related command authorities is key to developing the desired unity of effort for counterair operations.

b. If command relationships and support requirements (e.g., security and logistics) are not already provided for in existing agreements, the JFC should request to have such agreements concluded (memorandums of agreements, technical arrangements, status of forces agreements, etc.) between US and MNF members conducting counterair operations.

The authority to negotiate and conclude international agreements with MNF members is not an inherent aspect of the JFC's OPCON authority, and must be exercised only by those entities specifically delegated authority to negotiate and/or conclude international agreements (i.e., SecDef, Secretaries of the Military Departments, the Chairman of the Joint Chiefs of Staff [CJCS], CCDRs).

c. The JFC must be aware that many different interpretations of OPCON and TACON exist among MNF partners, and all must ensure complete understanding of the terms early during the planning of the operation. The JFACC/AADC may expect no more than TACON over MNF counterair units/capabilities, and very likely, may have simple support relationships based on mission-type orders.

Refer to JP 3-16, Multinational Operations, *for more details on organizing alliance and coalition command structures and headquarters.*

13. Organization

a. No matter how the MNF is organized, the organizational structure and command relationships must be clearly understood by all commanders and supported by the C2 capability.

b. Some significant organizational considerations affecting counterair include force capabilities and disparities, information and equipment security, unit procedural and organizational differences, cultural differences, language barriers (including differing use of common terms), and interoperability of the C2 systems of the MNF components. See Figure II-1 for a listing of some principal factors affecting national military capabilities.

(1) Each nation normally establishes a national center or cell as a focal point to ensure effective support and control of its forces, to include counterair forces.

(2) National intelligence systems should be integrated to ensure responsiveness to counterair operational needs. Because sharing intelligence and warning information is vital to unity of effort, any issues related to the release of intelligence information and products to MNF partners must be resolved early during planning. At all levels, the senior US officer needs to be concerned with the issues of foreign disclosure guidance and intelligence sharing early in the planning process to ensure the commander's requirements and intent have been clearly stated and understood.

Factors Affecting the Military Capabilities of Nations

- National interests
- Objectives
- Arms control limitations
- Doctrine
- Training
- Leader development

- Equipment
- History
- Defense budget
- Domestic politics
- Religion
- Culture

Figure II-1. Factors Affecting the Military Capabilities of Nations

(3) Some nations are particularly sensitive to certain force protection measures (use of flares, security patrols by national forces other than their own, arming of force protection personnel, limiting access of airfield support personnel to aircraft, etc.). These issues should be coordinated ahead of time, and agreements must be continually updated as situations warrant.

(4) Before assigning tasks to MNF units, the JFACC/AADC should ensure that all elements can make meaningful contributions to the overall counterair mission. Some partners may be restricted to the types of targets they are permitted to attack and the level of risk they are willing to accept due to domestic politics, arms limitation agreements, or their capabilities.

(5) The AADC should ensure that MNF ROE, engagement authorities, and procedures are consistent with the combined AADP and the MNF ability to identify friendly forces, in order to prevent gaps and ensure joint air forces are not subject to an increased risk of fratricide and MNF are not restricted from self-defense. When MNF ID and C2 capabilities are not consistent with joint capabilities, it may be necessary to implement additional ACM, procedural ID, and engagement control measures, or to limit MNF engagements to self-defense only. US liaison elements may be required at MNF AD or air operations facilities to ensure an adequate capability for ID and engagement control exists.

c. All critical forces and geopolitical areas should receive adequate protection from air and missile threats. Some MNF partners are not uniformly capable of defending against air and missile threats and may require DCA assets from another theater or nation.

d. **The JFACC/AADC should consider using liaison officers to assess and/or assist MNF partners' counterair capabilities and to maintain span of control and keep forces connected at the tactical level.** Also, depending upon the makeup of the MNF, the need for interpreters should be considered.

See JP 3-0, Joint Operations, and JP 3-16, Multinational Operations, for further detail concerning multinational operations.

SECTION C. COMMAND AND CONTROL SYSTEMS AND FUNCTIONS

14. General

Joint counterair operations require reliable C2 capabilities that allow the JFC/JFACC/AADC, component commanders, and subordinate forces to integrate and synchronize/deconflict OCA and DCA operations. Effective C2 systems facilitate centralized planning and direction and decentralized execution, helping commanders to synchronize geographically separated operations into a unified action. C2 systems must support OCA operations while at the same time detecting, identifying, and tracking threats in order to warn, cue, and coordinate DCA assets, including providing accurate warnings of enemy missile launches and impact points.

Refer to JP 6-0, Joint Communications System, *for details regarding planning communications systems for joint operations.*

15. Requirements, Infrastructure, and Resources

a. **Requirements.** The C2 systems should be capable of rapidly exchanging information, interfacing among components, and displaying a CTP to all participating components. The components typically are tasked to provide a CTP. The components' CTPs and information from the joint planning network contribute to a GCC's COP. The information flow should be as complete, reliable, secure, and as near real time (NRT) as possible to support commanders' decision-making cycles. These systems should be flexible enough to allow NRT retasking and coordination for attacks on TSTs. The C2 architecture among all levels of command should be survivable, interoperable, flexible, secure, and redundant to the maximum extent possible. C2 integration includes communications and data links for sensors, weapons systems, staffs and liaisons, and supporting agencies. Effective C2 systems support unity of effort during counterair operations by enabling commanders to fuse disparate databases and geographically separated offensive and defensive operations into a single COP/CTP that enhances situational awareness and understanding. For every operational element involved in counterair the C2 family of systems must support the following:

(1) Rapid communications and coordination links and procedures.

(2) Data fusion and decision-making nodes.

(3) Warning and cueing systems.

(4) Links to dedicated weapons systems, other MNF partners, and/or civilian authorities.

(5) Vertical, horizontal, technical, and procedural interoperability. **Counterair C2 processes are built using existing joint and Service systems and capabilities.**

b. **Infrastructure.** The C2 infrastructure should consist of interoperable systems that provide complete coverage for an integrated diverse force spread across a theater/JOA including considerations for any MNF assets. The systems will include large, fixed site C2 facilities, small remote relay sites, mobile land and maritime sites, and airborne systems. These systems should be connected to commanders at appropriate decision and execution levels to integrate forces and missions. The C2 architecture provides the timely intelligence and operational information needed to plan, employ, coordinate, deconflict, execute, and sustain joint counterair operations. These systems also facilitate the integration of counterair with other joint operations via rapid communications among commanders, staffs, sensors, weapon systems, and supporting agencies.

(1) Part of that infrastructure is the TAGS, a system of the various component air-ground systems integrated for planning and execution of air-ground operations. The TAGS consists of an overarching joint C2 architecture and Service coordination links. It is not a formal system in itself but rather the sum of the component air-ground systems operating in the theater. It is applicable to all theater operations to include air, ground, maritime, and amphibious operations.

Refer to FM 3-52.2/NTTP 3-56.2/AFTTP(I) 3-2.17, Multi-Service Tactics, Techniques, and Procedures for the Theater Air-Ground System, *for detailed discussion of the TAGS and the Service component contribution to the infrastructure.*

(2) For theater warning, the Theater Event System reports the launch (voice and data) in-theater over two types of satellite broadcast networks: the Integrated Broadcast Service-Simplex (IBS-S) and the Integrated Broadcast Service-Interactive (IBS-I). IBS-S transmits real-time data via the SECRET Internet Protocol Router Network (SIPRNET) or tactical terminal to the GCCS. IBS-I can provide timely intelligence information directly from collectors and associated ground processing facilities to the theater commanders for targeting, battle management, and overall situational awareness.

(3) The IADS is another part of the infrastructure that is not a formal system, but an integration of numerous systems that includes not only C2, but sensors, weapons, etc. Although primarily for DCA operations, some components of the IADS infrastructure and C2 architecture comprise a component of the TAGS.

Refer to FM 3-01.15/MCRP 3-25E/NTTP 3-01.8/AFTTP(I) 3-2.31, Multi-Service Tactics, Techniques, and Procedures for an Integrated Air Defense System, *for details regarding the IADS.*

c. **Resources.** Service components, the JFSOCC, and specialized joint communications elements provide the core of the communications capabilities for C2 for the joint force. The following summarize some of those capabilities that contribute to C2 for various aspects of counterair:

(1) **Air Force C2.** The Air Force TACS provides resources for a C2 infrastructure that can support the AFFOR or joint operations. The TACS includes the following elements that function under the tenets of centralized control and decentralized execution for joint air operations.

(a) The Air Force air and space operations center is the senior air operations element of the TACS with the primary function of planning, directing, coordinating, and controlling air operations. It is capable of operating as a JAOC for the JFACC.

(b) The CRC, as a worldwide deployable airspace control and battle management platform, is employed at the tactical level to support air operations planning and execution across the entire range of operations. The CRC operates independently or in combination with other tactical C2 elements (e.g., Joint Surveillance Target Attack Radar System [JSTARS], the air support operations center [ASOC], and AWACS). It supports horizontal integration with tactical resources and vertical integration with the Air Force air and space operations center. A CRC is capable of being a regional/sector AD center.

(c) The ASOC plans, coordinates, and directs air support for land forces, normally at corps level and below. It is directly subordinate to the Air Force air and space operations center and is responsible for the integration of air operations within its assigned corps sector to include CAS, air interdiction, air surveillance, reconnaissance, and targeting, SEAD, theater airlift, and personnel recovery.

(d) JSTARS E-8C aircraft provide NRT surveillance and targeting information on moving and stationary ground targets, slow-moving rotary and fixed-wing aircraft, and rotating antennae. These surveillance platforms also provide attack support to friendly offensive air elements in all ambient light and weather conditions. Based on the JFC's objectives, JSTARS supports the JFLCC's scheme of maneuver as well as the JFACC. JSTARS is a battle management, ISR, and C2 platform and is considered an HVAA.

(e) AWACS E-3B/C aircraft is a C2 platform with organic sensors that provides battle management and air surveillance functions, including airspace management, identifying and tracking friendly aircraft; detecting, identifying, and tracking enemy air threats for early warning and AD purposes; and it supports execution of the ATO. AWACS works directly with other Services' AD aircraft and SAM units supporting the joint defense against air breathing and to a limited extent, BM threats. An AWACS may be designated as a SADC if a CRC or other ground-based C2 node is not in the JOA/AOR. This is usually a short-term solution until a CRC deploys into theater, or if an operation is of limited scope or a short duration. AWACS is considered an HVAA.

(2) **Army C2 Assets.** The Army air-ground system (AAGS) is the control system for synchronizing, coordinating, and integrating air operations with an Army land force commander's scheme of maneuver. The AAGS initiates, receives, processes, and executes requests for air support and disseminates information and intelligence produced by aerial assets. Although some elements within AAGS (such as the tactical air control party [TACP]) belong to different Services or other nations, they function as a single entity in planning, coordinating, deconflicting, and integrating air support operations with ground operations. The Army elements of the AAGS consist of operations, fire support, AD, mission command, and coordination/liaison elements. The Army uses fires cells at all echelons to plan, coordinate, and execute joint fires and fire support within the Army/JFLCC's AO. **These elements can support OCA operations by advising the Army**

unit commander/JFLCC on capabilities and the effective use of assets and by assisting in the planning and coordination of attacks of OCA targets within the AO.

(a) **BCD.** The Army provides a BCD as the interface for selected battlefield functions between the ARFOR/JFLCC and the AFFOR/JFACC. Typically, a BCD is colocated with the JAOC. **The BCD supports OCA operations by advising the JFACC/JAOC on the capabilities and effective employment of ARFOR systems.** The BCD passes JFACC requests for ARFOR/JFLCC support for OCA. The BCD assists in the synchronization of joint air operations with Army/JFLCC maneuver and fires and the exchange of operational and intelligence data.

(b) **AAMDC.** For OCA, the AAMDC, through its attack operations cell, plans, analyzes, tracks, develops, and nominates enemy air and missile targets. The AAMDC should colocate with, or nearby the JAOC, or provide a liaison element to the JFACC. For DCA, the AAMDC is the senior Army air defender for both the theater Army commander/JFLCC (as the TAAMDCOORD) and the AADC (as the DAADC).

For more information on Army fire support C2 assets, see JP 3-09, Joint Fire Support.

(3) **Navy C2 Assets**

(a) **Navy Tactical Air Control System (NTACS).** NTACS is the principal air control system afloat. The senior Navy air control agency is the Navy TACC and the subordinate airborne element is the E-2 Hawkeye aircraft. The Navy TACC is responsible for planning and conducting naval air operations as well as coordinating operations that affect airspace. If the JFACC's command operations center is afloat, the Navy TACC may support operations as the JAOC. The link between the JFACC and naval commanders is the NALE located in the JAOC. The NALE assists in integrating naval air capabilities (including counterair) to help the JFACC meet JFC objectives through the NTACS.

(b) **CTF IAMD.** CTF IAMD provides a standardized C2 layer between the NFC with their associated MOC and subordinate maritime commanders. CTF IAMD is subordinate to the NFC and will support the NAVFOR and one or more assigned JFMCCs, as required. CTF IAMD is the JFMCC's tactical execution agent for supporting the JFACC's counterair mission by implementing the AADC's defense design for protecting the prioritized DAL.

(c) **E-2C Hawkeye.** The E-2C is an all-weather, aircraft carrier-capable tactical airborne early warning aircraft with comparable C2 capabilities to the AWACS E-3B/C. With its organic sensors (active and passive) as well as large communication and data link suite, it provides airborne battlefield C2 and air surveillance functions, including airspace management; identifying and tracking friendly aircraft; detecting, identifying, and tracking enemy air threats for early warning and AD purposes; and it supports execution of the ATO. The Hawkeye works directly with other Services' AD aircraft, C2 platforms, and SAM units supporting the joint defense against air breathing and to a limited extent, BM threats. Cooperative engagement capability-equipped Hawkeyes enhance early cueing of the Navy Aegis weapons system, dramatically extending the lethal range of the standard missile against airborne low-altitude, low-radar cross-section targets. E-2C crews train to act as a SADC if a CRC or other ground-based C2 node is not in the JOA/AOR. This is usually a short-term solution until a CRC deploys into theater or if an operation is of limited scope or a short duration. The limiting factor for the E-2 is on station time as it currently does not have the ability to refuel airborne. E-2 is considered an HVAA.

(4) **The Marine Air Command and Control System (MACCS).** The MACCS provides the Marine ACE commander with the capability to C2 and influence the application of Marine aviation assets. The Marine air C2 agencies involved in OCA and DCA are the tactical air command center (TACC) and the TAOC.

(a) The Marine TACC is the senior agency for the ACE commander and battle staff to plan, command, supervise, and direct MAGTF air operations. The TACC maintains complete information on the friendly situation, including an integrated air picture with ground combat information essential to the air effort. It can provide automated displays, ATO generation equipment, and data link feeds. Functionally, it is divided into four mutually supporting sections: current operations, future operations, future plans, and air combat intelligence. The TACC current operations section executes and assesses the daily ATO, while the TACC future operations section helps develop future ATOs and operation orders for the ACE. The TACC future plans section conducts aviation planning in support of the next mission, or potential mission, assigned to the MAGTF. The TACC air combat intelligence section supports the entire TACC by producing and disseminating aviation-specific all-source intelligence required to plan and execute air operations, to include counterair operations.

(b) The TAOC is the principal AD agency in the MAGTF. Subordinate to the TACC, the TAOC provides real-time surveillance, direction, positive control, and navigational assistance for friendly aircraft. It performs real-time direction and control of all antiair warfare operations, including manned interceptors and surface-to-air weapons. The TAOC has the capability to serve as a SADC.

(c) The MARFOR normally provides a MARLE to the JAOC to serve as the Service conduit to the JFACC/AADC.

(5) The SOF under a JFSOCC (or a CDRJSOTF designated for an operation) have their own joint force C2 architecture and are linked to and a part of the JFC's C2 architecture. The CDRJSOTF has at least one secure dedicated C2 network for their operations and other networks with the SOF Service components. Although SOF can play a significant role in OCA operations and they may share common operational areas with the JFACC (both routinely operate deep in enemy territory), the SOF only control their own operations or operations in which they are the supported command. The SOF have no capability for DCA. Therefore, SOF aviation and surface activities must be closely coordinated with all other joint operations, from planning through execution, to provide synchronization/deconfliction and to prevent fratricide. The SOLE serves as the JFSOCC's representative to the JFACC and coordinates, deconflicts, and integrates all SOF air and surface activity into the ATOs and ACOs.

(6) **Joint Interface Control Officer (JICO).** The JICO is the senior interface control officer in support of MTN operations and is the MTN coordinator for the JDN within the theater/JOA. The MTN is the primary feed/data source to support generation of a CTP. The CTP subsequently feeds the CCDR's theater COP. The JICO is responsible for planning, monitoring, and managing the architecture and technical integration of joint data and communications systems for the MTN. The MTN components are the TDLs such as Link 11, Link 11B, Link 16, etc. The JICO controls and acts as the coordinating authority for the joint interface control cell (JICC) and for any regional interface control officer (RICO)/sector interface control officer (SICO) for planning and executing TDL functions that cross regional and/or sector boundaries or impact the theater-wide MTN. When a JTF is formed, there will be only one JICO per JTF, and the JICO will normally be located in a C2 facility with connectivity to the primary TDLs (normally the JAOC). There may be Service component interface control officers located at the JICC.

(a) When regional/sector AD commands are established, the JICO will coordinate with the RICOs/SICOs designated for and normally located at those commands. The RICO/SICO coordinates with the JICO but is responsible to the RADC/SADC for TDL continuity at their level. RICOs/SICOs may require interface control cells depending upon the complexity of their TDL networks. See Figure II-2 for a depiction of a notional joint interface control officer functional/command relationship.

(b) The JICO is responsible to the JDNO for the MTN, which is one of four networks in the JDN. In turn, the JDNO is responsible to the JFC for integration of information from the sub-networks into a common track database used to generate the CTP. The JDN is the primary feed to support generation of the CTP. The CTP and information from the joint planning network contributes to the COP.

Refer to Chairman of the Joint Chiefs of Staff Manual (CJCSM) 3115.01B, Joint Data Network (JDN) Operations, *and CJCSM 6120.01D,* Joint Multi-Tactical Data Link (TDL) Operating Procedures, *for full details regarding the JICO and JDN and TDL operations.*

(c) Navy interface control officer for IAMD located at the MOC (with JFMCC or CTF IAMD) also requires connectivity to the primary TDLs as both a redundant capability to the JAOC JICO and in support of C2 of multi-mission Navy IAMD forces or as a RADC/SADC.

16. Situational Awareness

> *"When we started our deployment, we had only the most rudimentary communications infrastructure in Southwest Asia and the challenge of distance was daunting. Thanks to good planning and our understanding of the importance of satellites, we quickly and smoothly transitioned to a mature tactical theater network."*
>
> **General Colin L. Powell, United States Army,**
> **Chairman of the Joint Chiefs of Staff**
> **December 1990**

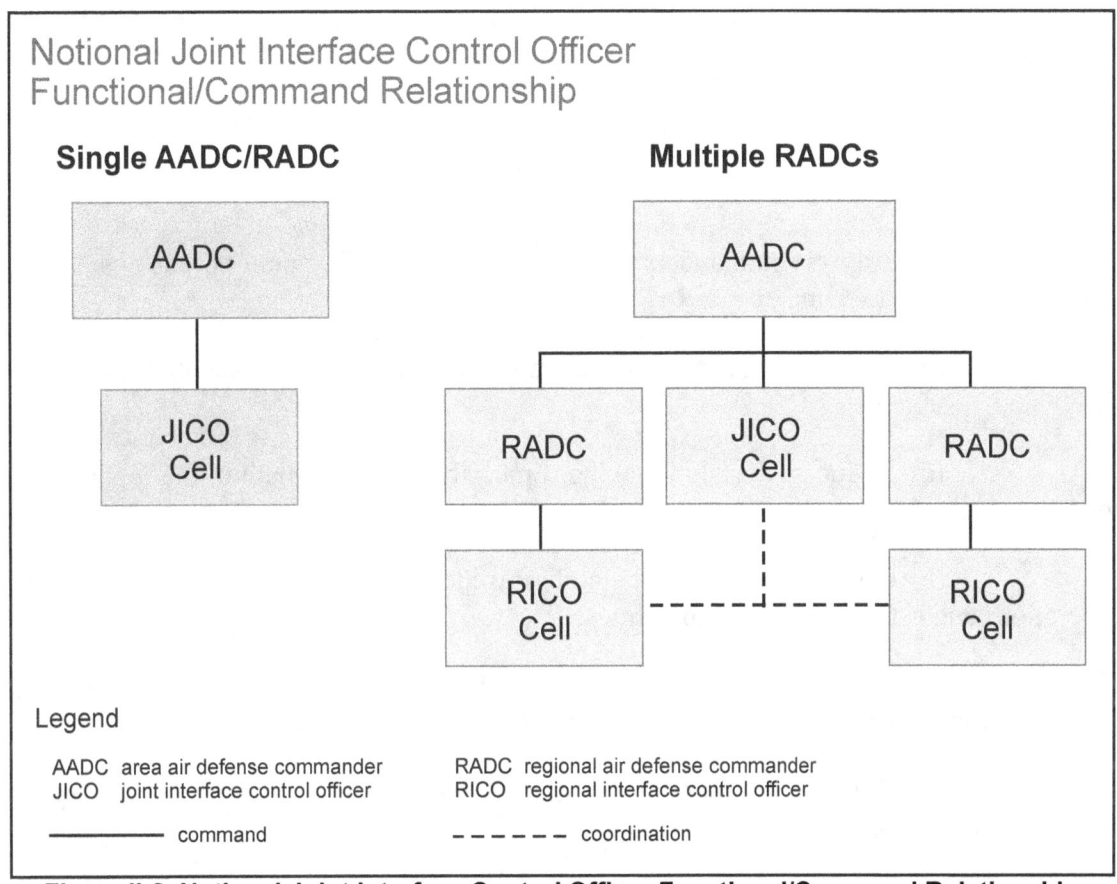

Figure II-2. Notional Joint Interface Control Officer Functional/Command Relationship

a. A primary objective the staff seeks to attain for the commander and for subordinate commanders is **situational awareness, a prerequisite for commanders to understand and anticipate counterair opportunities and challenges.** In simplest terms, this results in the ability "to see first, understand first, and act first" across the full range of military operations. Therefore, supporting situational awareness at this level dictates technical integration of joint data and communications systems for the MTN. True understanding should be the basis for information provided to commanders in order to make decisions. Knowledge of friendly capabilities and enemy capabilities, intentions, and likely COAs enables commanders to focus joint counterair efforts where they best and most directly contribute to achieving air superiority objectives. Further, the JFC's situational awareness must be broad to include the relevant actions and intentions of MNF partners, civilian agencies, adjacent commands, higher headquarters, and HN authorities.

b. The CCDR uses the COP and CTP for theater situational awareness. A subordinate JFC uses the COP and CTP as graphic depictions of the situation within the theater/JOA. There may be multiple CTP inputs to the COP. The COP and CTP normally indicate position location information of significant friendly, neutral, unknown, and enemy forces. The COP and CTP are normally shared with the component commands. The COP is at best NRT. Currently, the COP is the picture provided in the GCCS, supplemented by Command and Control Battle Management and Communications System-provided BMD situation awareness at key locations. A COP facilitates collaborative counterair planning and assists all echelons to achieve situational awareness. A theater JFACC may have the COP at the JAOC.

(1) For counterair situational awareness, a properly managed CTP:

(a) Reduces the degree of operational uncertainty.

(b) Allows commanders to create and control the dynamics of the operational area and not react to them.

(c) Gives commanders more situational awareness of the operational tempo of MNF and US forces.

(d) Reduces decision-making time, thereby dominating the opponent's decision cycle.

(e) Gives commanders the ability to identify, focus, and control counterair operations against the enemy's capabilities.

(f) Allows the commander to monitor the execution phase of counterair operations and assess how well the operations are progressing in accordance with the plan.

(g) Provides commanders with shared situational awareness to coordinate joint counterair operations.

(2) An accurate CTP requires proper track management that is the responsibility of the GCC or a designated representative, typically one of the component commanders (e.g., JFACC). For a subordinate joint force, track managers are assigned at the headquarters and component commands who are responsible for their reporting and database management. Track information from the components is consolidated in the CTP utilizing data link interfaces.

(3) The data link interfaces used for consolidating the track information for CTP are the responsibility of the JICO who subsequently works with the JFACC's CJE for air/space track data and JFMCC's CJE for maritime track data and subsequent data inputs to the JFC's CTP/COP. The JICO and the JICO cell normally reside at the JAOC to manage all theater/JOA data link interfaces. There may be Service component interface control officers located at the JICO cell, or at their respective Service headquarters, and there may be subordinate interface control officers designated at regional/sector AD commands to manage links for the RADC/SADC who report counterair related tracks up to the JAOC. When designated as a RADC, CTF IAMD requires access to voice, data, and chat circuits required for DCA coordination and execution across the joint force and with multinational partners. TDL access should include all available frequencies and networks. To ensure quality of service and assured C2 connectivity, CTF IAMD requires the ability to manage fleet or joint TDL network access, to include redundant and alternate communication paths, and support disadvantaged end users. Due to the nature of force orders and real-time data coordination, TDL capability must be verified to be reliable and validated for tactical operation.

(4) To provide effective support to the JFACC's JICO, Service component interface control officers, and in the case of the Navy, the maritime RICO normally located at the MOC, are tasked with providing persistent monitoring and management of maritime MTN health and participant status, and verification of operational adherence to communications planning and execution documents such as the operations task link (OPTASKLINK) message.

c. Additional counterair situational awareness is provided by the theater joint intelligence operations center by processing information from surveillance and reconnaissance sensors for display on various mediums, including on the COP.

d. At the tactical level, the CTP is a source of situational awareness. The CTP is a current depiction of the operational environment in the JOA within the GCC's AOR. The CTP is an accurate and complete display of relevant tactical data that integrates tactical information from the MTN, composite tracking network, intelligence network, and ground digital network. The CTP enables C2, situational awareness, and CID. It supports the tactical elements of all joint mission areas, to include counterair operations and supports the development of the COP.

17. Battle Management

a. **Battle management** is the management of activities within the operational environment based on the commands, direction, and guidance given by appropriate authority. C2, including battle management, is the binding element that integrates capabilities and operations within and among joint force commands.

b. Battle management entails visualizing where, when, and with which forces to apply capabilities against specific threats. The dynamics of the counterair mission often require flexibility during decentralized execution that normally takes place at the tactical level. This flexibility accomplished through battle management allows the direct, often real-time monitoring and execution of operations based on the intent and within the scope of the operational-level commander's orders. Some counterair examples: AWACS aircraft, with an air battle manager, may provide battle management of an OCA multistage attack against TSTs using Tomahawk land attack missiles (TLAM) and aircraft; an AWACS assisting the air-to-air interception of enemy fighter-bombers beyond visual range (BVR); or the SADC (at a CRC) using battle management of friendly fighters and SAMs to defend assets in the sector against an air attack by enemy aircraft and CMs.

c. Successful counterair battle management supports synchronization and integration of active and passive AD efforts with other air operations, supporting unity of effort and reducing the expenditure of resources and the risks of fratricide. For subordinate commanders and controllers, **effective battle management requires situational awareness, managing available resources, directing and controlling the correct action in a timely manner, and monitoring and assessing the execution.**

d. Based on the principles of centralized planning and direction and decentralized execution, the JFC typically delegates commit, ID, and engagement authority to the

JFACC/AADC and authorizes further delegation to the optimum level for mission accomplishment consistent with the ROE. The responsibilities and authorities assigned to battle managers should be clear and unambiguous, and may be limited in time, scope, or by specific operations/activities.

e. Automated battle management aids can assist operators in sensor management and weapons pairings, allowing operators to manage by exception. The speed of the engagement process and the complexity of sensor-weapons performances and integration may require some degree of automation to assist in effective intercepts. Automated systems are not infallible, and weapons systems operators must maintain situational awareness and exercise sound judgment in accordance with ROE to prevent fratricide.

CHAPTER III
COUNTERAIR PLANNING

"If you know the enemy and know yourself, you need not fear the result of a hundred battles."

Sun Tzu, *The Art of War*

1. General

a. The JFC develops an operation/campaign plan focused on the enemy centers of gravity (COGs) while ensuring that friendly COGs are protected. Counterair operations strive for the degree of air superiority and protection required by the JFC's COA to attain the desired objectives.

b. Counterair requires a combination of OCA and DCA operations based on the JFC's air apportionment decisions and balanced against the enemy's potential COAs and air and missile threats. The integration and synchronization of OCA and DCA, in conjunction with the other joint missions supporting the JFC, are the basis for counterair planning.

c. This chapter discusses counterair planning in the context of preparation, major considerations, and enabling capabilities that support both OCA and DCA. This discussion assumes a JFACC is responsible for counterair (specifically OCA operations) and an AADC is responsible for DCA operations, whether or not the JFACC is designated as both the AADC and ACA. The joint air operations plan (JAOP) and the AADP, as well as other detailed planning factors, will be discussed in the respective chapters for OCA and DCA.

d. Counterair planning considerations include accurate joint intelligence preparation of the operational environment (JIPOE) and intelligence preparation of the battlespace (IPB), airspace control, ROE, ID and CID requirements, and some major enabling capabilities.

e. GBMD planning complements coordination of cross-AOR aspects of counterair operations. This process enhances a GCC's ability to employ forces and capabilities within their AOR in support of another GCC. Planners must balance competing requirements for potentially scarce resources. GBMD planning tools assist planners in both preparing and validating defense designs. See Appendix E, "Global Ballistic Missile Defense Synchronization."

SECTION A. INTELLIGENCE PREPARATION

2. General

Knowledge of the potential enemy is one of the fundamentals of joint warfare. JIPOE and IPB are the analytical processes and methodologies employed by joint commands and Services to produce intelligence assessments, estimates, and other intelligence products to support the commander's decision making. JIPOE and IPB generally differ in terms of their relative purpose, focus, and level of detail. JIPOE is focused at the JFC level, while IPB is focused at the joint force component command and Service level. To support the decision-making process, the JIPOE effort also must remain dynamic, constantly integrating new information into the initial set of facts and assumptions. The JIPOE effort must be fully integrated and coordinated with the separate IPB efforts of the component commands and Service intelligence centers. JIPOE and IPB should begin as early as possible during the planning process, preferably during peacetime.

3. Joint Intelligence Preparation of the Operational Environment and Intelligence Preparation of the Battlespace

a. JIPOE is described as the continuous, analytical process used by joint intelligence organizations to produce intelligence assessments, estimates, and other intelligence products to support the JFC's decision-making process and all joint force planning. The JIPOE process assists JFCs and their staffs in achieving information superiority by providing predictive intelligence and focusing intelligence collection at the right time and place. JIPOE helps the JFC to react faster and make better decisions than the adversary, or simply stated, to stay inside the enemy's decision-making cycle. JIPOE provides the basis for intelligence direction, collection management, and synchronization that supports not only the COA selected by the JFC, but all joint force planning. JIPOE supports counterair planning by identifying adversary air and missile capabilities and their likely employment. JIPOE products are used by JFC and component staffs in preparing their estimates and analysis, selection of friendly COAs, and continuing planning requirements (e.g., development of a viable CONOPS.) The process for JIPOE involves four basic steps:

(1) Defining the operational environment.

(2) Describing the impact of the operational environment.

(3) Evaluating the adversary.

(4) Determining adversary COAs, particularly the adversary's most likely COA and the COA most dangerous to friendly forces and mission accomplishment. During analysis of the adversary's potential COAs, consideration must be given to the escalation potential when attacking adversary's C2 and other strategic systems.

b. JIPOE and IPB products generally differ in terms of their relative purpose, focus, and level of detail. JIPOE supports the JFC by using a macro-analytic approach to identify an adversary's strategic vulnerabilities and COGs, whereas IPB requires micro-analysis to support an operational level component command. JIPOE and IPB analyses are intended to support each other while avoiding a duplication of analytic effort.

c. The components' IPB focuses on the adversary's forces and operations necessary to accomplish the most likely and most dangerous COAs identified by JIPOE. Certain factors of operation planning are particularly important when conducting the IPB process, and failure to properly consider an adversary's most likely and most dangerous COAs can have serious consequences. This is a focal point of OCA/DCA integration, and procedures must be developed to rapidly share data between OCA and DCA forces.

d. IPB assists the counterair planner in visualizing the operational environment, assessing adversary air and missile capabilities, and identifying the adversary's probable intent and attack locations. IPB is not simply enumeration of adversary air and missile systems, but must describe how the adversary air and missile forces operate.

e. JIPOE/IPB for counterair relates to any information about adversary air and missile threats and supporting infrastructure, including information on enemy ADs, C2 networks, radar coverage, and other early warning/detection systems, etc. JIPOE/IPB will provide available information on the following:

(1) Location, status, and disposition of WMD and the capabilities for employing them.

(2) Aircraft operating bases and dispersal sites, to include aircraft carriers and other air capable ships.

(3) Missile target systems, including their infrastructure, storage and operating locations, launch platforms, C2 nodes, missile stocks, forward operating locations/bases (FOLs/FOBs), transload sites, reloading/refueling sites, terrain and road infrastructure (bridges, tunnels) where their destruction could interrupt enemy missile operations and logistics. For example, intelligence will identify BM operating areas where an adversary's missile C2, infrastructure, and forces may operate.

(4) Order of battle of adversary IADS (i.e., aircraft, SAMs, airfields, and antiaircraft artillery [AAA]), including C2 systems (i.e., early warning/ground control intercept [GCI] sites and facilities), communication links, and any associated facilities.

(5) Signals intelligence capabilities and EW assets, including operating instructions, vulnerabilities, redundancies, capabilities, and locations.

(6) Changes by adversary in direct and indirect threat emitters, including wartime reserve modes and reprogramming of target sensing weapon systems.

(7) Climate and terrain within the JOA and their effects on friendly and enemy operations.

(8) Overall assessment of the strengths and vulnerabilities of adversary offensive and defensive air systems, including location and status of all key nodes and targets that affect their ability to sustain air operations.

(9) Analysis of adversary's potential escalation COAs if their leadership, national C2, and other strategic systems are attacked.

(10) Adversary preparations, including camouflage, concealment, and deception; movement of noncombatants and civilians; ID of no-strike sites; indications of hidden enemy capabilities; etc.

Details regarding the JIPOE and IPB processes can be found in JP 2-01.3, Joint Intelligence Preparation of the Operational Environment.

SECTION B. AIRSPACE CONTROL CONSIDERATIONS

4. General

a. The primary goal of joint airspace control is to enhance combat effectiveness of the joint force. Airspace control should maximize the effectiveness of combat operations without adding undue restrictions and with minimal adverse impact on the capabilities of any Service/functional component. For counterair, all components of the joint force may potentially share a part of the theater/JOA airspace for offensive/defensive operations. This environment becomes increasingly complex with the addition of civilian, nongovernmental and intergovernmental organizations, interagency, HN, and MNF users. Airspace control procedures and planning considerations must allow for a transition from peacetime operations to combat operations and back to peacetime operations.

b. Airspace control is provided to reduce the risk of friendly fire, enhance AD operations, and permit greater flexibility of operations. Although airspace control is the responsibility of the ACA, the controlling authority of the ACA does not infringe on the command authorities vested in commanders to approve, disapprove, or deny combat operations. The ACA recommends and the JFC approves the boundaries within which airspace control is exercised and provides priorities and restrictions regarding its use. **Airspace control requires positive and procedural controls.**

(1) Positive control is a method of airspace control that relies on positive ID, tracking, and direction of aircraft within an airspace and is conducted with electronic means by an agency having the authority and responsibility therein.

(2) Procedural control is the method of airspace control that relies on a combination of previously agreed and promulgated orders and procedures.

c. **Airspace Control System.** The ACA establishes an ACS that is responsive to the needs of the JFC and integrates when appropriate the ACS with that of the HN. The ACS is an arrangement of those organizations, personnel, policies, procedures, and facilities required to perform airspace control functions. Airspace control should be executed through a responsive theater/tactical air control system capable of real-time control that includes surface and airborne assets, as necessary (e.g., CRC and AWACS). The ACS requires timely exchange of information through reliable, secure, and interoperable communications networks. Elements of the ACS may have dual roles as DCA assets (e.g., a CRC can be a RADC/SADC).

d. **Airspace Control Plan.** Beginning with an ACP approved by the JFC, the ACA develops broad policies and procedures for airspace control and for the coordination required among units within the theater/JOA. **The ACP establishes the procedures for the ACS in the operational area.** The ACP must consider procedures and interfaces with the international or regional air traffic systems because the ACP is designed to identify all airspace users, facilitate the engagement of hostile air and missile threats, and expedite the safe passage of friendly and neutral forces.

e. **Airspace Control Orders.** Implementation of the general guidance of the ACP is accomplished through ACOs that provide specific airspace control procedures applicable for defined periods of time. ACOs are designed to deconflict and identify all airspace users as well as eliminate fratricide. **The ACO is an order that provides the details of the approved requests for ACMs.** It is published either as part of the ATO or as a separate document and must be adhered to by all components. It defines and establishes airspace for military operations. It notifies all agencies of the effective time of activation and the composite structure of the airspace to be used. The ACO may include ACMs, such as air routes, base defense zones, drop zones, pickup points, restricted areas, etc., and fire support coordination measures (FSCMs), such as the fire support coordination line (FSCL), no-fire areas, and restrictive fire areas. A change to the ACO should be distributed whenever a new area is established or an existing area deleted or modified.

f. **Airspace Coordinating Measures.** ACMs are designed to facilitate the efficient use of airspace to accomplish missions and simultaneously provide safeguards for friendly forces. ACMs may take several forms and will be discussed in paragraph 6.

g. **Integration of the ACP with the AADP.** The ACP facilitates synchronization and deconfliction of joint operations. Prioritization of airspace users for deconfliction/synchronization is essential. The ACP must be integrated with the AADP because airspace control areas/sectors normally coincide with AD areas/sectors, and there are DCA operations and procedures that could interfere with other airspace control procedures. **Both plans should complement available C2 systems and capabilities.** JFC-approved ACMs help integrate the two plans. Airspace control must be flexible enough to meet rapid changes such as the real-time retasking of OCA forces against TSTs.

5. Planning and Coordination Requirements

a. **Planning for Airspace Control in the Combat Zone.** Every JTF is different and each operational area has specific operational requirements for airspace. These requirements must be determined as early as possible and incorporated in the overall joint force planning effort. Political constraints and national and military airspace management systems and procedures and their capabilities and limitations are important considerations. ROE, disposition of AD weapons, fire support plans, and procedures for ID of US and MNF aircraft are also important items to consider. **The following broad principles of planning** (see Figure III-1) **are essential for effective airspace control:**

(1) **Interoperability.** Plans for airspace control should be exercised in the joint and multinational environments during peacetime and in conflict. Planning should strive to maximize the interoperability of equipment, personnel, and terminology and facilitate continuous, detailed coordination. **The ACS must function with the AMD families of systems and may include dual tasking of certain radar, sensor, and C2 assets.** Interoperability is essential to effective operations, conservation of force, and to prevent fratricide.

Principles for Planning Airspace Control

- Interoperability
- Unity of effort
- Mass and timing
- Integrated planning cycles
- Degraded operations

Figure III-1. Principles for Planning Airspace Control

(2) **Unity of Effort.** The ACS must be integrated and coordinated with the AMD system, including dual tasking of assets as necessary. Integration of an HN AD system (as part of an IADS) and air traffic control (ATC) system should be properly planned. Proper liaison is essential and should be identified and exercised prior to hostilities when integrating HN and joint force airspace control.

(3) **Mass and Timing.** Planning should consider the aircraft traffic volume and timing to fully integrate DCA with OCA and other joint missions. Constraints may require changes in positive or procedural control measures.

(4) **Integrated Planning Cycles.** The airspace control planning cycle must be integrated with the joint operation/campaign planning cycle, and more specifically, the AADP planning cycle. The ACP normally is added as an appendix to the operations annex of the joint OPLAN or operation order.

(5) **Degraded Operations.** The ACP must anticipate degraded operations of airspace control and AD systems as the results of attacks (combat losses) and enemy EW efforts. Loss of communications can dramatically degrade positive control measures. Effective plans should span the spectrum from minimal to full degradation and consider the effects of adverse weather and night operations.

Refer to JP 3-52, Joint Airspace Control, *for detailed information regarding airspace control, the ACP, and the ACO.*

b. Military ATC facilities and radar control units (e.g., Marine TAOC, or Air Force CRC) normally will provide flight following and monitoring throughout the airspace control area. If an HN ATC system is used before hostilities, then procedures must be in place to revert to the military system when required. The urgent exchange of information between the ATC facilities, radar control units, and airspace users requires reliable voice and data nets; radars; identification, friend or foe (IFF); and selective ID features. **Accurate and timely ID enhances engagement of enemy aircraft and missiles, conserves friendly resources, and reduces risk to friendly forces.**

c. Key factors to consider when developing the ACP are as follows:

(1) The ACP should be coordinated with the HN and any partner nations if it includes their airspace or their systems.

(2) When developing the ACP, combine familiarity with the basic OPLAN or operation order, knowledge of host and multinational constraints and restraints, capabilities and procedures of HN civil and military airspace management systems, and general locations of friendly and enemy forces.

(3) The ACP needs to support an orderly transition between peacetime and combat operations. Such a transition could occur during a period of increasing tensions or suddenly without warning.

(4) The ACP specifies ACMs to be used in the operational area and how these measures will be distributed and implemented. The ACP should provide guidance on what FSCMs will be placed on the ACO. The ACP also should provide guidance on component-unique ACMs, terms, or graphics that may be included in the ACO.

(5) The ACP provides procedures to fully integrate the resources of military ATC facilities responsible for terminal area airspace control or en route ATC. ATC facilities should be interfaced and linked with ACS communications to form a system that ensures the safe and efficient flow of air traffic.

(6) The ACP should include processes for establishing procedural ACMs, including activating/deactivating weapon engagement zones (WEZs) and minimum-risk routes (MRRs) and procedures for AD and air control operations in a degraded communications environment. Detailed engagement procedures and decentralized weapons control procedures (as applied to AD) are key to counterair operations in a degraded environment. The geographic placement of weapons, the location of specific AD operations, and specific procedures for ID of aircraft and missiles are critical factors to include in the ACP.

(7) The ACP and AADP must be distributed to all joint force components, applicable HN, MNF, and interagency partners, as well as those commands providing direct delivery (intertheater) and/or intratheater support to the theater/JOA. **Not understanding or following the ACP and AADP may result in hazardous air traffic situations, cause confusion between aircraft and control agencies, and increase the risk of fratricide.**

d. Some specific counterair requirements that must be accounted for in the ACP or through ACMs include:

(1) General orbit locations for DCA combat air patrols (CAPs), airborne warning and control, C2, surveillance, reconnaissance, air refueling (AR), and EW platforms.

(2) Coordinating authorities for controlled airspace and their responsibilities and coverage areas, including the RADCs/SADCs and other C2 nodes.

(3) WEZs and their activation procedures.

(4) Procedures for positive and procedural airspace controls.

(5) Positive ID and procedural ID criteria and procedures.

(6) Procedures to expeditiously route outbound OCA packages through friendly airspace. This will become more complex in a multinational environment.

(7) Develop airspace control procedures for OCA missions including the communications conduits (e.g., airborne C2 or satellite communications) for missions that may occur beyond the visual/communications range of ground-based C2 agencies.

(8) Locations and procedures for MRRs, for turning on/off IFF equipment, air defense ID, and areas for sanitizing returning OCA packages from enemy aircraft.

(9) Procedures to support planned responses for AD emergencies.

(10) Procedures to support immediate attacks on TSTs by aircraft or long-range surface fires such as SSMs, rockets, and CMs.

(11) Identify airspace control tasks for airborne elements of the TACS (e.g., AWACS). The sensor capability of airborne platforms makes them well suited for providing airspace control for real-time execution of OCA and DCA operations.

(12) Procedures to recover aircraft unable to self-identify and unmanned aircraft systems (UASs) recovering autonomously.

(13) Identify potential ACMs and FSCMs that allow aircraft and surface fires to simultaneously engage ground targets in support of the land forces—the aircraft being above the airspace required for supporting surface fires.

(14) Identify potential ACMs to minimize hazards to aircraft from outbound long-range interceptors transiting to MEZs/joint engagement zones (JEZs).

6. Airspace Coordinating Measures

a. ACMs are employed to facilitate the efficient use of airspace to accomplish missions and simultaneously provide safeguards for friendly forces. Airspace control requires a combination of positive and procedural controls that rely on proper ID of the users. ID is discussed in Section D, "Identification." Positive control requires radar or other sensor tracking and direct communications between the airspace controller and the user. Procedural controls are established through ACMs.

b. ACMs not established in the ACP are normally forwarded through a component command's senior airspace control element to the ACA for processing and approval. Approved ACMs are normally promulgated through ACOs and, when necessary, in the ATO. Some ACMs are planned, requested, and approved, but not promulgated or activated until required.

c. **For standardization, more than a hundred ACMs have been categorized and defined/described with applicable uses and planning considerations.** Those ACMs have been grouped in the following categories: AD areas, AD operations areas, ATC, air corridors/routes, procedural controls, reference points, restricted operations zones, and special use airspace.

d. A good example of the use of ACMs for integrating procedural airspace control with DCA operations is the WEZ. In AD, a WEZ is airspace of defined dimensions within which the responsibility for engagement of air threats normally rests with a particular weapons system. WEZs include fighter engagement zone (FEZ), high-altitude missile engagement zone (HIMEZ), low-altitude missile engagement zone (LOMEZ), and short-range AD engagement zone (SHORADEZ), each of which is established by an ACM. WEZs are discussed in more detail in Chapter V, "Defensive Counterair Planning and Operations."

Refer to JP 3-52, Joint Airspace Control, *for more details regarding ACMs, including a representative airspace control request format for a procedural ACM, and for the list of the most common ACMs.*

7. Other Considerations

a. Maritime strike groups are not static; they are usually a "moving JEZ." In a littoral environment, an amphibious operations area may encompass a sector of a land AO and include a MEZ. In this case, maritime combatants may be restricted by geography when defending selected coastal assets. **Linking land-based SAM systems with search and fire control data from maritime forces, or vice versa, can result in improved ability to defend littoral areas of the theater.** Without that kind of close coordination between land and maritime air defenders, a seam may be found in the AMDs.

b. Operations along the edges of WEZs, sectors, or other geographically defined areas of airspace with separate controlling units/commands may create seams and present commanders with extensive coordination challenges. Enemy aircraft may cross into adjacent sectors during engagement or may fly through friendly corridors or attack targets in one sector or WEZ from an adjacent area. The following are some considerations that may facilitate coordination:

(1) Establish procedures to coordinate handoffs of flight operations between sectors and regions that grant permissions to enter and depart airspace and coordinate combat zone control activities with HN ATC services. A dedicated communications network/line for the regions/sectors is a must if real-time handoffs are required.

(2) Liaison officers should be located at ATC centers that provide positive control for areas overlapping or adjacent to AD areas.

(3) Designate buffer zones in which one AD region/sector can authorize engagement in an adjacent area.

(4) Whenever possible, establish friendly air corridors outside the ranges of friendly AD forces that rely only on visual ID to reduce the risk of fratricide, since visually aimed surface weapons often have no capability to readily identify airspace boundaries or control measures in their portion of the operational environment. The ACA and AADC must collectively plan to address the issue.

c. During forcible entry operations or in undeveloped theaters, C2 should be simple and facilitate the joint force's ability to respond to a given threat. **The ACP must be continuously assessed through feedback from commanders to ensure it adequately supports operational requirements in a potentially dynamic operational environment.** The initial architectures may need to be modified based on the situation and/or additional assets arriving into the operational area.

SECTION C. RULES OF ENGAGEMENT

8. General

ROE are directives issued by a competent military authority that delineate the circumstances and limitations under which US forces will initiate and/or continue combat engagement with other forces encountered. Standing ROE, including rules on the inherent right of self-defense and supplemental measures for mission accomplishment, as approved by SecDef, are found in Chairman of the Joint Chiefs of Staff Instruction (CJCSI) 3121.01, *Standing Rules of Engagement/Standing Rules for the Use of Force for US Forces.* Approved ROE for mission accomplishment, applicable to a specific mission, are typically found in the mission's respective warning order, execute orders, operations order/plan, ROE serials, and/or special instructions (SPINS) section of the ATO.

a. With SecDef approval, CCDRs may augment the standing rules of engagement (SROE)/standing rules for the use of force (SRUF) with theater-specific ROE and with supplemental instructions. The JFC and commanders at every echelon are responsible for establishing/implementing ROE, but their ROE cannot be less restrictive than that approved for a superior commander.

b. The JFC implements the approved SROE/SRUF/theater ROE and may request more specific ROE for the JOA/mission. The JFC normally requests inputs from subordinate commanders when developing the ROE. To prevent violations or misunderstandings, ROE should be clear, concise, and unambiguous. The JFACC/AADC should offer ROE recommendations to the JFC in anticipation of the need, or when requested to do so. In conjunction with ROE recommendations, engagement authority and its delegation and other authorities must be considered and may be part of the ROE. MNF operations may further complicate processes for establishing and executing ROE. **The key is to anticipate the requirement so the changes may be staffed and approved at the appropriate level for implementation when needed at a specific time or for a special circumstance.** When planning counterair operations, the component commanders must ensure they comply with the established ROE for the theater/JOA that may include special (and somewhat different) ROE for separate operations. ROE can limit or restrict certain options, targets, and methods. For example, the air ROE may restrict firing of air-to-air weapons if the target is BVR or across an international boundary. ROE are promulgated through command channels by numerous means and normally can be found in the SPINS section of the ATO. **Commanders must not only promulgate ROE to the joint force, but must also train the joint force on the ROE.**

c. For MNF operations, nations may have specific ROE that cannot be changed or overruled by alliance or coalition chains of command. These national procedures must be identified, published, and understood by all other nations and command echelons within the MNF.

9. Criteria

a. **Obligation and Responsibility for Defense.** Unit commanders always retain the inherent right and obligation to exercise unit self-defense in response to a hostile act or a demonstrated hostile intent. Self-defense includes defense of other US military forces in the vicinity, as well as defense of any others identified in the mission-specific ROE. The commanders of all US forces must ensure that the ROE as established do not place constraints on a unit's ability to defend itself. Upon commission of a hostile act or demonstration of hostile intent, all necessary means available and all appropriate actions may be used in self-defense. If time and circumstances permit, forces should attempt to deescalate the situation. In addition, force used in self-defense should be proportional; that is, sufficient to respond decisively. Force used may exceed that of the hostile act or hostile intent, but the nature, duration, and scope of force should not exceed what is required to respond decisively.

b. **Functional Rules.** Commanders should also develop functional rules as to how ROE are to be tactically implemented. Some examples are **arming orders,** which specify circumstances under which commanders will permit loading or arming of munitions and **border crossing authority (BCA).** National borders are sovereign and cannot be crossed without specific authorization. Permission to violate borders may be pre-delegated to the JFC after hostilities or under specific conditions or restrictions to enable force protection. BCA also applies to aerial reconnaissance. Space platforms are not restricted as the United States adheres to a policy of freedom of navigation in space based on treaty and customary international law.

c. **Integration with the ACP and AADP.** The ROE are an integral part of the AADP and the ACP. Commanders and their staffs must ensure that the AADP contains specific instructions that implement the ROE. It is an important point to ensure the ACP, AADP, and the ROE are consistent with regard to aircraft in international air corridors. These corridors are usable by civilian aircraft, even those operated by an adversary, until the international governing body or an appropriate authority closes a route and a notice to airmen is issued. Commanders must ensure the proper response is made when penetrations of the friendly airspace occur under the auspices of international air flight.

10. Planning

a. Normally, the initial ROE are already established by higher authority or an existing plan. The JFC is responsible for implementing the ROE and anticipating changes to ROE based on operational necessity such as changing phases of an operation. The ROE are an integral part of the operations planning process, and the J-3 is responsible for their integration for the JFC. Centrally planned ROE, ID, and engagement procedures are vital for minimizing duplication of effort and the potential for fratricide/friendly fire while providing necessary flexibility to engage.

b. The current SROE recognizes a fundamental difference between the two sets of supplemental measures. Measures that are reserved to the President, SecDef, or CCDRs are generally **permissive;** that is, the particular operation, tactic, or weapon is generally restricted, and the President, SecDef, or CCDR approves the supplemental measure to specifically permit the particular operation, tactic, or weapon. In contrast, the remainder of the supplemental ROE measures (i.e., those delegated to subordinate commanders) are all **restrictive** in nature. Absent implementation of supplemental measures, commanders are generally allowed to use any weapon or tactic available and to employ reasonable force to accomplish the mission, without having to get permission first. Only when enacted will these supplemental ROE measures restrict a particular operation, tactic, or weapon.

c. ROE may be permissive or restrictive, depending on the circumstances. For example, ROE may allow use of BVR weapons to engage hostile targets as early as possible. Permissive ROE would entail instructions directing decentralized execution by the joint force to immediately engage any incoming BMs. However, that same ROE may restrict retaliatory or preemptive attacks against the launcher that may result in its destruction but permit the use of nonlethal capabilities that disable or neutralize the launch system. JFCs may elect to include any category of CM or antiship missiles for accelerated engagement as the situation warrants.

d. When developing their ROE recommendations, commanders and staffs must coordinate with their staff judge advocates (SJAs) for compliance with US and customary international law, as well as treaties and conventions to which the US is a signatory. Once the ROE are approved, commanders, assisted by their SJAs, are responsible for promulgating the ROE and ensuring that all subordinate forces understand the ROE. Commanders must also maintain close coordination with the public affairs office to ensure their awareness of any command or strategic messaging considerations.

e. Lower echelon MNFCs and local HN commanders may lack the authority to speak on behalf of their nations in the ROE development process. Complete consensus or standardization of ROE should be sought, but obtaining concurrence for ROE from other national authorities can be a time-consuming process.

f. US forces participating in MNF operations will follow the ROE established by the MNFC if authorized by SecDef. US forces will be under the control of an MNFC only if SecDef determines that the ROE for that MNF are consistent with the policy guidance on unit self-defense and with the rules of individual self-defense contained in the SROE/SRUF. If the MNFC has not issued ROE, US forces will operate under the SROE/SRUF.

SECTION D. IDENTIFICATION

11. General

a. ID is the process of determining the friendly or hostile character of an unknown detected contact and the product (classification) of that process. Assigning ID requires ID authority and criteria. ID authority is the authority to assign an identity classification to an unknown contact, if possible. This authority is inherent within the C2 chain. The JFC normally delegates ID authority to JFACC/AADC and authorizes further delegation to subordinate commanders for decentralized execution as allowed by ROE and necessitated by the operational situation. ID authority and ID criteria should be stated and discussed in the AADP and ACP for approval by the JFC. **Both ID authority and criteria may require modification, sometimes in conjunction with ROE, in a dynamic operational environment and/or with changes in phases of the campaign.**

b. ID is an essential and inseparable part of airspace control and AD operations. Comprehensive surveillance and accurate and persistent tracking combined with accurate, timely, and consistent ID enhances situational awareness, improves weapons employment options, helps conserve friendly resources, and reduces the risk of fratricide.

c. The CID process complements the ID process to support application of weapons resources and other military options. For counterair, CID should be accomplished with NRT or better exchange of information between airspace control/AD units and airspace users to meet the time and accuracy demands of combat operations. CID is discussed separately in paragraph 14, "Combat Identification."

12. Methods of Identification

a. For the purposes of counterair, the intent of an ID process is to either facilitate airspace control or to support an engagement decision through CID. The objective of CID is to obtain the highest confidence, positive ID possible. Lacking positive ID, the objective is to reach the level of confidence in an ID that can be supported by the ROE for an engagement authority to make a decision. ID can be accomplished through several recognized methods. The JFC approves the procedures used for ID and designates who may be delegated that authority in the AADP and ACP.

b. **Positive ID.** Positive ID is ID derived from visual recognition, electronic support systems, noncooperative target recognition techniques, IFF systems, or other physics-based ID techniques. Positive ID does not assume identity solely based on location or adherence to airspace procedures. To prevent fratricide or undesired engagements, positive ID normally is required by ROE as a basis for CID for engagement (shoot/no-shoot) decisions for air threats. Normally, a positive ID means much more than a simple "lack of friend" or "lack of enemy" level of accuracy. The degree of accuracy of a positive ID method is specific to that method and should remain a constant, whereas CID criteria can be changed by the JFC based on ROE. Positive ID ACMs should be established in the AADP and ACP and can be modified through ACMs promulgated by ACOs and the SPINS.

c. **Procedural ID.** Procedural ID is based on adherence to airspace control measures and rules. ID is assumed to be friendly as long as rules are followed, but ID is assumed hostile if rules are not followed and the suspect vehicle is not otherwise positively identified. Procedural ID separates airspace users by geography, altitude, heading, time, and/or maneuver. Normally, a combination of positive and procedural ID is used to identify friendly and hostile tracks. Procedural ID can be advantageous for some missions and scenarios, but generally not for engagement decisions for which positive ID is normally required because of the risk of fratricide. **The AADP should include a matrix with criteria developed by the AADC in coordination with the components and approved by the JFC that can be used to establish a track ID for a detected object.** The ID matrix is a logic tree for categorizing a track (e.g., friendly, hostile, unknown, or neutral) and following it throughout its life in the AOR/JOA. The ID matrix applies logical steps to ID a track using all available means in the operational area. By following the criteria in the matrix, users assess the identity of an unknown for tracking and additional action, if necessary. If not identified as friendly, an object being tracked may require further assessment based on position, the ROE, and weapons control status (WCS). WCS will be discussed in Chapter V, "Defensive Counterair Planning and Operations," paragraph 11, "Active Air and Missile Defense."

d. **Auto-ID Systems.** Some weapon systems have the capability to execute an auto-ID function (e.g., aircraft carrier auto-ID, Aegis-equipped ships, and PATRIOT missile systems). Use of auto-ID can reduce the workload (no man in the loop) and improve the timeliness of the ID process in an extremely dynamic/saturated AD environment, but it also can result in mistaken ID and fratricide, engagement of noncombatants, or inadvertent protection for the enemy. The CID and ROE criteria for engagement should explicitly discuss when and what types of auto-ID are allowed. Automation should enhance, and not replace, the judgment of operators in a tactical situation and should be used only to keep the operators from being so overwhelmed they become ineffective and cannot make enough knowledgeable decisions.

e. **Formation assessment,** applicable to both friendly and hostile formations, is a procedural ID method used to apply the ID (from positive or procedural means) of one air track to other aircraft operating in mutual support as determined by their spatial relationship. That spatial relationship (horizontal range, altitude separation, speed, and course), called formation criteria, must be determined by the AADC and ACA, approved by the JFC, and published in the AADP and ACP. Formation criteria may vary by theater/JOA. See Figure III-2 for a depiction of that spatial relationship. These formation criteria are a procedural ACM to help manage the volume of tracks (and operator workload) that must be displayed on the joint TDL and elsewhere (e.g., COP). Formation strength information may be handled in various ways by those surveillance elements of the IADS that contribute to the MTN. To declutter the air tracking displays of surveillance systems, a single track is carried with the number of objects meeting the formation criteria entered as a number on the track information associated with the ID symbol. Referred to by various systems as strength/flight size/raid numbers/composition, the process is described as formation tracking. The purpose of formation assessment is to provide timely and accurate track ID to engagement platforms (airborne or surface-based AD assets) to support engagement decisions for hostiles yet minimize the chances of fratricide. The use of formation assessment presumes that a formation track has been established and that an ID has been placed upon the formation track by competent ID authority. Also, the same formation assessment criteria must be applied to the other local tracks (non-TDL tracks) as was used by the surveillance system used to create the formation track to ensure integrity of the process. Failure to use the same specified criteria for formation tracking and formation assessment may mistakenly result in the application of "friend protection" to hostile aircraft or engagement of friendly aircraft by

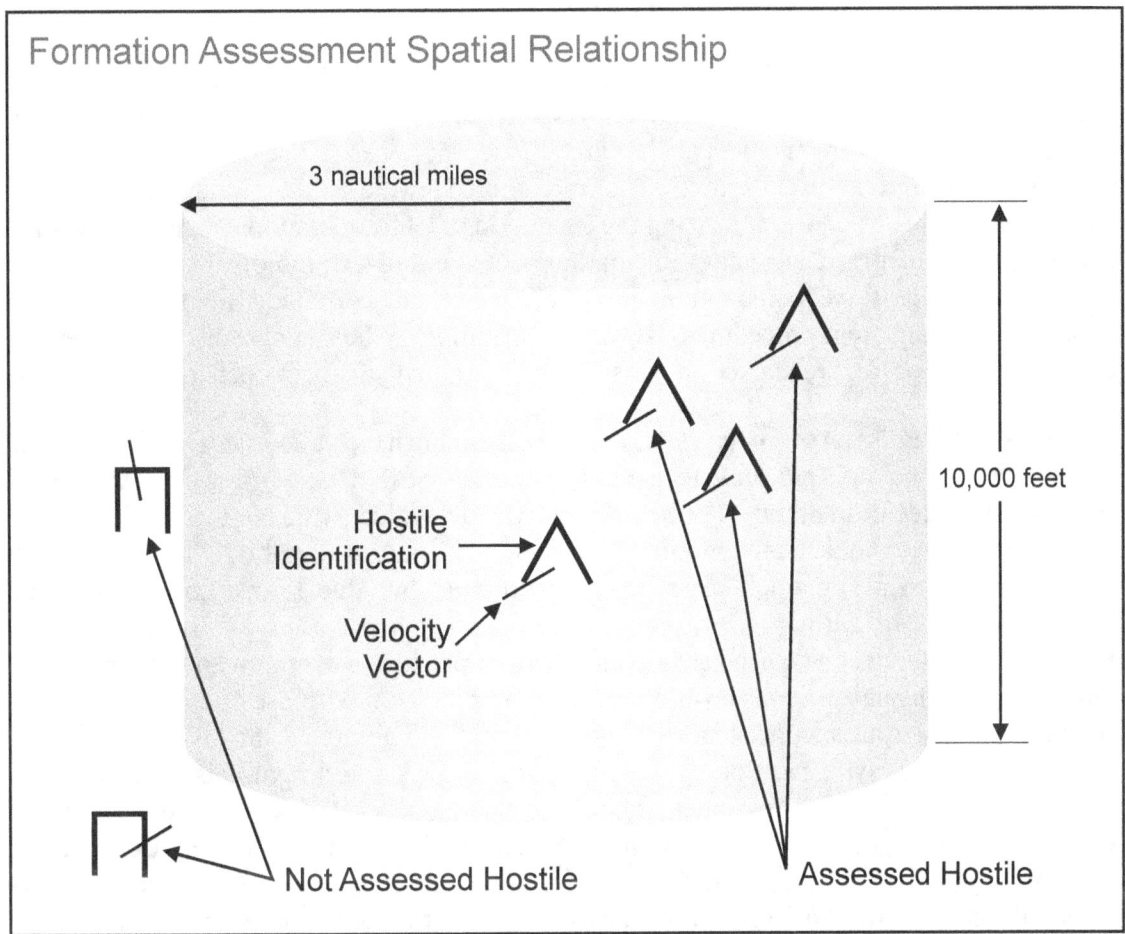

Figure III-2. Formation Assessment Spatial Relationship

friendly weapons platforms. The risk of friendly engagements and friendly protection to hostile aircraft is greater with formation assessment in effect, but to help mitigate this risk, care should be taken in the development of the spatial criteria used for the formation assessment.

f. **Formation Tracking.** Formation tracking is the use of a single data link air track (with a strength field indicating the number or estimated number of aerial vehicles comprising the formation) to represent a formation of two or more aerial vehicles. To qualify for formation tracking, the aircraft in the formation must maintain a consistent relationship with each other (horizontal and vertical separation, speed, and course). Air surveillance systems selectively employ formation tracking when displaying air tracks. Formation tracks are displayed to the operators and transmitted to other air surveillance and AD systems via joint TDL. Formation tracking reduces operator workload, allows older C2 systems to handle larger surveillance responsibilities, and reduces the number of transmitted tracks required to represent the entire air picture.

13. Identification, Commitment, and Engagement Authorities

a. The AADC has certain authorities, delegated by the JFC, that must be understood and may be delegated to subordinate commanders such as a RADC/SADC. The authorities of ID, commitment, and engagement are required for decisions based on established criteria that may be tied to operational capability and are rooted in the ROE. Delegation of those authorities is a means of decentralizing the execution of DCA operations. In joint and MNF operations, subtle differences may exist in the processes and terminology used to authorize the employment of weapons. It is imperative that the command lines, engagement authorities, engagement procedures, ROE, and terminology be standardized, documented, clearly understood, and rehearsed (if possible) before an engagement decision is necessary.

b. **Identification Authority.** The AADC will establish the policy for ID authority, with JFC approval, and will promulgate it via the AADP, SPINS, and/or an OPTASKLINK supplement. Execution of the ID policy normally is delegated to the tactical level, but care must be taken that the tactical commander is capable of performing the ID function in real time. There are seven track classification symbols, but due to varying host-system implementations of Military Standard 6016D, *Tactical Data Link (TDL) 16 Message Standard*, only three can be used across the IADS to produce a common and unambiguous (unique) track display: friend, hostile, and unknown. The next closest unique symbol is "neutral," but there are inconsistencies in how "neutral" is interpreted and displayed by some Service component systems. Some systems implement variations in symbols such that use of "pending," "suspect," and "assumed friend" carry a significant risk of system-to-system variance and will produce an uncommon MTN picture. Proper and consistent execution of the ID policy is extremely important to minimize fratricide and prevent enemy tracks misidentified as friendly/neutral from successfully penetrating the defenses for an attack.

(1) The criteria for track classifications and the meanings of those classifications are approved by the JFC as part of the AADP, and any changes, especially those regarding ROE (e.g., meaning of hostile and engagement criteria) would be promulgated on the current SPINS and through ROE serial changes. **An ID of hostile, subsequently placed on the TDL with a hostile symbol, normally does not constitute authority to engage (employ weapons).** Engagement criteria are a product of threat analysis, risk management, and collateral damage assessment as determined by the JFC. Based on the ROE, **a positive engagement order normally is required,** such as a voice or specific electronic direction to engage. An ID of hostile may be assigned a track based on procedural ID, but the engagement decision normally is based on positive ID or affirming hostile intent or a hostile act. **To avoid fratricide and potential TDL ambiguities, any uncertainty as to what specifically constitutes engagement authority must be resolved within tactical timelines before allowing weapons employment (engagement).**

(2) Once identified, a track is followed until it is no longer of significance (friendly or neutral) or required to be engaged (confirmed hostile by CID or hostile intent). It is not uncommon for a procedural ID of a track to be changed, based on better information, such as a later positive ID or a change in the determined intent.

(3) Proper application of ID authority and classification may impact AMD units based on their assigned WCS (free, tight, or hold/safe). AMD units often rely on linked track data until tracks are within range of their sensors. For example, under weapons hold or tight, a positive hostile ID and a command to engage is typically required, but under a weapons free state, presence of a track not positively identified as friendly may be engaged.

c. **Commit Authority.** Commit authority may be used (and delegated) by the AADC as a battle management tool. The AD echelon with commit authority is permitted to authorize assets to **prepare to engage** an entity (e.g., position a DCA fighter to intercept or direct an ADA unit to track and target). **Commit authority does not imply engagement authority.** Further permission is required to engage an entity that has been committed upon. If the unit with commit authority also holds engagement authority, the engagement decision is still separate and unique. Commit and engagement authorities are typically split during the transition phase of a major campaign or during containment and show of force operations to avoid accidental escalation of conflict. For example, during a deter/engage phase, the JFC may approve delegation of commit authority down to the tactical level (e.g., RADC/SADC) but retain engagement authority with the AADC or the JFC to prevent inadvertent escalation by a lower level command.

d. **Engagement Authority.** The JFC is vested with authority to prosecute engagements within the theater/JOA consistent with ROE currently in effect. The AD authority with engagement authority is permitted to authorize engagement of an air or missile threat. For AD engagements within the IADS, the authority normally is delegated to the AADC who may further delegate the engagement authority to tactical levels (e.g., RADC/SADC). The degree of delegation must be consistent with the ROE, the DAL, and the inherent right of self-defense. In addition to engagement authority, the process and means of ordering engagements (shoot/no-shoot) must be clearly stated in the AADP or ACO and SPINS. For example, a TDL track identified and carried as hostile (by symbol) and passed from one sector to another remains hostile, but normally cannot be engaged without further assessment (CID or known hostile act or intent) and a real-time engagement order by the controlling AD command with engagement authority.

14. Combat Identification

a. **CID is the process of attaining an accurate characterization of detected objects in the operational environment sufficient to support an engagement decision.** Ideally, the CID process uses the most positive ID methods available to allow the highest confidence required for that decision, because it normally is one of the most critical decisions to be made. Some commanders use the CID process as the basis for high confidence, timely application of other military options, and not just for the employment of weapons.

b. The CID process is determined by the JFC (normally in coordination with subordinate commanders), supported by the ROE, and may be situational dependent and/or time-sensitive. CID allows the commander to balance the level of confidence in the ID method against the risk associated with an erroneous ID. While high confidence-low risk is always desired, the commander may face situations when the absence of positive ID requires procedural ID be used with a recognized increase in the risk of fratricide or to mis-ID an enemy (i.e., low confidence-high risk). This remains a commander's decision. For example, during DCA operations against numerous simultaneous attacks by enemy aircraft and CMs, potentially with WMD, it may be necessary to accept lower confidence ID methods for hostiles and increased risk of fratricide to minimize the risk of a "leaker" getting through to the target. Unambiguous lines of command and clarity of ROE are particularly important to the CID process, especially when delegating authority for engagement decisions during decentralized execution.

c. **The CID process is for all joint forces and for defensive action as well as offensive.** For example, CID may provide a positive ID of friendly SOF positioned in close proximity to a high-priority target system deep in enemy territory being attacked from the air. The leader/battle manager of the attacking force would use that CID when making an engagement decision on that target.

d. A CID matrix is a good tool for the CID process for counterair. To that end, the CID matrix should mirror the ID criteria and the CID process contained in the counterair plans and must be coordinated to ensure no conflicts arise during joint operations.

See Appendix A, "Combat Identification," for additional discussion of CID and a sample ID process matrix.

15. Multinational Considerations

a. Special attention must be paid to establishing a workable CID system during MNF operations. A mix of units with dissimilar capabilities and differing electronic systems, fire control doctrine, and training can present the AADC with an extremely difficult AD situation. Advanced planning may be required to compensate for a "patchwork" of separate MNF CID capabilities, not just for the surface AD and air control units, but for their aircraft as well.

b. No matter how well integrated a CID system is, as much training as possible should be conducted to facilitate the CID processes. Means of positive ID should be stressed as early in the planning phases as possible and every effort made to devise a system of positive ID for each MNF members' aircraft when airborne.

c. In addition to the ID/CID obstacles, the AADC must ensure the promulgation of that data throughout the MNF. While US joint forces may have TDL, many MNF may not have the same TDL interoperability.

SECTION E. ASSET PROTECTION

16. General

a. The JFC and staff, normally the plans directorate of a joint staff, develops a prioritized critical asset list (CAL) (see Figure III-3) for each general phase of an operation with inputs from the components and based on the theater level protection required to support tasks/missions assigned by the JFC. Within each general phase (e.g., seize initiative phase), subordinate JFCs or component commanders may establish additional phases that fit

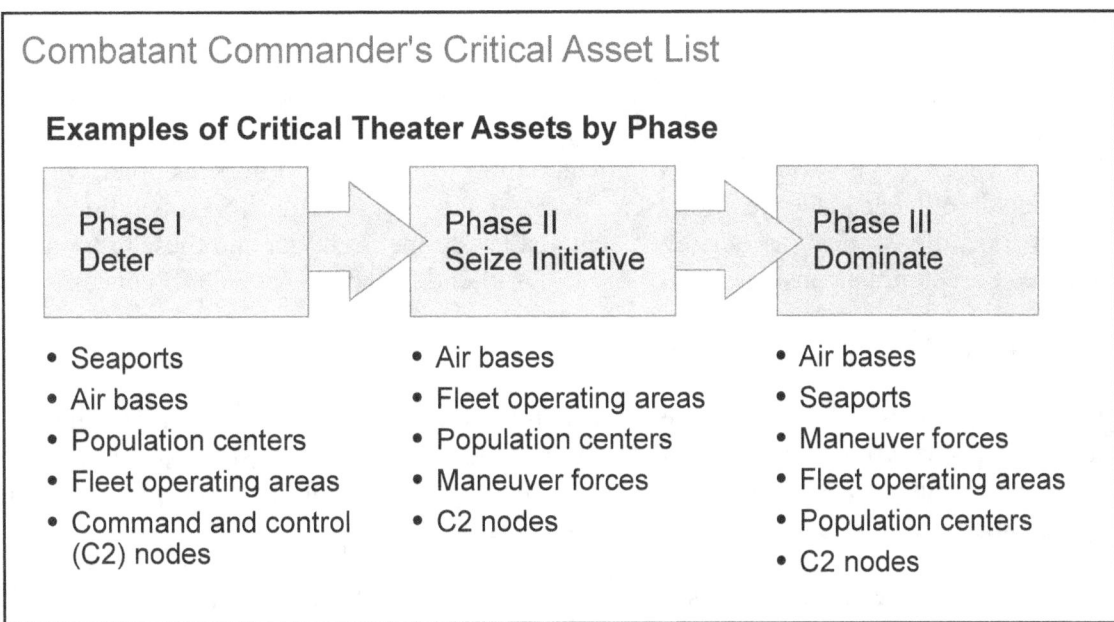

Figure III-3. Combatant Commander's Critical Asset List

their CONOPS (e.g., phase I, deploy; phase II, forcible entry; phase III, defense; phase IV, offense) for which there may be separate CALs. The task CAL maintained by a GCC's Defense Critical Infrastructure Program office may be useful in providing a preliminary baseline for JFCs for various operational scenarios within a JOA. The CAL should include designated assets and areas within the joint security areas (JSAs) of the JOA. Protection for JSAs outside the JOA, but within the AOR, normally remains the responsibility of the supported GCC. Protection of the lines of communication outside the AOR and vulnerable to enemy (or their ally's) air and missile attack must be coordinated with the responsible CCDRs by the supported GCC. **For DCA protection, the joint security coordinator designated by the JFC normally coordinates with the AADC to ensure the JSAs are appropriately covered by the AADP.** Usually the number of assets requiring some level of AMD will be greater than the resources available to defend them. Also, due to the dynamics of joint operations, priorities may change over the course of the operation or campaign.

b. The completed CAL is forwarded to AADC, who will allocate available active AMD forces to defend the prioritized assets listed. The product of this effort is the DAL. **The DAL is a list of those assets on the CAL that can be covered by JFC AMD forces and capabilities.** Each defended asset on the DAL should be prioritized as requiring active AD or appropriate passive measures if that is all that is available. After initial active AD allocation, commanders should consider "clustering" to conserve AMD forces and assess if passive measures alone satisfy an assets' required defensive posture. If passive measures alone are insufficient to defend an asset on the DAL, the issue should be resolved by the JFC. **Once completed, the DAL is approved by the JFC.**

See JP 5-0, Joint Operation Planning, *for additional details regarding plan phases.*

17. Critical Asset List Development

a. All assets nominated for the CAL usually are prioritized based on a methodology of assessing the three major factors of criticality, vulnerability (includes recoverability), and the threat (CVT). This is called the "CVT methodology." The CVT process is objective and considers intelligence, air operations, ground combat operations, maritime operations, and support operations. Each asset is evaluated against defined criteria, and these criteria are weighed based on the consideration of the JFC's intent, CONOPS, and COG concerns.

b. **CAL Development Factors**

(1) **Criticality** is the degree to which an asset is essential to accomplishing the mission. It is determined by assessing the impact that damage to or destruction of the asset will have on the success of the operation/campaign. Damage to an asset may **prevent, significantly delay,** or **have no impact** on success of the plan.

(2) **Vulnerability** consists of two parts: **susceptibility** (the degree an asset is susceptible to surveillance, attack, or damage), and **recoverability,** if attacked and damaged. Recoverability, once a factor itself, is now a subset of vulnerability and is the degree and ability to recover/reconstitute from inflicted damage in terms of time, equipment, and manpower and to continue the mission. Commanders should consider the time to replace personnel, equipment, or entire units, as well as whether other forces can perform the same mission. The following factors should be considered when assessing vulnerability:

(a) Survivability and cover (hardening).

(b) Camouflage, concealment, and deception.

(c) Mobility and dispersion.

(d) Ability to adequately defend itself from air/missile threats.

(3) **Threat.** Assess the probability an asset will be targeted for surveillance or attack by a credible/capable adversary. Determination of adversary intent and capability are key determinants of assessing the probability of attack. A thorough JIPOE oriented specifically on adversary air and missile capabilities is key to an accurate threat assessment. Examples include targeting information provided by intelligence estimates, past adversary surveillance and attack methods, and threat doctrine.

c. **High Value Assets (HVAs).** HVAs are classified as friendly critical assets requiring protection. They may be any forces, facilities, or area, etc., the friendly commander requires for the successful completion of the mission. They are categorized as follows:

(1) **High Value Geopolitical Assets.** Those assets so important that the loss of even one could seriously impact the JFC's operation/campaign. In addition, the political ramifications of destroying one of these assets could provide the adversary with a tremendous propaganda victory.

(2) **HVAA**

(a) Include all major airborne platforms for C2, reconnaissance and surveillance, targeting, AR, and EW (e.g., AWACS, Rivet Joint, JSTARS, Compass Call, Cobra Ball, U-2, E-2C, and EP-3). Depending on the defensive situation, other special mission aircraft also may be considered.

(b) Active protection for an HVAA normally is performed by fighter escorts, a fighter CAP between the HVAA and all potential air-to-air threats, or surface-based AD systems between the HVAA and the enemy.

(c) Passive protection includes positioning HVAA stations or orbits beyond SAM range and where an enemy interceptor attack can be detected in time to retrograde the HVAA out of harm's way.

(3) **High Value Units**

(a) Maritime assets include aircraft carriers, maritime pre-positioning ships, combat logistics force ships, and amphibious ships conducting amphibious assaults and landings. Maritime HVAA include the E-2C or EP-3 aircraft.

(b) Active protection normally is provided by maritime AMD capable systems (e.g., fleet AD assets).

(c) Passive protection is accomplished by operating outside of the range of the enemy's weapons envelope.

(d) Land assets include air and surface ports of debarkation, major supply route checkpoints, early entry forces, operations centers, and logistical centers.

(e) Active protection normally is provided by SAMs and/or airborne interceptors.

(f) Passive protection is accomplished by cover and concealment, dispersal, hardening, and operating outside the envelope of the enemy's weapons capabilities.

18. Defended Asset List Development

a. **DAL Development Considerations.** The DAL is developed through the process of applying the CVT methodology, AMD resources, and defense design to the CAL while identifying the risk. It identifies the prioritized assets from the CAL to be actually defended with resources available. For prioritizing the DAL, the following are those considerations for levels of protection and levels of engagement effectiveness.

(1) **Levels of Protection.** A level of protection is an aggregated probability that an asset will not suffer mission critical damage from an air or missile attack. It encompasses all joint force capabilities used to defeat the air and missile threat. Levels of protection are assigned to each entry on the CAL list based upon the outcome of the CVT analysis.

(a) **Level 1.** Level 1 provides the highest level of protection to assigned assets. It is a primary driver for resource positioning, planned methods of fire/integration of fires, and initialization of DCA systems to obtain the highest feasible probability of protection against specific threats.

(b) **Level 2.** Level 2 provides the highest protection achievable while maintaining the highest level of protection for highest ranked assets.

(c) **Level 3.** Level 3 provides the highest protection achievable while maintaining directed level for higher ranked assets.

(2) **Levels of Engagement Effectiveness.** There are five levels of operational engagement effectiveness. The AADC normally implements the JFC-directed protection level for each defended asset on the DAL based on the threat capabilities and proximities, terrain and weather, support available–time available, and civil considerations. Implementation may include active and passive AMD measures. After a level is established, the defense design and firing parameters are developed. Levels of engagement effectiveness 0-4 are employed using tiers or methods of coverage with some employing multiple tiers and a variety of active and passive measures. Tiers are commonly categorized as upper and lower. The AADC should recommend OCA attack operations against the anticipated threats when an asset cannot be adequately defended from an attack due to the threat composition, strength, or proximity.

(a) **Level 0 (None)**—described as the commander's decision to accept maximum risk where active AD forces provide no tiers of protection.

(b) **Level 1 (Low)**—for commanders that wish to provide some level of protection throughout their defended areas. One tier of protection will be used.

(c) **Level 2 (Medium)**—the normal level of defense used to provide specific military assets using a single tier of protection. While a single tier operating alone normally provides Level 2, it may employ two integrated tiers of defense.

(d) **Level 3 (High)**—described as the appropriate level of defense for assets that require a more robust level of protection than Level 2. Level 3 normally employs two tiers but may use one tier operating independently. This also may include areas where coordination between upper and lower tiers is used to defend a common asset.

(e) **Level 4 (Very High)**—described as the maximum defense for high priority assets. This level normally requires two tiers operating together in an integrated defense. This may include areas where coordination between upper and lower tiers is used to defend a common asset.

b. The DAL must be continuously assessed, especially in a dynamic, multi-phased campaign. The AADC normally delegates further assessment of the DAL to a working group/coordination board with appropriate staff and component representation (e.g., a DAL reprioritization board or DAL synchronization board). The assessment and recommended adjustments to the DAL are presented to the AADC for concurrence and forwarding to the

JFC for final approval. Changes to the DAL should be anticipated with changes in phases of an operation/campaign due to changes in the priority of defended assets by phase, loss of AMD assets due to attrition, inventory depletion, or the arrival of additional AMD forces. Normally, DAADC will chair the working group/board for assessing the DAL for changes.

See FM 3-01.94, Army Air and Missile Defense Command Operations, *for detailed discussion of CAL and DAL, including sample worksheets for the CVT process.*

SECTION F. ENABLING CAPABILITIES

19. Special Operations

SOF core operations and activities should be considered when planning counterair operations. SOF can aid counterair operations by providing information or by destroying or disrupting air and missile assets, bases, logistic sites, and C2 facilities. For example, SOF can locate enemy assets (especially those being concealed/camouflaged) behind the lines, provide terminal guidance (e.g., laser target designation) for joint air attacks, and provide post-attack assessment. They may be used for OCA operations, but they are not a recognized DCA asset. To ensure proper ID and reduce the potential for fratricide, SOF liaisons must ensure proper procedures are in place for CID of SOF teams and aircraft during cross-border operations or those considered behind enemy lines or in enemy rear areas. Often special liaison or trusted agents will coordinate/facilitate SOF movements, including using ACMs for activation of joint special operations areas or restricted fire areas.

For more detailed information on SOF, refer to JP 3-05, Special Operations.

20. Information Operations

a. Counterair operations are most effective when they are conducted from a position of information superiority. IO can provide significant capabilities against OCA target sets such as C2 systems, AD nodes, missile sites, and airfields/operating bases. Adversary IO vulnerabilities related to their offensive and defensive air and missile systems should be identified as early as possible in the planning process. Denying the adversary knowledge of friendly counterair capabilities and their locations is integral to effective counterair operations and is achieved via the full range of IO measures, such as operations security (OPSEC), military deception, and EW.

b. IO can be employed offensively to degrade the adversary's situational awareness and their decision-making processes, disrupt vital AD information transmissions and their capability to synchronize AMDs, disrupt their ability to coordinate attacks, and deny them reconnaissance and surveillance capabilities. Military deception can be used to lead the adversary into making erroneous decisions and wasting resources, or to mask friendly force intentions.

c. EW is normally a multifaceted very high demand/low density capability. EW aircraft are especially heavily tasked to support a myriad of joint missions. **An EW coordination cell (EWCC), or its functional equivalent, is required within the JAOC, separated from but integrated with the IO cell, to coordinate requirements, set priorities for EW assets,**

and take advantage of reachback capabilities within the reprogramming centers that support specialized and self-protection EW systems. Airborne EW is especially important to SEAD operations throughout a campaign.

d. The development and updating of the joint restricted frequency list (JRFL) is critical to successful counterair operations because of the EW and IO implications. All joint operations require a JRFL to identify and deconflict/synchronize friendly force use of frequencies. This list is a critical tool in the management of the use of the electromagnetic spectrum, and it specifies protected frequencies that should not be disrupted either because of friendly use or friendly exploitation. The JRFL is maintained and promulgated by the J-6 through the joint frequency management office (JFMO) in coordination with the J-2, J-3, and the JFC's EW staff or an EWCC, if delegated. The JFMO must manage all frequencies used by the joint force. For defensive purposes, the JRFL is a means of preventing radio frequency interference among friendly users. Frequency deconfliction through the use of the JRFL is also a key to a successful coordinated defense against enemy C2-attack operations. EW planners must know what frequencies to protect from enemy EW action. The JRFL is constantly being modified, and a daily EW deconfliction message normally is used to protect frequencies from jamming or other forms of manipulation. Experience has shown that during intense SEAD operations, friendly forces have been erroneously attacked because their electronic emitters were not recognized as friendly.

For more details regarding the JFRL and JFMO and in-depth discussion on EW, see JP 3-13.1, Electronic Warfare.

For more information on IO, see JP 3-13, Information Operations.

21. Space Operations

a. The enabling capabilities that space operations bring to the joint force are significant for countering air and missile threats. Space forces provide BM launch warnings and attack assessments, engagement sensor cueing, launch locations, predicted headings and impact areas, global and theater-/JOA-wide communications, current and forecast weather information, space based ISR, global positioning system (and navigation and timing assets for accuracy of precision munitions), and theater-/JOA-wide ID/CID systems support. Space assets also may be used to facilitate emission control and jamming/spoofing when conducting SEAD missions.

b. The JFC normally designates a lower echelon commander as the SCA to serve as the focal point for coordinating user requirements for space support with USSTRATCOM. Each GCC has a network of space operators resident on staffs at multiple echelons. Their primary purpose is to serve as theater advisors for space systems (national, civil, commercial, military, and foreign) and for integrating space capabilities into joint force planning and employment. These individuals concentrate primarily on working the detailed activities of theater space operations.

For more information on space operations, see JP 3-14, Space Operations.

22. Intelligence Support

a. Intelligence support for counterair operations begins with the JIPOE and IPB processes. Ongoing intelligence support provides current, integrated, accurate, and timely all-source intelligence of adversary capabilities and activities developed from interface with existing national and theater intelligence sources. The intelligence system is vital to decision making and must support the status, assessment, planning, warning, and JIPOE and IPB functions, as well as target prioritization and engagement decisions. Intelligence elements should be tailored to support real-time operations as well as deliberate planning. Intelligence functions include collection management; combat assessment, including battle damage assessment from OCA efforts, indications and warning/early warning/launch warning, assessing weather effects, and providing the NRT data on enemy targets; operating bases; missile launch sites and hide sites; EW systems; C2 facilities; surveillance and control systems; and logistic and infrastructure support.

b. The JFC normally will be supported by a joint intelligence element where appropriate and possibly by a national intelligence support team. Although the functional systems (sensors, decision support, or fusion centers and firing units) may be dissimilar, interoperable communications and software must be possible, including making allowances for systems of MNF members. Issues regarding the release of intelligence to MNF partners must be addressed as early as possible during counterair planning.

c. Increasing the readiness posture includes performing the vital operating functions that prepare weapon systems, ISR assets, and C2 nodes for the level of hostile activity anticipated. Once enemy air and missile activities are detected, the preparation and planning measures provide a capability for parallel defensive and offensive responses. Hostile air and missile activity observed and identified through sensor and surveillance systems (national, theater, and tactical) keys the C2 process that uses communications interfaces to provide NRT DCA and OCA responses. Data is made available in NRT to C2 centers, systems, and forces supporting counterair operations. Simultaneously, while enemy air and missiles are in flight, updated enemy launch locations and target database information are passed to the appropriate C2 and attack systems, and launch warnings are provided to all units or commands within the theater.

For more information, see JP 2-01, Joint and National Intelligence Support to Military Operations, *and JP 2-03,* Geospatial Intelligence Support to Joint Operations.

23. Intelligence, Surveillance, and Reconnaissance

a. Situational awareness relies on joint force ISR and associated processing, exploitation, and dissemination capabilities. Those capabilities are provided by air-, land-, space-, and sea-based platforms. As a group, ISR platforms with multidimensional sensors provide the most accurate "picture" of the adversary. Many ISR assets are high demand/low density and require careful planning for their utilization.

b. The backbone of ISR capabilities is a theater ISR CONOPS based on a coherent collection strategy that fully integrates and optimizes the use of all organic, multinational, commercial, and requested national or interagency ISR assets. The capabilities include both periodic reconnaissance and continuous surveillance of the operational area. While some of the information requires processing for intelligence, other producers can be directly linked to commanders and OCA or DCA forces as required. This is especially true for time-sensitive targeting and decision making. Depending on the capabilities of the sensor and surveillance systems and the source and quality of the intelligence, cueing of additional systems may be necessary to provide more refined adversary air and missile threat data to ensure accurate targeting and assessment. National or theater sensor and surveillance assets may be able to detect, footprint, or search areas that will then require more refined ISR activities by theater and tactical assets. Friendly aerial reconnaissance, ground surveillance systems, and other intelligence assets requiring cueing are focused rapidly to achieve the necessary accuracy for IPB targeting objectives.

c. The JFACC normally is responsible for airborne ISR for the JFC, and the JAOC has an ISR division for planning and execution. The GCC is responsible for theater-level ISR, to include ISR support to the subordinate JFC. Typically, the GCC manages ISR operations via the joint reconnaissance center and ISR collection management via the intelligence directorate collection management staff entity. At the national and the Department of Defense (DOD) levels, USSTRATCOM identifies, develops, and recommends sourcing solutions for DOD ISR and associated processing, exploitation, and dissemination capabilities to satisfy combatant command and national operational and intelligence requirements while synchronizing operational ISR plans and allocation strategies to integrate national and theater capabilities.

Refer to JP 2-01, Joint and National Intelligence Support to Military Operations, *and JP 2-03,* Geospatial Intelligence Support to Joint Operations, *for more details regarding ISR.*

24. Air Refueling

a. AR is an important force multiplier and enabling function for counterair and joint air operations. AR greatly increases the range, endurance, and payloads of aircraft conducting counterair and other joint air operations.

b. During a combat operation, the highest priority for intratheater AR units is normally supporting combat and combat support aircraft executing joint air operations. This is especially true during the initial phases of a conflict. Theater AR assets bolster the security of air assets by allowing them to be based beyond the range of enemy threats. AR increases the endurance of air combat support assets such as AWACS type aircraft, and JSTARS aircraft and are among the many crucial airborne platforms used to help manage, direct, and conduct combat operations. Depending upon the operation, extending range or endurance could reduce the number of sorties required, decrease ground support requirements at forward locations, and may reduce the number of aircraft required to be deployed to a theater.

c. AR not only allows combat aircraft to greatly extend their range of operation (which may allow them to operate from bases further away from the conflict that may be more secure and have existing infrastructure and logistic capabilities that are critical to military operations) and endurance (making possible longer "on-station" times, thereby decreasing the number of aircraft needed to meet objectives), but may also allow some types of aircraft to carry a larger payload on initial takeoff by decreasing the amount of onboard fuel required. Fuel necessary for mission range requirements is on-loaded after takeoff by either pre-strike or post-strike refueling (or both). The ability to increase an aircraft's weapons load multiplies the combat force and combat efficiency of that aircraft. **A lack of airspace for AR tracks can limit the amount of combat and combat support sorties the JFACC/AADC is able to schedule and execute. AR support is essential for both DCA and OCA.**

Refer to JP 3-17, Air Mobility Operations, *for more details regarding AR operations.*

Intentionally Blank

CHAPTER IV
OFFENSIVE COUNTERAIR PLANNING AND OPERATIONS

"After all, the great defense against aerial menace is to attack the enemy's aircraft as near as possible to their point of departure."

Winston Churchill
Memo of 5 September 1914

1. General

OCA operations normally have a high priority as long as the enemy has the air and missile capability to threaten friendly forces and the JFC does not have the degree of air superiority desired to accomplish the objectives required for the end state. OCA operations reduce the risk of air and missile attacks, allowing friendly forces to focus on their mission objectives. The preferred method of countering air and missile threats is to destroy or disrupt them prior to launch using OCA operations.

SECTION A. OFFENSIVE COUNTERAIR PLANNING

2. General

a. OCA planning begins with JIPOE and IPB and considers the JFC's assessment of the overall air and missile threat, the predicted effectiveness of the defense design, target database, ROE, objectives, priorities, missions, available friendly capabilities, and the weight of effort or force apportionment decision. IPB enhances the commanders' ability to find targets, task attack forces, and assess their effectiveness. Considerations include the enemy's air and missile operating areas, signatures, capabilities, and deployment and employment procedures. IPB attempts to provide a comprehensive picture of the enemy activity, terrain, and weather within the theater/JOA and generally requires planning for surveillance and reconnaissance in support of intelligence collection.

b. Through centralized planning and direction, the JFACC synchronizes OCA operations with DCA and other joint operations and relies on robust C2 systems for decentralized execution. Decentralized execution allows components and units to exercise initiative, responsiveness, and flexibility within their command authorities to accomplish their tasks. Operations against fixed targets require emphasis on preplanning, accurate and timely intelligence, target selection, time over target, and published ROE. OCA operations against mobile targets or TSTs (e.g., SAMs, BM or CM launchers) also require preplanned procedures that can be implemented or modified quickly to assign the optimum weapon system relying on integrated C2 systems for as close to real time control as possible. This emphasis on planning enhances mission effectiveness while minimizing potential for fratricide and interference with other operations.

c. Reliable and secure C2 systems are needed to ensure timely and accurate integration, planning, responsiveness, and close coordination. **These systems represent the collective**

threads that tie all joint forces together, and those C2 systems must be aggressively protected from enemy interference.

d. Planning should include the use of longer range attack operations against deep threats. These should be included in planning contingencies developed under the collaborative planning process with other CCDRs.

3. Offensive Counterair and the Joint Air Operations Plan

a. The preponderance of OCA operations are conducted with joint air forces/capabilities that are integrated in action through the JAOP. OCA planning is an integral part of this overall joint air operations planning. The air estimate process has six phases that result in the JAOP. While the phases are presented in sequential order, they can be worked either concurrently or sequentially. The phases are integrated and the products of each phase are checked and verified for coherence. Figure IV-1 illustrates the six phases. The following explains the process in regards to OCA planning, not each phase:

(1) The process begins with mission analysis (i.e., analyzing the JFC guidance, the situation, resources, and risks involved). Mission analysis provides the data that is used to answer the essential question about an operation. The JFACC uses the mission analysis to produce air objectives that support the JFC's objectives. In general terms, the focus of OCA is to attain and maintain the JFC's desired degree of air superiority in the operational area. This requires that both an enemy's offensive and defensive air and missile capability be made combat ineffective to some degree. **Specific OCA objectives and desired effects**

Joint Air Estimate Process

Mission Analysis

Intelligence preparation of the battlespace (IPB) is initiated. Phase focuses on analyzing the joint force commander's guidance.

Situation and Course of Action (COA) Development

IPB is refined to include adversary COAs. Adversary and friendly centers of gravity are analyzed. Multiple air COAs or one air COA with significant branches and sequels are developed.

COA Analysis

Friendly COAs are wargamed against adversary COAs.

COA Comparison

Wargaming results are used to compare COAs against predetermined criteria.

COA Selection

Decision brief to joint force air component commander (JFACC) with COA recommendation. JFACC selects COA.

Joint Air Operations Plan (JAOP) Development

Selected COA is developed into a JAOP.

Figure IV-1. Joint Air Estimate Process

must be clearly defined and measurable so the JFACC can assess whether or not OCA operations are achieving the objectives while avoiding undesired effects.

(2) After establishing OCA objectives, the JFACC uses the data from the mission analysis to examine resources and risks, as well as enemy COA (both known and anticipated) to arrive at the best option for integrating OCA into the JFACC's COA for joint air operations.

(3) The JFACC's COA is approved or amended by the JFC and gets translated into the final JAOP that includes details on the integration of OCA into the overall air operations plan. The JAOP should identify objectives by priority order, describing in what order they should be attacked or otherwise neutralized, the desired effects, and the weight of effort required to achieve them. For OCA operations, the JAOP should account for current and potential offensive and defensive threats and indicate the phasing of joint air operations. The results of the planning process also are incorporated into the daily master air attack plan (MAAP).

(4) The MAAP forms the basis of the daily ATO. During MAAP development OCA resources are allocated to accomplish specific tasks. OCA planning considers the operational context and environment and the results from current operations. Planners will work with specialty teams, component liaisons, and unit representatives, incorporating and synchronizing OCA aspects of the air operations directive, joint prioritized integrated target list, threat situation, joint prioritized collection, forecast weather, weapons system availability, AR, and weapons employment options. The MAAP has sufficient flexibility to adapt to the changing situation throughout the theater/JOA. Planners adjust to the changing availability of joint assets to ensure each task or target is assigned the best available capability.

b. OCA planning includes targeting enemy air and missile threats and their C2 and supporting infrastructure. Targeting is the process of selecting targets and matching the appropriate response to them, accounting for operational requirements and capabilities. The following seven criteria are normally used to establish targets and their priorities:

(1) Objective—the degree to which targets contribute to the OCA objectives.

(2) Threat—determining the need and urgency to counter the threat posed by the target.

(3) Expected Effect—the degree the enemy capability can reasonably be expected to be affected by a successful action.

(4) Delay in Effect—the time between the initial engagement and the desired effect.

(5) Risk Calculation—the probable risk to attacking forces.

(6) Forces Available—the composition of forces required to achieve the desired results.

(7) Assessment—the ability to determine the effect of an attack on enemy capability.

Refer to JP 3-60, Joint Targeting, *for a detailed discussion of the targeting process.*

c. OCA targets should be attacked on the surface prior to launch and as close to their source as possible. However, based on the JFC's priorities and ROE, many mobile targets, especially TSTs, may be sought and attacked wherever and whenever they are found. Target ID and planning should start prior to hostilities, but target data should be as current as the latest intelligence. Target defenses, to include active and passive systems, also should be evaluated to determine vulnerability. Commanders should consider the following target systems for OCA operations:

IRAQI INTEGRATED AIR DEFENSE SYSTEM DURING DESERT STORM

"The underlying principle of the suppression of enemy air defense (SEAD) plan was to attack KARI [nickname for Iraqi integrated air defense system] as a whole. It would not be necessary to kill all the surface-to-air missile (SAM) sites; it would be enough, if the coalition SEAD assets intimidated the Iraqis to the point that those running SAM sites would refrain from turning radar on. Finally, the plan to suppress enemy air defenses aimed to defeat the SAM threat, so that allied aircraft could operate at medium altitudes which would minimize the threat posed by Iraqi antiaircraft artillery. In effect, planners looked to maximize the inherent inefficiencies and frictions within KARI. They believed that the Iraqis could not operate effectively without centralized direction; once the system began to break down at the center, it would no longer function at all."

SOURCE: The Gulf War Air Power Survey, Volume II

---

(1) **WMD.** The engagement of targets involved with the production, storage, and delivery of WMD present the JFC with significant and unique challenges. When tackling these challenges, the JFC must consider targeting priorities, reviewing and revising existing ROE where needed, and developing clear guidance for WMD targeting. When planning OCA against WMD targets, risk assessments should consider the unique nature of the collateral damage. Escalation concerns may place some enemy WMD and delivery capabilities on the restricted target or no-strike lists.

See JP 3-40, Combating Weapons of Mass Destruction, *for further guidance on combating WMD planning.*

(2) **Missiles and Support Infrastructure.** OCA operations are most effective against missiles prior to their launch. The destruction of missiles, launch facilities, storage facilities, and other support infrastructure greatly limits subsequent missile attacks. OCA assets may also be rapidly retasked to destroy TSTs such as mobile launchers.

(3) **Airfields and Operating Bases.** Destruction of hangars, shelters, maintenance facilities, and other storage areas as well as petroleum, oils, and lubricants will reduce the enemy's capability to generate aircraft sorties. Runway or taxiway closures often prevent use of the airfield for short periods, thus preventing subsequent takeoffs and forcing returning aircraft to more vulnerable or distant locations. Direct attacks on crews and maintenance personnel facilities may reduce sortie generation rates longer than attacks on the infrastructure of airfields and operating bases.

(4) **Aircraft.** Target aircraft include enemy fixed-wing and rotary-wing aircraft (manned or unmanned), whether in flight or on the ground. Destruction of these targets will limit enemy attacks, observation, and defensive capability.

(5) **C2 Systems.** C2 systems are critical to the employment of forces and should be given a high priority during OCA operations. Remember the desired effect may be to take away the enemy's C2 capability while retaining the ability to reconstitute it after the conflict. C2 systems include intelligence gathering, warning and control systems (i.e., GCI sites, early warning and acquisition radars, space-based systems, and other sensors), as well as their supporting facilities. Fixed site, hardened facilities are usually easier to locate than mobile systems. Attacks against fixed sites can also be preplanned with appropriate weapons to increase the probability of kill (P_k). Attacks should also be considered against airborne, maritime, and ground-based C2 platforms, as well as against systems supporting space-based platforms. IO capabilities should be employed offensively for the desired effects whenever possible.

(6) **Naval Platforms.** Enemy naval platforms capable of employing aircraft, long-range SAMs, or missiles are also important OCA targets. Destruction of these platforms limits the enemy's ability to conduct air and missile attacks in the littoral or possibly influence vital sea lines of communications.

(7) **AD Systems and Enemy Forces.** Disruption or destruction of enemy AD systems and the personnel who control, maintain, and operate them significantly limit enemy self-defense efforts.

4. **Offensive Counterair Assets**

a. The effectiveness of OCA operations depends on the availability and capabilities of friendly assets. The choice of a particular weapon system or capability may depend upon the situation, target characteristics, desired effects, threats, weather, and available intelligence. Whenever possible and within the ROE, commanders should employ weapon systems that minimize the risk to friendly forces and noncombatants.

b. **Aircraft.** Offensive aircraft provide the advantages of air-refuelable manned systems (flexibility of control), night and all-weather capable, long ranges, tailorable weapons loads, precision weapons, and most are capable of self-defense. Offensive aircraft include bombers, air-to-air fighters, fighter-attack, EW aircraft, and fighters especially configured for SEAD. Additionally, there are the warning and control, reconnaissance, aerial tankers, special operations, and airlift aircraft that directly support the offensive aircraft or other forces capable of OCA operations.

c. **UA.** UA can be used for attacks, surveillance, reconnaissance, deception, jamming, and decoy of enemy forces and AD systems. UA are preprogrammed or remotely piloted and often provide intelligence to friendly forces while providing confusing and erroneous information to the enemy. Some UA are night-capable and carry precision guided weapons. UA may cause the enemy to expend weapons and other AD resources to evaluate or attack them. Airspace control can be a problem when mixing UA and manned aircraft in close proximity.

d. **Missiles.** Missiles that may be used for OCA include surface-to-surface, air-to-surface, and air-to-air guided missiles as well as air-, land-, and sea-launched cruise missiles (SLCMs). CMs provide the capability to attack very heavily defended targets when the risk to aircrews is not acceptable.

e. **SOF.** SOF conduct direct action, provide terminal guidance, observe attacks, and collect intelligence through special reconnaissance. SOF may strike enemy targets that are normally beyond the capability of other conventional munitions. Examples include targets concealed by difficult terrain, underground facilities, or "safe haven" targets. SOF may also be used to locate, positively identify, and designate targets for other forces. Coordination with the SOLE at the JAOC is critical to synchronize/deconflict operations and avoid fratricide for SOF working behind the lines and/or in the land/maritime AO.

f. **Surface Fire Support.** Artillery and naval surface fire support may be used during OCA operations if enemy targets are within range. Surface fire may provide the safest and fastest method of attacking targets.

g. **Antisubmarine Warfare Forces.** Sea- and land-based antisubmarine capabilities may be employed against some enemy CM and BM submarines, based on approved ROE. Employment is dependent upon whether the enemy presents an operational threat and the commander's desires regarding conflict escalation.

h. **Armed Helicopters.** When apportioned by the JFC and made available for tasking, these assets may be placed in direct support of the JFACC with mission-type orders for attack operations. Army attack helicopters are considered maneuver units for the land forces.

i. **C2 Systems.** C2 support for OCA includes early warning and surveillance systems, radars, ID/CID systems, communications systems, and other surface-, air-, and space-based sensors. These systems provide indications and warning, intelligence, targeting data, and C2. C2 systems are vital to counterair.

j. **IO. IO can generate nonlethal effects that have proven to be essential to OCA operations.** The employment of information-related capabilities can save valuable aircraft sorties during a high-tempo air war. Many OCA targets, such as C2 nodes, missiles, and support infrastructure, and airfields/operating bases can be affected by various IO actions that include computer network operations and EW. Some information-related capabilities afford the JFACC access to targets that may be inaccessible by other means.

5. Enemy Air Defenses

a. Enemy ADs may range from autonomous AAA to the most advanced IADS. An enemy IADS could include detection, C2, and weapon systems integrated to protect those assets critical to achieving their strategic, operational, and tactical objectives. An enemy IADS attempts to provide a seamless capability to destroy, disrupt, or neutralize ISR and air and missile attacks or other penetrations of their airspace. To degrade effectiveness of friendly OCA operations, enemy defensive tactics may include jamming aircraft navigation, communications, target acquisition systems, and precision weapons guidance systems. IADSs have become increasingly complex and can differ widely in terms of organization, sophistication, and operational procedures. As a target system or number of target systems, enemy IADSs need to be analyzed in depth to neutralize or avoid their strengths and exploit their weaknesses.

b. **C2.** Traditionally, many potential adversaries exercise rigid centralized control over AD activities. ADCs located in centralized C2 posts provide warning and cueing, assign targets, and control weapons readiness using overlapping and redundant communication links. However, some potential adversaries may employ a decentralized system where multiple nodes may have the redundancy to direct the entire IADS. Radio-based C2 is now being supplemented by combinations of communications over landline (cable/fiber optics), microwave, cellular, satellite, and Internet systems.

c. **Employment.** Mobile AD elements allow forces to echelon in depth and include tactical and strategic SAM and AAA systems. Technologies are now available that allow passive detection with little warning prior to weapon engagements. Known adversaries are adept at camouflage, concealment, and deception, complicating the targeting process. SAM forces have become more mobile and lethal, with some systems demonstrating a "shoot-and-move" time in minutes rather than hours or days. Modern SAM systems have been dramatically improved in both range and capability and some older systems have received substantial upgrades that continue to make them serious threats to US forces. Long-range SAMs are usually located near high-value targets and provide area and point defense coverage. However, their range and mobility mean these systems could provide AD coverage over the forward edge of the battlefield at various stages of the conflict and threaten friendly airborne warning and control, surveillance, and reconnaissance and targeting platforms well into friendly airspace. Point defenses and maneuver units may use short-range air defenses (SHORADs) including SAMs, multiple calibers of AAA, and MANPADS that may be guided by infrared or radio frequency methods. For enemy maneuver units, the SHORAD will probably present a primary threat against air assault, air mobility, and CAS operations. The proliferation and lack of warning of some SHORAD systems make them a serious threat to all fixed- and rotary-wing aircraft operating at low and medium altitudes, especially during takeoff and landing. OCA planners should expect MANPADS and AAA coverage wherever enemy forces are encountered.

SECTION B. OFFENSIVE COUNTERAIR OPERATIONS

6. General

a. The preferred counterair employment strategy is to execute OCA operations prior to the launch of air and missile threats and as close to their source as possible. Prior planning and accurate and timely intelligence are keys to locating and attacking OCA targets as well as their supporting elements. Under decentralized execution, units tasked for OCA operations should have the latitude to plan, coordinate, and execute their operations. OCA operations may be conducted by any component of the joint force with the requisite capability using aircraft, missiles, SOF, surface fires, C2 systems, or ground forces.

b. OCA operations can be preemptive or reactive, and may be planned using deliberate or dynamic targeting. Missions using deliberate targeting are scheduled or on-call targets and included in the ATO and rely on continuous and accurate intelligence to identify them at particular locations and times. Missions using dynamic targeting are unanticipated/unplanned targets, such as mobile TSTs, that fall outside the ATO cycle and require immediate action. Minutes often define the timeline when these targets are vulnerable to attack. Those targets requiring immediate action cannot be effectively attacked unless responsiveness and flexibility is built into the targeting process and the ATO. OCA may require provisions for ground/airborne alert aircraft, on-call surface fire support, and diverting aircraft with suitable weapons for the target/target system.

c. To ensure unity of effort, conservation of force, and fratricide prevention, attacks within a designated surface AO require coordination with that supported component commander, as designated by the JFC. For a land AO, the land force commander normally establishes a fire support coordination line (FSCL) as a permissive FSCM. Attacks short of the FSCL are controlled by the land force commander. Beyond the FSCL, coordination and restrictive measures are used to avoid conflicting or redundant operations. Forces attacking targets beyond the FSCL must coordinate with all affected commanders to allow necessary reaction and avoid fratricide, both in the air and on the ground. Generally, the ATO process provides sufficient coordination for scheduled and on-call targets beyond the FSCL. If permitted by specific JFC guidance, ROE, and preplanned procedures, unanticipated/unplanned targets may be attacked quickly using whatever information and coordination that can be provided through the C2 system. Liaison elements can be very useful for coordination of operations against unanticipated/unplanned targets. Under exceptional circumstances, if approved by the JFC, the inability to perform coordination may not preclude attacking the target, with the commander of the attacking force assuming the increased risk of fratricide. Therefore, the component commanders must plan and coordinate procedures for operations against unanticipated/unplanned targets, especially those in the land or maritime component AOs. OCA operations include attack operations, SEAD, fighter escort, and fighter sweep, shown in Figure IV-2.

Primary Offensive Counterair Missions

- Attack operations
- Suppression of enemy air defenses
- Fighter escort
- Fighter sweep

Figure IV-2. Primary Offensive Counterair Missions

7. Attack Operations

a. OCA attack operations are offensive actions against surface targets that contribute to the enemy's air and missile capabilities. All components normally have forces capable of supporting attack operations. Some Service components refer to attack operations as strikes. The objective of attack operations is to prevent the hostile use of enemy aircraft and missiles by attacking them and their supporting elements and infrastructure with the fires necessary to create the desired effects.

DESERT STORM OFFENSIVE COUNTERAIR

The Iraqi Air Force posed both a defensive threat to Coalition air operations and an offensive threat to Coalition forces in the region. In addition to a defensive capability, the Iraqi Air Force had a chemical weapons delivery capability and had used precision-guided missiles.

Initial targeting of the Iraqi Air Force during Operation DESERT STORM emphasized the suppression of air operations at airfields by cratering and mining runways, bombing aircraft, maintenance and storage facilities, and attacking [command, control, and communications] facilities. Coalition planners anticipated the Iraqis initially would attempt to fly large numbers of defensive sorties, requiring an extensive counterair effort. Air commanders also expected the Iraqis to house and protect aircraft in hardened shelters. An attempt to fly some aircraft to sanctuary in a neighboring country also was expected, although the safe haven was thought to be Jordan, rather than Iran.

SOURCE: Final Report to Congress
Conduct of the Persian Gulf War, April 1992

---

b. **OCA Attack Operation Targets.** Attack operations target the following components of enemy air and missile capability (not in a prioritized order):

(1) Air and missile unit C2 nodes/centers.

(2) Aircraft on airfields and in shelters.

(3) CMs and BMs on fixed and mobile launchers.

(4) Airfield runways, taxiways, and underground facilities entrances.

---

(5) Major IADS C2 facilities.

(6) Operations and maintenance facilities, equipment, and personnel.

(7) Logistic support (e.g., fuel storage, munitions depots, electrical power generation and transmission).

(8) ISR and target acquisition systems.

(9) Transportation infrastructure serving garrisons/deployment sites for mobile/moveable missiles (e.g., bridges, tunnel adits, rail choke points).

(10) Aircraft carriers and sea-based offensive missile and AMD platforms.

c. **Resources**

(1) Assets used to support OCA attack operations include fixed- and rotary-wing aircraft, CMs, SOF, other surface-to-surface fires, ground maneuver forces, EW and other IO capabilities, and ISR systems. Also, when required, long-range strike capabilities may be available to support the OCA effort.

(2) Attack operations are highly dependent upon predictive and developed intelligence. Because of the difficulty in detecting highly mobile launch systems, a seamless network of C2 systems and sensors should be employed to share information and support NRT targeting and attack. National sensor systems normally will be required to augment theater air and surface based systems. Space systems provide tactical information to assist in determining enemy missile launch points and tracking. Additionally, intelligence collected by these systems can enable theater forces to anticipate hostile air and missile operations and determine their unit locations.

d. **Execution.** In addition to the JFACC's own Service component forces, the JFC may apportion additional component force/capabilities to the JFACC to support theater-/JOA-wide attack operations. The JFACC's recommendation and the JFC's decision on apportionment determine the amount of effort made available for OCA attack operations. Attack operations are generally planned against scheduled and on-call targets, but some flexibility must be planned for unanticipated/unplanned targets of opportunity.

(1) **Planned Scheduled Targets.** Normally, OCA targets are nominated and prioritized through the joint targeting process that results in planned targets; that may include a list of approved TSTs that must be attacked at the onset of hostilities, or even prior to the onset of hostilities. **Typically, JFCs organize a joint targeting coordination board (JTCB) for determining apportionment of operational fires and shaping the operational environment in the theater/JOA, including fires supporting OCA attack operations.** The JTCB normally simultaneously addresses at least three ATO cycles that are either being planned, about to be executed, or in execution.

(2) **Planned On-Call Targets.** The quicker the joint force can locate, identify, and target the enemy air and missile threats, the quicker they can be attacked and defeated. On-

call missions are conducted against on-call targets, those emerging mobile targets and TSTs that require the execution of mutually supporting tasks (e.g., detection, acquisition, ID, tracking, attack, and assessment). These operations rely on sensor systems, a responsive NRT sensor management and communications network, and weapon systems capable of attacking targets as soon as adequate targeting information is available.

(3) **Target Acquisition.** Acquisition and tracking systems may utilize cueing from wide-area and local surveillance systems and receive warning data from other intelligence sources. Acquisition supports target ID, discrimination, and timely engagement by accurately locating and monitoring targets and transmitting information relative to their movements.

(a) **Target Detection.** In the case of BMs and CMs, detection can be accomplished through identifying launch signatures or intelligence sources such as measurement and signature intelligence or signals intelligence. To support attack operations in all environments, joint forces should minimize the effects of enemy countermeasures while capitalizing on distinctive equipment signatures. Surveillance capabilities should integrate national level intelligence with theater level capabilities. Space-, sea-, air-, and ground-based area and point surveillance sensors also will be key to establishing a comprehensive surveillance network. Detection involves a systemic search of areas of interest identified during the IPB. After detection, warning or location data should be passed immediately to joint and component intelligence and operations centers, executing units, and air and surface search equipment. Simultaneously, tactical warnings also should be provided to potential friendly targeted assets.

(b) **ID.** ID of aircraft and missiles and their supporting nodes requires management of target movement data, determination of the type of system employed, and discrimination of the launch and support systems from decoys. Target ID also requires the use of predictive intelligence, including the ID of potential future target locations, area limitation analysis, and automated cueing of sensors to threatening targets.

(4) **Attack.** Observed enemy activity should trigger timely counterair execution. Targets identified in the IPB database are included in the JFC's plan for preemptive strikes or operations at the onset of hostilities. **Targets acquired are attacked in accordance with JFC guidance that normally allows attack of unanticipated/unplanned targets as they present themselves.**

(5) **ATO.** The ATO should be flexible enough to deal with immediate attack operations. The combat operations division of the JAOC is responsible for adjusting the ATO in order to deal with real-time developments in the operational area. One method to permit this flexibility is designating selected forces in the ATO as either ground alert or airborne alert. These on-call assets can then be tasked real time against immediate counterair targets.

(6) **TSTs.** Prior planning, delegating authority, and having the appropriate C2 systems can streamline decision cycles for attacking counterair TSTs.

Refer to JP 3-60, Joint Targeting, *for a discussion of targeting and TSTs.*

8. Suppression of Enemy Air Defenses

a. SEAD is activity that neutralizes, destroys, or temporarily degrades surface-based enemy ADs by destructive or disruptive means. SEAD must be an integral part of all planning and air operations, but the SEAD requirement will vary according to mission objectives, system capabilities, and threat complexity. SEAD operations are based upon the JAOP and the components' suppression needs, target priorities, and availability of SEAD assets.

b. SEAD objectives are specified by the JFC, who will consider the unique capabilities of each component to contribute to counterair operations. Traditionally, there are three categories of SEAD, each of which reduces attrition and creates more favorable conditions for friendly air operations: AOR-/JOA-wide joint AD system suppression, localized suppression, and opportune suppression. For each category, there are two means of executing SEAD, destructive and disruptive.

c. SEAD assets are often used in conjunction with other air operations/missions (i.e., air interdiction, OCA attack, airborne operations) when surface ADs are a factor. Specially trained aircrew and specially equipped aircraft are designed for SEAD missions, especially against an IADS. SEAD dedicated aircraft normally are equipped with special electronic detection and electronic countermeasures (ECM) equipment, deceptive expendables (chaff, flares, or decoys), and antiradiation missiles (ARMs) for use against emitting radars. During major operations, SEAD assets normally are too valuable to be used for missions without a SEAD requirement. Other fighter-attack and multi-role fighter crews normally are trained to support the SEAD mission, especially against the enemy AD infrastructure.

d. **Threat.** AD threats can encompass many national or multinational systems normally integrated into an IADS. Potential adversaries' IADSs have become increasingly complex and can differ widely from country to country in terms of organization, sophistication, and operational procedures. An adversary's IADS needs to be analyzed in-depth with an eye to potential strengths and weaknesses, especially seams in coverage. The goal is to identify command structure, AD doctrine, early warning and tracking capabilities, C2 reliability/redundancy, and defensive weapons systems. SEAD operations target the following components of an IADS:

(1) IADS C2 nodes/centers.

(2) SAM sites.

(3) AAA.

(4) Early warning and fire control radars and GCI sites.

(5) SAM carriers and storage bunkers.

(6) AD operations and maintenance personnel.

e. **Resources.** Each component has its own capabilities for SEAD. Most are normally oriented toward their mission areas, and they assume the immediate responsibility for suppressing enemy AD threats expected against their forces. The components with dedicated, specialized aircraft and aircrews have the best potential and options for SEAD. Some of these options include aircraft with special detectors, jammers, and ECM equipment, ARMs, and terminally guided munitions (TGMs). Dedicated SEAD forces may be supported by aircraft with TGMs or unguided air-to-surface munitions. Land forces may use EW equipment, attack helicopters, and direct or indirect fires (including mortars, artillery, missiles, or naval surface fire support). SOF may be used for direct action (attack) or providing terminal guidance for air attacks. Additionally, space assets may also be used to facilitate emission control and jamming/spoofing when conducting SEAD missions.

f. **Means of SEAD Execution.** SEAD operations are accomplished through destructive and disruptive means.

(1) **Destructive Means.** Destructive means seek the destruction of the target system or operating personnel.

(2) **Disruptive Means.** Disruptive means temporarily deny, degrade, deceive, delay, or neutralize enemy surface AD systems. Disruptive means may be either active or passive.

(a) Active means include EA, directed energy, electromagnetic jamming, electromagnetic deception, expendables (chaff, flares, and decoys), and tactics such as deception, avoidance, or evasive flight profiles. In addition, UASs can be used to actively employ disruptive means.

(b) Passive means include emission control, camouflage, infrared shielding, warning receivers, and material design features, to include stealth technology.

g. **Categories of SEAD Execution**

(1) **AOR-/JOA-wide AD System Suppression.** AOR-/JOA-wide suppression is conducted against specific enemy AD systems throughout the AOR/JOA to degrade or destroy their major capabilities/effectiveness. It targets high payoff AD assets that result in the greatest degradation of the enemy's total system. It normally is a major effort to destroy/disrupt the whole enemy IADS and therefore may have a higher priority than localized suppression. **Typically, destruction of key C2 nodes has the most disruptive effect on an IADS.** In conjunction with SEAD, efforts are normally made to destroy/disrupt enemy equivalent AWACS aircraft. The immediate objective is to destroy or disrupt the integration and synchronization of the enemy AMDs. The duration and level of disruption depends upon the JFC's objectives and the sophistication of the IADS.

(2) **Localized Suppression.** Localized suppression operations normally are confined to geographic areas associated with specific targets or transit routes for a specific time. Under localized suppression, SEAD aircraft normally escort other aircraft to protect them from a surface-based air defense threat in that sector. Localized suppression normally takes place in different areas and times throughout the AOR/JOA. Although planned to

protect specific operations or missions, localized suppression may also support AOR-/JOA-wide AD suppression.

(a) **Planned Localized Suppression.** Localized SEAD coordination occurs at all echelons. Localized suppression requests are processed from the lowest echelon of command to the highest using the appropriate air control system. Liaison elements located in the JAOC aid this effort. A requesting echelon or component must first consider what organic SEAD systems are available. When the requirements exceed the capability or availability of organic systems, the requesting component passes the requirements through its respective chain of command to the JFACC for resolution. Units requesting air support are required to identify known or suspected AD systems that could threaten the mission. SEAD requests also will include these defensive systems and identify other supporting targets that likewise cannot be engaged with organic capabilities/forces.

(b) **Immediate Localized Suppression.** Threat assessment and suppression requirements, usually destructive, must be made quickly when processing a request for this type of SEAD support. Procedures for requesting immediate localized suppression are similar to immediate requests for CAS. If a surface force cannot support the SEAD requirement, their component control center passes the request to the JFACC through the appropriate air control system for immediate SEAD support considerations.

(3) **Opportune Suppression.** Opportune suppression is unplanned and includes aircrew self-defense and attack against surface-AD targets of opportunity. The proliferation of highly mobile AD weapon systems, coupled with deception and defensive tactics, will lead to an increase of opportune suppression. Any movement by air defense systems from targeted locations will change localized suppression into opportune suppression. The JFC will establish ROE for opportune suppression because SEAD operations require correct ID of enemy systems to prevent fratricide, especially when launching ARMs against sources of unknown, spurious electronic signals. **Realizing that the window to engage highly mobile targets may be fleeting, concern should be given to establishing ROE and detailed planning that will allow the rapid prosecution of threats before they have the opportunity to move or conceal themselves again.** Opportune suppression is a continuous operation involving immediate response to acquired targets of opportunity. In cases where air assets are not available or not required, the component commander establishes priorities for opportune suppression. These priorities are forwarded from the designated fire support coordinator at component-level headquarters to the executing commands. The following are the different types of opportune suppression:

(a) **Aircrew Self-defense.** An aircraft commander has the inherent authority and is obligated to use all necessary means available and to take all appropriate actions in self-defense of the aircraft and other US forces in the vicinity. Nothing in the SROE, theater-specific ROE, or SPINSs limit this inherent right and obligation. However, for clarity and understanding, commanders may establish parameters for certain self-defense situations, and the allowable responses based on the operational environment. For further guidance, see CJCSI 3121.01B, *Standing Rules of Engagement/Standing Rules for the Use of Force for US Forces.*

(b) **Targets of Opportunity.** SEAD targets of opportunity are those enemy air defense systems detected by surface or airborne sensors or observers within range of available weapons and not yet targeted. Many SEAD efforts by surface forces may be against targets of opportunity. Surface and air weapon systems may suppress AD targets of opportunity whenever capabilities, mission priorities, and ROE permit. Such suppression operations must be in accordance with established rules and FSCMs. The purpose of SEAD ROE is to enhance effective SEAD while minimizing risks to friendly forces.

(c) **Targets Acquired by Observers or Controllers.** Combat elements may often be in good position to acquire SEAD targets of opportunity. Observers, spotters, controllers, and liaison officers from the components have the authority to request suppression for SEAD targets of opportunity. Such personnel may include joint terminal attack controllers, airborne controllers and observers, TACPs, Marine assault support coordinators, artillery forward observers, UA operators, Army fire support teams and combat observation/lasing teams, and STRYKER platoons. The observers or controllers will forward these requests through their respective fire support channels. Requirements should first be passed to suppression systems that belong to or support the unit acquiring the target because they can respond immediately. If the suppression requirement exceeds the capabilities of the ground forces, the immediate request will be sent via the air request net to the component control centers.

(d) **Targets Acquired by Aircrews.** When aircrews have acquired SEAD targets of opportunity but have not engaged them because of mission priorities, weapons limitations, or SEAD ROE, they pass the information to the agency controlling their mission. **This agency should immediately pass the targeting data through the appropriate C2 channels to the battle manager/operations center of the force component capable of targeting the threat.**

h. **Surface Component SEAD Capabilities.** Based on the JFC guidance, the land and maritime surface components' fires cells, fire support elements and fire support coordination centers will determine the weapon systems available to conduct SEAD. Examples of these capabilities/forces include field artillery, mortars, naval surface fire, attack helicopters, EW, and SSMs. To ensure unity of effort and conservation of force, components need to coordinate their SEAD activities within their AOs with the JFACC to ensure they meet mission requirements and do not interfere with other planned operations. Component liaison elements, such as the BCD located in the JAOC, can assist localized suppression operations by coordinating the means to request surface fire support. **A rapid and free exchange of SEAD target information between the JFACC and other component commanders is required for effective surface suppression.**

(1) Component commanders will use their organic assets to locate, identify, and attack SEAD targets within their AOs and areas of interest whenever possible. They continually update lists of potential SEAD targets, including target location, desired effects, timing, and sequence of attack. In many cases, however, only the JFACC has assets to specifically find and identify or attack certain SEAD targets so the components must request SEAD support. Component liaison elements normally are responsible for consolidating their component's SEAD requirements and priorities for action.

(2) An air support request (ASR) should identify known or suspected enemy air defense threats to, from, and around the target area. Within their capabilities, each echelon handling the request refines and updates threat data. The ASR contains this updated data, along with the type of suppression desired by the requesting component. For example, during the planning and execution of CAS, TACPs and other fire support agencies identify potential local SEAD targets and request SEAD fire support.

Refer to FM 3-01.4/MCRP 3-22.2A/NTTP 3-01.42/AFTTP(I) 3-2.28, Multi-Service Tactics, Techniques, and Procedures for Suppression of Enemy Air Defenses, *for additional detailed information regarding SEAD.*

9. Fighter Escort

a. Fighter escort missions are often essential to offensive air operations and for protection of HVAAs. As an OCA mission, fighter escort sorties are normally flown over

---

SUPPRESSION OF ENEMY AIR DEFENSES IN "THE STORM"

On the morning of 17 January [1991], an EA-6B from Marine Tactical Electronic Warfare Squadron Two provided electronic warfare support for Marine, Navy, and Royal Air Force strike packages attacking strategic targets at the Al-'Amarah and Az-Zubayr command and control sites, as well as the Az-Zubayr railroad yards and the Al-Basrah bridges across the Tigris River. These targets were heavily defended by interlocking belts of surface-to-air missiles (SAMs) and antiaircraft artillery (AAA). Iraqi fighters also were a potential threat. This was a dangerous mission— among the first daylight strikes of the war. Long before they approached the targets, the EA-6B crew started to work. The first enemy radar that came up was quickly jammed. Shortly after, however, additional radars were noted searching for the strike groups. Jamming of Iraqi long-range early warning radars allowed the strikers to approach undetected. However, Iraqi ground control intercept radars as well as target tracking radars simultaneously began probing the Coalition strike package. The EA-6B crew quickly introduced intense electronic jamming into all modes of the Iraqi air defense system, which prevented the vectoring of enemy fighters. They also forced SAM and AAA systems into autonomous operation, uncoordinated by the command and control system which greatly reduced their ability to locate and track Coalition aircraft. To accomplish this, the EA-6B crew did not attempt evasive action but placed themselves into a predictable, wings-level orbit which highlighted their position amidst the beaconing (sic) and jamming strobes of the enemy radars. The severe degradation to radio transmissions caused by jamming interference limited the EA-6B's ability to receive threat calls, making it vulnerable to enemy aircraft. Nonetheless, the crew remained on station, enabling all Coalition aircraft to strike the targets, accomplish the missions, and return home without loss or damage.

SOURCE: 3rd Marine Aircraft Wing Award Citation
cited in DOD Final Report to Congress,
Conduct of the Persian Gulf War, April 1992

---

enemy territory to protect other primary mission aircraft from enemy fighters en route to and from a target area during offensive missions (i.e., for air interdiction, OCA attack, SEAD, an airborne operation). Fighter escorts may protect airlift, AR, EW, C2, search and rescue, and SOF aircraft from enemy fighters. Fighter escorts also may be used as a DCA mission, as in the case of HVAA protection. Air planners, along with JFACC/JAOC intelligence staff, must evaluate the threat posed by the adversary counterair forces and determine the type and size of fighter escort force required, because the same air assets are usually shared for DCA operations. The planners also must coordinate the support required by the escort force (i.e., AR, EW, C2).

b. **Offensive Fighter Escorts.** Joint air operations may require air-to-air capable fighters to be used as escorts to protect friendly aircraft over enemy territory from attacks by enemy fighters. After considering the mission requirements, the required capabilities of the fighter escorts (i.e., speed, sophistication of weaponry, data links, guns) are determined by the operational/tactical commanders responsible for air operations. Those air operations packages also may be supported by specially equipped and trained SEAD assets when surface AD threats are also a concern.

c. **Defensive Fighter Escorts.** Fighter escort missions may be planned as DCA missions to protect HVAAs (i.e., AWACS, JSTARS, Rivet Joint, Compass Call, E-2C) from potential enemy fighter attack over neutral or friendly territory.

d. **Threats/Targets.** The primary threats for fighter escorts include any enemy aircraft with a capability to attack and disrupt/destroy the primary mission aircraft. Escort fighters target only those airborne aircraft that threaten the primary mission. Fighter escorts in conjunction with their supported aircraft must avoid the direct threat of enemy surface-based ADs (unless the fighters are escorting a SEAD package). If SAM/AAA threats cannot be avoided, the threat and risk to the primary mission and fighter escorts require SEAD support.

e. **Resources.** Dedicated air-to-air or multi-role fighters are best suited for the escort mission. Escort missions are more effective when ground and airborne early warning or GCI radar assets are available for situational awareness and threat warnings. Airborne C2 (battle management) assets normally are required for rapidly synchronized/complex air operations. The duration of the escort mission may require AR support for the escorts, even if the primary mission or other support aircraft do not. IO support, apart from SEAD support, also may be required to disrupt the effectiveness of enemy communications and information systems that support their acquisition, tracking, and interception capabilities.

f. **Execution.** The specific responsibilities of the fighter escort force must be clear to all participants. In direct support, their mission is to protect the primary mission force and not necessarily attrite enemy aircraft. **If the enemy chooses not to attack because a fighter escort is present, then the objective of the fighter escort has been met.** Conversely, escort fighters must exercise caution against being drawn away from the escorted force by diversion or decoys, thereby leaving that force vulnerable to other enemy aircraft.

10. Fighter Sweep

a. The fighter sweep is an offensive mission by fighter aircraft to seek out and destroy enemy aircraft or targets of opportunity in a designated area.

b. Fighter sweeps are conducted by fighter/fighter-attack/multi-role fighter aircraft. Normally, fighter sweeps are conducted in order to achieve local or JOA air superiority. Based on the targeting potential, AWACS and ISR assets should be used in support for more effective acquisition of targets.

c. The need for fighter sweep missions versus attack operations will depend on the air and missile threat and the objectives of the JAOP. Intelligence should help OCA planners determine the proper force mix (air-to-air and air-to-ground) for a fighter sweep in a given sector.

d. **Threats/Targets.** The fighter sweep is a flexible air mission because threats/targets can be anywhere in the allotted sector. Fighter sweeps should normally be planned into areas where the threat from surface-based ADs is minimized, through tactics or attrition. This enables the concentration of OCA assets on the destruction of enemy aircraft, missiles, missile launchers, and other such soft targets of opportunity.

e. **Resources.** Package aircraft normally are those fighter/bomber aircraft used for OCA attack, air interdiction, CAS, strategic attack, and fighter escort missions. Friendly early warning and GCI radar sites and AWACS aircraft should be tasked to support the mission. This may be especially important when aircraft with BVR ID systems and weapons are used or when significant numbers of enemy aircraft may be encountered. SEAD requirements will be determined by enemy surface-based AD capabilities and the JFC's acceptable level of risk. Based on mission duration and distances, AR also may be required. EW may be used to enhance the element of surprise/disruption and give the attacking force a tactical advantage.

f. **Execution.** Although a flexible air mission, the fighter sweep involves employing fighter aircraft over hostile territory. Fighter sweep missions normally should follow a series of OCA attack and SEAD operations aimed at neutralizing/destroying the enemy offensive and defensive aircraft and missile threats. However, a sweep may be synchronized with a rapid series of OCA operations (including attack, SEAD, and escort missions), or into other offensive air operations (i.e., air interdiction, strategic attack). Ground or airborne warning and control assets enhance overall effectiveness, but if those supporting resources are not available, execution of autonomous fighter sweeps with fighters using only their own fire control radar and ID systems are possible. Flexibility being key, some fighter sweeps may be just air-to-air capable fighters looking for airborne targets; others can be multi-role fighters hunting air and ground targets.

58TFS FIGHTER SWEEP/ESCORT DURING DESERT STORM

"The plan's essence—as far as the 58th was concerned—was that twenty F15s, in line with strategically positioned four ships (four-ship flights of aircraft) from several squadrons, were going to be the first air-to-air fighters to sweep across the Iraqi border after the STEALTHs, F-15E bombers, and TOMAHAWK missiles had made a surprise attack mostly on Baghdad's vital command and communications centers, hopefully knocking them out and, with them, the country's air defenses.

Then, as the bombers, done with their surprise missions, sped back to safety south over the border, the EAGLES, including two four ships from the 58th would charge in over their top, engaging any enemy fighters...and clearing a path for the waves of conventional nonstealth bombers and other warplanes that would be following."

SOURCE: *Wings of Fury* by Robert Wilcox, 1996, pp. 220–221

Intentionally Blank

CHAPTER V
DEFENSIVE COUNTERAIR PLANNING AND OPERATIONS

"Find the enemy and shoot him down, anything else is nonsense."

Captain Manfred Baron von Richtofen
The Red Baron, **1917**

1. General

a. DCA operations consist of active and passive AMD measures executed through a joint C2 infrastructure. The AADC normally is responsible for developing an IADS by integrating the capabilities of different components with a robust C2 architecture. **Because of their time-sensitive nature, DCA operations require streamlined coordination and decision-making processes.**

b. The AADC uses assigned operation/campaign plan tasks to develop the AADP with the coordination of component commanders, MNF partners, and the JFC's staff. (See Appendix B, "Area Air Defense Plan Format"). The AADP prescribes the integration of active AD design, passive AD measures, and the C2 system to provide a comprehensive approach to defending against the threat. The AADP builds upon the DCA Estimate (see Appendix C, "Defensive Counterair Estimate Format") and should address command relationships, the adversary and friendly situations, the AADC's intent, concept of operation, and logistics and C2 requirements, as well as detailed weapons control and engagement procedures. The AADP must be closely integrated with the ACP and should facilitate a streamlined decision and coordination process for DCA operations. Due to the dynamic nature of joint counterair operations, the AADP may need to be continually modified. Ideally, as the JFC's operation/campaign progresses and the AADP is refined, the combination of DCA and OCA operations should diminish the enemy's ability to conduct air and missile attacks, reducing the requirement for DCA operations and the threat to the JFC's freedom of action.

c. This chapter discusses AMD from the perspective of an AADC being responsible for DCA operations, whether or not a JFACC is also designated as the AADC and/or ACA.

SECTION A. DEFENSIVE COUNTERAIR PLANNING

2. General

a. Through promulgation of the AADP, the AADC implements theater-/JOA-wide DCA priorities, authorities, procedures, tasks, and actions approved by the JFC. The AADP is designed to be a plan of action for DCA operations, and the RADCs/SADCs, if established, may be required or may wish to provide supplements to the AADP to reflect additional guidance or intentions.

b. DCA planning should adhere to the following principles and ideals:

(1) **Centralized Planning and Direction.** Centralized planning and direction is essential for coordinating the efforts of the DCA forces. The JFACC/AADC maintains unity of effort and optimizes the contributions of all forces.

(2) **Decentralized Execution.** Decentralized execution permits timely, decisive action by tactical commanders without compromising the ability of operational-level commanders to direct DCA operations. Decentralized execution is essential due to the high tempo of DCA operations and because no one commander can control the detailed actions of a large number of units or individuals during a complex operation. The AADC-RADC-SADC organizational structure with delegated commit, ID, and engagement authority enables this principle.

(3) **Planned Responses.** Planned responses support prompt, decisive tactical action by exploiting prior development, testing, and rehearsal of DCA operations. Use of planned responses is especially important for BMD operations due to compressed timelines.

(4) **Effective and Efficient Communications.** In addition to being fully interoperable and efficient, COMNETs require superior information management processes for timely data and information exchanges. An optimized, effective network that avoids unnecessary communications will both provide for an improved operational tempo and support key decision making.

(5) **Layered Defense.** A layered defense should provide multiple engagement opportunities, ideally beginning at the maximum range from friendly forces and areas, before attacking aircraft release their weapons and missile warheads can impact. This includes interception of enemy surveillance and reconnaissance/targeting aircraft. The layered defense normally includes land- or sea-based aircraft, long- and medium-range SAMs, and SHORADs (including AAA and close-in weapons systems). The layered defense normally includes support by necessary surface and airborne early detection, warning, and tracking assets and electronic decoys/jammers and chaff.

(6) **360-Degree Coverage.** 360-degree coverage guards against unpredictable targets, pop-up targets, and multithreat/multiaxis attacks by aircraft (including ASMs) or CMs. Since the flight profiles of most BMs are very predictable, the specialized assets used for BM defense normally cover specific launch-space sectors or BM operating areas rather than 360 degrees.

(7) **ID and Tracking.** Early detection, location, ID, and tracking support prompt attack warnings and timely cueing of not only AMD, but they also enable prompt, informed decision support for determining launch sites and engaging targeting of TSTs (e.g., deployed enemy BMs).

(8) **Alert and Warning.** Design, administer, and implement alert and warning procedures and networks, which influence combat system and weapons readiness conditions.

(9) **Establish Modes of Control.** For tactical AMD forces, these modes are key to operations. In AD, centralized control is the mode whereby a higher echelon makes direct target assignments to fire units, and decentralized control is the normal mode whereby a

higher echelon monitors unit actions, making direct target assignments to units only when necessary to ensure proper fire distribution or to prevent engagement of friendly aircraft.

3. Defensive Counterair Assets

a. DCA operations employ a mix of weapon, sensor, communications, and C2 systems integrated from all components into an IADS to protect friendly forces, assets, population centers, and interests from air and missile threats.

b. The integration of AMD systems provides efficient control and exchange of information to all DCA forces. Assets used in conducting DCA operations normally include air-to-air capable fixed-wing aircraft; SAMs; AAA; surface-, air-, and space-based sensors; EW systems; and C2 systems; all networked into an IADS using a redundant and flexible C2 architecture with interoperable data links, voice command circuits, and common displays. If OCA is not possible before threat aircraft or missiles are launched, and because DCA is by nature reactive, the enemy may gain the early initiative; the IADS must be flexible enough to respond to the most challenging threats.

c. **BMD Assets.** BMD systems provide lower-and-upper tier intercept capabilities to counter BMs of all ranges. The objective of BMD is an integrated, "layered" architecture that provides multiple opportunities to destroy missiles and their warheads before they can reach their targets.

d. Land-based and sea-based AMD forces possess the following type of SAM capabilities:

(1) ARFOR ADA battalions are task organized under ADA BDEs to protect JFC and/or ARFOR critical assets. AMD forces have short-range and medium- to high-altitude AD capabilities. They normally are configured with two-four missile battalions (high-to-medium-altitude air defense [HIMAD]) and/or a SHORAD capability. In addition, theater-level BDEs, with HIMAD and/or exo-atmospheric assets normally will be made available to the AADC for DAL protection, usually under C2 of the commander, AAMDC.

(2) Varying with the size of the MAGTF, MARFOR are equipped with long-range radars, SHORAD weapons, and extensive C2 facilities.

(3) NAVFOR AMD capabilities include SAMs and the C2 suitable for regional/sector AD commands. Aegis-equipped cruisers and destroyers will provide area (e.g., high-to-medium altitude AD and BMD) and point (e.g., SHORAD) AMD. In addition to those AMD capable ships, all surface combatants are provided with some self-defense capability (guns and/or missiles). Area defense capable ships normally will deploy as part of a carrier strike group but may also be attached to amphibious ready groups or deploy independently. Some of the Aegis-equipped/command ships may be made available and assigned tasks in support of the AADC for C2 of AD in a maritime or littoral area while remaining under the OPCON/TACON of the appropriate NAVFOR commander. The AMDC may be established by a composite warfare commander/officer in tactical command (CWC/OTC) to conduct AD within the task group/task force assigned operational area. CTF IAMD coordinates with the AMDC through the CWC/OTC to ensure seamless integration of

maritime forces in the execution of the AADP. Maritime assets assigned to DCA missions within the sphere of influence of a strike group commander will operate within the CWC structure. Maritime assets assigned to DCA missions outside of a strike group may be TACON to CTF IAMD. Planning for the AMD of maritime assets performing other missions outside of a strike group will be the responsibility of CTF IAMD.

e. **Interceptor Aircraft.** The AFFOR, NAVFOR, and MARFOR possess fixed-wing aircraft capable of an AD role. However, both the multi-role and air-to-air capable aircraft normally can be tasked against both DCA and OCA operations, dependent upon the JFC's daily air apportionment decision.

f. Other aircraft that are critical to DCA include the airborne C2, AR, signals intelligence, and EW aircraft.

g. When operating with an MNF, a multitude of AMD capabilities (aircraft, interceptors, sensors, SAMs, ISR, and C2) from simple legacy to state-of-the-art is possible. Integration of those capabilities without creating a seam or hole in the AMD coverage is the challenge.

h. In addition to EW, IO assets and procedures can be essential to DCA operations because of the critical reliance on electronic and computer systems for sensing, passing, and displaying air and missile threat and defense information. Understanding that reliance, an enemy may attempt offensive IO against DCA assets.

4. **Integrated Air Defense Systems**

a. An IADS is not a formal system in itself but the aggregate of Service/functional component AMD systems comprising sensors, weapons, C2, communications, intelligence systems, and personnel operating in a theater/JOA under the command of an AADC. However, the IADS typically depends on support and enabling functions from national assets and systems not controlled by the JFC. Because the IADS is normally composed of different components, it requires significant integration and interoperability of communications and TDL architectures to generate its expected synergistic effects for the JFC. An IADS requires planning that begins with organizing the AMD forces and determining command relationships through the establishment of the COMNET for C2 of all the weapon systems integrated for DCA operations.

b. To ensure counterair situational awareness and enable decision making, plans for an IADS must include the requirement for a reliable, consistent COP/CTP available in all major and supporting C2 facilities.

c. The heart of the IADS is the integrated forces/capabilities controlled by, made available to, or in direct support of the AADC, and the actions planned and executed in accordance with the JFC's AADP. Subject to the authority of the JFC, each component commander within a joint force does the following in support of DCA operations:

(1) Coordinates and prioritizes their DCA operations and needs with the JFC and other component commanders through the AADC.

Note: The commander responsible for the JSAs within the JOA will coordinate with the AADC to ensure those areas are covered by the AADP, and should provide a joint security coordinator liaison officer to JAOC or whichever facility is the prominent C2 node for the IADS.

(2) Employs AMD weapons in accordance with the ROE and the AADP.

(3) Identifies AADP capability shortfalls to AADC and requests OCA and other support to mitigate gaps.

(4) Coordinates and deconflicts the employment of forces with other subordinate commands. Coordination for airspace control may be facilitated by colocating key airspace control facilities, AMD, and fire support coordination organizations.

(5) Coordinates/provides airspace control, as required, in designated areas in accordance with the ACP. Is prepared to assume airspace control in other areas when combat or other factors degrade the ACS.

(6) Forwards requests for ACMs in accordance with the ACP.

(7) Develops detailed airspace control instructions, plans, and procedures in accordance with ACP guidance. Keeps these detailed instructions, plans, and procedures consistent with JFC-approved ACP.

(8) In support of the IADS, provides necessary facilities and personnel for airspace control functions in assigned areas and identifies those facilities and personnel for inclusion in the ACP.

d. It is the responsibility of the JFC's communications system officer, the J-6, to plan, oversee, and maintain the IADS C2 architecture. This includes all voice communications networks and the JDN.

(1) **JDN.** The JDN is essential to the IADS. The JDNO is responsible to the JFC, through the J-3 with support from the J-6, for all JDN operations, including the intelligence network, ground network, sensor network, and MTN and integrating data from the component commands into the common database used to generate the CTP. Each of those networks has a responsible manager as do the components (i.e., the CJE). The JDNO ensures interoperability and integrates joint force information systems that provide the input to the CTPs and the COP. Although closely associated with DCA operations, the networks administered by the JDNO are critical to tasks throughout the entire operational area and for every component. The JDNO may be located with the JFC or JFACC.

(2) **JICO.** The JICO cell is responsible for planning, establishing, and maintaining the MTN and provides a CTP input to the JDN for integration into the COP. The JFC, with recommendations from the JICO through the JFACC/AADC, may require a RICO/SICO for each RADC/SADC. The RICO/SICO reports to the RADC/SADC to develop and maintain their portion of the CTP and ultimately for the COP. RICOs/SICOs will coordinate with and answer to the JICO for planning and execution functions that cross regional boundaries or

impact the theater-wide JDN. The JICO may recommend resolution of architectural and data coordination issues between RICO/SICO cells.

For more detailed information on the JICO, see CJCSM 3115.01B, Joint Data Networks (JDN) Operations.

Refer to FM 3-01.15/MCRP 3-25E/NTTP 3-01.8/AFTTP(I) 3-2.31, Multi-Service Tactics, Techniques, and Procedures for an Integrated Air Defense System, *for a discussion of IADS.*

5. **Enemy Air and Missile Threats**

    a. Enemy threats comprise two main elements: air threats, including manned and UA and CM, and BM.

        (1) **Air.** Air threats can include bombers, fighter-attack, fighter escorts, ISR, SEAD, EW, airlift (for airborne attacks), helicopters, CMs, ASMs, manned suicide bombers, airborne early warning, UA, and AR aircraft. It should be noted that UA are being developed with more technologically advanced systems and capabilities. They can duplicate some of the capabilities of manned aircraft for both surveillance/reconnaissance and attack missions. They can be small enough and/or slow enough to elude detection by standard early warning sensor systems and could pose a formidable threat to friendly forces.

        (2) **BMs.** BMs pose a significant challenge since they are often difficult to detect and destroy after launch. They can be employed from long ranges across AOR boundaries and in all types of weather. BMs, whether employed in high or low altitude trajectories, also present unique problems, including high velocities and short reaction times for the defender. BMs include short, medium, intermediate, and long range/intercontinental and have trajectories that are commonly divided into four phases of flight: boost, ascent, midcourse, and terminal.

Additional information is provided in Appendix D, "Threat Missile Systems," and Appendix E, "Global Ballistic Missile Defense Synchronization."

    b. C2 facilities, like other infrastructure targets (e.g., ammunition storage), are vital links in the enemy's system that enable them to generate combat power and attack through the air domain.

    c. Air and missile threats vary in technological sophistication and capabilities; additionally, technology transfers and weapons proliferation complicate the ability to assess all potential threats with certainty. Many countries possess and continually upgrade modern combat aircraft, but an air force and its sustainment can be very expensive in comparison to a missile force. Based on improved technologies and increases in the number of available missile systems, the number of countries with both short- and long-range missile capabilities is likely to increase. Also, a mobile missile force can be dispersed to complicate its being targeted and employed from remote sites without the infrastructure, support, and manpower required for aircraft. The proliferation of CMs, BMs, and UASs complicates the tasks of providing force protection and attaining air superiority.

d. GCCs should specifically focus intelligence efforts on potential adversaries and their air and missile threats in their theaters and adjacent areas of interest, and assess the vulnerability to cross-AOR threats from outside an established JOA/theater of operations. Emphasis should be placed on WMD capabilities and potential aircraft and missile delivery systems. Intelligence developed during peacetime planning and collected regularly, or as necessary, should prevent the strategic or tactical surprise of an unanticipated capability by a potential adversary. Intelligence can support ROE decision points for proactive AMD protection measures based on imminent hostilities.

6. Identification and Tracking

a. ID and tracking relies on surveillance and reporting. Execution of efficient DCA operations requires a continuous surveillance and reporting system capable of NRT production and dissemination of the tracking data necessary for effective decision making. Target track production is a sequential process that begins with the surveillance function. NRT surveillance and threat analysis is dependent upon the ability to merge all-source sensor data into an accurate theater/JOA attack assessment, whether from ground-, sea-, or air-based radars, or space-based sensors. As a track is detected, it is identified and labeled and this information is disseminated as rapidly as possible. The track data provided is sufficiently detailed and timely to allow decision makers to evaluate the track, determine the significance of the threat, and either designate DCA forces for interception or engagement or advise units of the passage of friendly aircraft.

b. **Surveillance Planning and Execution Considerations.** Detection, tracking, and ID are dependent upon the surveillance plan. The three most commonly accepted plans include mutual support (preferred method), track/report by exception, and track production areas (or a combination). Each has advantages, depending on the mix of surveillance sensors and platforms and their degree of interoperability.

(1) **Detection.** Tracking begins with detection. The types of sensors and their placement determine the detection capability of the IADS. Sensor placement is affected by the threat, threat axis, terrain, weather, time-distance analysis, defended assets, desired engagement zone, and surveillance requirements. Sensor placement also must consider accessibility, connectivity, force protection, mutual interference, and HN support.

(2) **Tracking.** The surveillance plan will contribute directly to the ability of the IADS to continuously and efficiently track airborne objects. Regardless of the surveillance plan adopted, interoperability for effective tracking and reporting can be difficult because of a number of anomalies in the systems. The surveillance and data link (reporting) planners must consider the following factors to minimize the effects of gaps in interoperability:

(a) **Track Deconfliction.** More than one sensor may detect and track a target. The assumption that all C2 participants will always see the same tracks, with the same identity, and in the same place, is not valid and leads to misunderstanding and mistakes. Robust voice communication among C2 agencies (ID authorities) is critical to resolving track discrepancies. Differences in sensor platforms can aggravate preexisting problems of miscorrelation and dual tracking. The following problems may result:

<u>1.</u> Tracks not updating/tracking aircraft.

<u>2.</u> Tracks appear to be tracking aircraft but are not.

<u>3.</u> Tracks that "swap" or "jump" from one aircraft to another.

<u>4.</u> IFF modes and codes swapped among tracks, conflicting their IDs.

<u>5.</u> Dual tracks. "Dualing" is the occurrence of multiple tracks on one target resulting in an air picture with more tracks than actual objects of interest. This occurs frequently within the IADS. Failure of some surveillance systems to correlate contacts with precise participant location and identification (PPLI) data (symbols) can also cause dual tracking.

(b) **Track Correlation Problems.** Correlation problems include varying size of correlation windows, auto-correlation system differences (or lack thereof), radar-measured altitude differences between systems, IFF conflicts by systems, sensor registration/gridlock problems, and lack of familiarization of the other Service system's capabilities and operations. Track correlation problems can create ID conflicts, which are dangerous and can result in loss of situational awareness and contribute to the risk of fratricide. **All combat systems introduce a certain amount of ambiguity into the "link" and although TDL message standards are common to all Services, the implementation of those standards may be inconsistent and selective. Combat system software baselines and ID doctrine also can introduce uncertainty into shared data.**

(3) **ID.** ID is used to support current ROE in light of weapon systems capabilities. The AADC is responsible for developing IADS ID criteria (both procedural and positive) for JFC approval in the AADP, with specific instructions in the ATO and/or SPINS. Not all IADS participants may see the same ID-related information. This is dependent primarily on TDL system implementation, J-series versus M-series message standards, and operator display capabilities. Because of the different implementation of TDL messages, planners should consider limiting the number of track classification symbols (ID symbols) to reduce confusion and the potential for fratricide. Positive ID (either on-board or off-board) or visual ID nearly always will be part of the ID process. The AADC may use the following considerations when developing ID criteria consistent with and in support of the current ROE:

(a) IFF Modes (1-5 per the ATO).

(b) PPLI.

(c) Procedural measures (e.g., MRRs).

(d) A radar contact correlated with a voice (position) report from an air or ground control agency.

(e) Off-board/on-board CID systems.

(f) Visual ID.

(g) Point of origin.

(h) Track maneuvers (e.g., noncompliance with ACMs).

(i) Validated speed, direction, altitude, and hostile intent/act.

(j) Formation assessment ("guilt by association"). Formation assessment is a procedural ID that can be used to identify all members in a group of targets. This group ID is based on the ID of at least one member of the group (using ID criteria). Factors such as similarity to known threat tactical formations and relative spatial relationships (distance, speed, and altitude) contribute to the formation assessment ID of the group. Once the group has been identified and the group is observed to split, all contacts in each of the resulting groups maintain the ID. This ID methodology requires that one or more radar systems (e.g., fighter or surface) continuously monitor the group or groups during the split. The group is considered "continuously tracked" if not lost/faded for more than one radar sweep/cycle.

Note: Army ADA systems (with the exception of Patriot) do not use group IDs and each track is evaluated using current ID criteria.

c. It is incumbent on the combat system making the ID (having ID authority) and the TDL operator to ensure tracks are correctly identified. Every opportunity within tactical timelines should be taken to resolve all track and ID ambiguities prior to engagement by firing units. Evaluation reports with details of tracking shortfalls may be researched at the Joint Deployable Analysis Team (JDAT). See the JDAT Web site at https://jdat.eglin.af.mil.

d. During plans development, the parameters and details for positive and procedural ID, auto-ID systems, formation assessment, and CID should be developed and approved by the JFC along with the ROE and promulgated as discussed in Chapter III, "Counterair Planning," Section D, "Identification."

Refer to FM 3-01.15/MCRP 3-25E/NTTP 3-01.8/AFTTP(I) 3-2.31, Multi-Service Tactics, Techniques, and Procedures for an Integrated Air Defense System, *for a detailed discussion of the ID/CID process within an IADS.*

7. **Area Air Defense Planning**

a. **Planning Considerations.** Development of the AADP and planning DCA operations involves integrating friendly force capabilities and limitations against adversary vulnerabilities to achieve optimum results in a dynamic tactical environment. Factors that should be taken into consideration for planning include:

(1) **Mission Analysis.** The mission statement is the AADC's expression of what DCA forces must accomplish and why. During mission analysis, the AADC translates specified and implied tasks into missions for the component and subordinate commands with DCA assets. Intent of the JFC, the current situation, resources available, and the desired end state contribute to the mission statement.

(2) **DCA Estimate.** Planners use the DCA estimate to evaluate how factors in each field of interest will influence the potential COAs, to provide information regarding their supportability, to recommend DCA priorities, and to form a basis for the AADP. The estimate provides the basis for planning current and future DCA operations and is developed in concert with the JFC's staff. See Appendix C, "Defensive Counterair Estimate Format."

(3) **Objectives.** The AADC develops an AADP to achieve DCA objectives that support the counterair effort to gain and maintain the degree of air superiority and protection required by the JFC to satisfy overall campaign objectives.

(4) **Force Requirements.** The AADC determines the type and number of forces needed to sustain the DCA effort until the objectives are accomplished, understanding that some assets may be shared with and lost between OCA, DCA, and other operations.

(5) **Logistics.** A comprehensive analysis of logistic capability is integral to support of DCA requirements. Planners must anticipate losses of critical items (e.g., fuel storage) and be aware of any agreements or CCDR directives that significantly alter responsibilities for logistic support.

(6) **Synchronization/Timing.** Synchronizing/deconflicting employment of capabilities/forces and matching appropriate weapons against enemy critical vulnerabilities are essential functions for the AADC.

(7) **Weapons Availability and Pairing.** Airborne targets may seem vulnerable to attack but may be impervious to certain weapons or EW systems. Planners must have a detailed understanding of enemy capabilities and friendly force DCA weapons and systems capabilities. They must analyze the threat from the perspective of correctly paired target-shooter adequacy of the DCA force. This will feed into logistic planning, CAL/DAL force allocation, and forces requests.

(8) **Force Availability.** Careful planning is required to ensure timely arrival and quick integration of DCA forces and to synchronize use of assets for DCA, OCA, and other operations.

(9) **Economy of Force.** In conjunction with planned responses, proper sizing and composition of responses to enemy attacks/penetrations of friendly airspace are essential. Economy of force includes analysis of the probability of destruction/disruption, distances, weather, weapon system reliability, etc.

(10) **Operational Assessment.** A comprehensive, continuous operational assessment is an essential part of DCA planning. The AADC's staff must determine how to evaluate the results of OCA and DCA operations to assist in ID of the decision points (e.g., points of attrition of enemy missiles or aircraft) regarding achievement of the operational objectives.

b. **Weapon Engagement Zones.** WEZs are a critical part of DCA planning because they represent part of the current defense posture against the air and missile threats. WEZs are established through the AADP and ACMs and can be changed as necessary. WEZs also represent the integration of airspace control with AMDs.

(1) WEZ. In AD, airspace of defined dimensions within which the responsibility for engagement of air threats normally rests with a particular weapon system.

(a) FEZ. In AD, that airspace of defined dimensions within which the responsibility for engagement of air threats normally rests with fighter aircraft.

(b) HIMEZ. In AD, that airspace of defined dimensions within which the responsibility for engagement of air threats normally rests with high-altitude SAMs.

(c) LOMEZ. In AD, that airspace of defined dimensions within which the responsibility for engagement of air threats normally rests with low- to medium-altitude surface-to-air missiles.

(d) SHORADEZ. In AD, that airspace of defined dimensions within which the responsibility for engagement of air threats normally rests with SHORAD weapons. It may be established within a low- or high-altitude missile engagement zone.

(e) JEZ. In AD, that airspace of defined dimensions within which multiple AD systems (SAMs and aircraft) are simultaneously employed to engage air threats. The JEZ construct blends MEZ and FEZ constructs into a more flexible engagement zone that can concurrently support operations against enemy airborne targets, including BMs.

(2) A MEZ can include one or more HIMEZs, LOMEZs, and/or SHORADEZs.

Note: By definition, a SHORADEZ may be established within a LOMEZ or HIMEZ because the SHORADEZ has SHORAD weapons (e.g., short-range SAMs, AAA, and small arms).

c. **Active AD Design.** DCA operations require not only the integration of all appropriate DCA forces/capabilities within a theater/JOA, but also their efficient and effective employment to protect selected assets and forces from attack. These operations are subject to the weapons control procedures established by the AADC. Defense against BMs, CMs, ASMs, and aircraft each have unique requirements for active ADs. During planning, multiple options should be developed using various combinations of weapon systems and WEZs allowing the flexibility to defend all critical assets, although there may be resources shortfalls. When possible, the AADC should design a layered defense to allow multiple engagement opportunities for friendly forces.

(1) An active AD includes the following types of defensive coverage:

(a) **Area Defense.** Area defense uses a combination of weapon systems (e.g., aircraft and SAMs) or various combinations of airborne and ground-based sensors and shooters to defend broad areas.

(b) **Point Defense.** Point defense protects limited areas, normally in defense of vital elements of forces or installations. For example, a SAM or AAA unit positioned to protect an airfield is considered point defense.

(c) **Self-Defense.** Self-defense operations allow friendly units to defend themselves against direct attacks or threats of attack through the use of organic weapons and systems. The right of self-defense is inherent to all ROE and weapons control procedures.

(d) **HVAA Protection.** HVAA protection defends airborne assets that are so important that the loss of even one could seriously impact US warfighting capabilities. HVAA protection is normally performed by fighter aircraft using various CAP or escort tactics, but can also be accomplished by surface-based assets such as Aegis ships.

(2) The following tasks also should be considered when planning active ADs:

(a) **Determine Surveillance Coverage Areas.** Defended airspace must be under continuous surveillance to facilitate early warning. The DCA planner should use a combination of air-, surface-, and space-based detection assets to achieve this requirement. Adequate early warning of air and missile attacks provides the reaction time necessary for friendly forces to seek shelter or take appropriate action. Early warning of hostile air and missile attacks is vital for a layered defense.

(b) **Develop the Active AMD Fire Plan.** The objective is to provide the required level of protection specified in the CAL. Defense resources involve applying a mix of the following six employment guidelines, because not all may be required or possible to defend dependent upon the threat and DCA assets available:

<u>1</u>. **Mutual Support.** Weapons are positioned so that the fires of one weapon can engage targets within the dead zone of the adjacent weapon systems. For gun systems, this dead zone is usually small. For missile systems, the dead zone may be large and mutual support is a critical element. Mutual support can also cover non-operational units or units at lower states of readiness.

<u>2</u>. **Overlapping Fires.** Weapons are positioned so that their engagement envelopes overlap. Because of the many altitudes from which the enemy can attack or conduct surveillance operations, defense planners must apply mutual supporting and overlapping fires vertically and horizontally.

<u>3</u>. **Balanced Fires.** Weapons are positioned to deliver an equal volume of fires in all directions. This is necessary for AD in an area where the terrain does not canalize the enemy or when the avenue of approach is unpredictable.

<u>4</u>. **Weighted Coverage.** Weapons are positioned to concentrate fires toward the most likely threat direction of attack. Based on the tactical situation, a commander may risk leaving one direction of attack unprotected or lightly protected to weight coverage in a more likely direction.

<u>5</u>. **Early Engagement.** Sensors and weapons are positioned to maximize early warning and to engage and destroy aircraft and missiles before they acquire and fire on or damage the defended asset.

<u>6</u>. **Defense in Depth.** AMD sensors and weapons are positioned to enable multiple engagement opportunities and deliver an increasing volume of fire as an enemy air or missile threat approaches the protected asset. Defense in depth reduces the probability that "leakers" will reach the defended asset or force.

(c) **Plan a MEZ.** Proper sequencing in the establishment of WEZs is critical to an effective IADS and DCA operations. MEZs established for surface defense are based on specific boundaries and weapons system capabilities. For the organic SAM capability of a surface force, the MEZ boundaries should be within the component AO, and for direct support the MEZ should cover the defended asset/area. The MEZ area should be large enough to allow early engagement of threats: ASM launch platforms should be destroyed or neutralized before they can launch standoff munitions, UA before they reach sensor/weapon range of defended assets, and BMs prior to maneuver or submunitions release. To the maximum extent possible, all targets should have multiple, layered engagement opportunities to ensure an effective defense. The AADP, ACMs, and SPINS should specify what targets can be engaged in the MEZ and the weapons to be used.

(d) Consider the fact that maritime forces are not "static" and they usually employ a "moving MEZ" with separate operational areas for air operations. In a littoral environment, amphibious operations may encompass a portion of the land AO and function as a MEZ. In this case, maritime combatants may be restricted by geography when defending selected coastal assets. Linking land-based SAM systems with maritime force generated search and fire control data and vice versa can result in improved ability to defend the littoral areas.

(e) **Determine Surface-Based Defenses C2 Coverage and Fire Control.** DCA operations depend upon effective and redundant C2 planning. The IADS should integrate the ground- and sea-based C2 nodes, airborne C2 platforms, and the surface force AD fire direction centers. As a minimum, the following is required:

<u>1</u>. Designate RADCs/SADCs as required and incorporate into the IADS architecture.

<u>2</u>. Specify required data links between C2 nodes and forces.

<u>3</u>. Designate primary and secondary C2 centers for all active AMD forces.

<u>4</u>. Align control centers with their operational forces whenever possible.

<u>5</u>. Establish an intelligence and warning architecture; ensure remote units and separate forces are addressed.

6. Delegate necessary authorities and establish conditions for automatic permissions, transfers of function, or other means to establish and sustain a responsive defense.

7. **Determine level of control (engagement authority).** This describes the AD echelon permitted to authorize engagement of an air or missile threat. It can be the AADC, RADC, SADC, ADA battalion fire direction center, or the individual fire unit. Engagement authority, originating with the JFC and normally delegated to the AADC, may be delegated to the RADC/SADC to allow for decentralized execution. Further delegation of engagement authority depends on operational necessity and ROE for DCA operations. **The AD element with engagement authority makes the decision whether to commit weapons to a particular air or missile threat.** Engagement authority may be established at different levels for fixed-wing aircraft, rotary-wing aircraft, UA, and missiles, and the levels of control may change over the course of an operation. For example, engagement authority is delegated to the lowest level SHORAD fire units for CMs and UA, to SAM fire units for BM engagements, and normally remains at SADC or higher for enemy aircraft.

8. **Determine modes of control.** For certain surface-based AD the two modes of control are centralized and decentralized. The mode of control will depend upon the capabilities of the C2 systems being employed and both the friendly and enemy air situations. **Centralized control** is when a higher echelon must authorize target engagements by fire units. **Permission to engage each track must be requested by the fire unit from that higher echelon.** Centralized control is used to minimize the likelihood of engaging friendly aircraft while permitting engagements of hostile aircraft and missiles only when specific orders are issued to initiate the engagement. Normally, centralized control is used for engaging aircraft. **Decentralized control** is the mode of control used when a higher echelon monitors unit actions, **making direct target assignments on a management by exception basis** to units only when necessary to ensure proper fire distribution, to prevent engagement of friendly air platforms, and **to prevent simultaneous engagements of hostile air targets. Decentralized control is used to increase the likelihood that a hostile aircraft or missile will be engaged as soon as it comes within range of a given weapon.** Surface-based AD forces (including SHORAD units) will comply with established ROE and WCS as directed by the designated ADC for their operational area.

9. Determine specific trigger events, when they should be changed, and who has the authority to change them, such as **autonomous operations** when a firing unit has lost both voice and data link (i.e., all communications) to higher tactical headquarters. The firing unit commander assumes full responsibility for control of weapons and engagement of hostile targets in accordance with existing ROE, WCS, and previously received directives.

(f) **Establish CAP Stations.** One method of employing fighters is the CAP. Fighter aircraft normally perform CAPs during DCA operations. CAP stations usually contain two to four fighter aircraft armed for air-to-air engagements. The following considerations apply when planning a CAP:

<u>1.</u> Assign barrier CAPs for the defense of a broad area when protecting multiple assets.

<u>2.</u> Assign a CAP to a specific asset (e.g., high value surface or airborne asset).

<u>3.</u> Assign CAPs to special missions, as appropriate. For example, a barrier CAP may be tasked to inspect or "sanitize" returning strike packages to ensure enemy aircraft do not shadow friendly aircraft back to friendly areas/bases.

<u>4.</u> If made available for tasking for DCA, consider Navy and Marine CAPs as not only defending maritime forces, but also for defense of land-based assets by positioning them over land during littoral operations.

<u>5.</u> Consider employing a CAP if defense is still required and inventory depletion or combat losses result in gaps in SAM coverage in MEZs, or if specific SAM interceptor inventory must be conserved for defense against BM threats rather than used against air threats.

(g) **Establish a FEZ.** Establish a FEZ to support CAP operations after the surface MEZs are established.

<u>1.</u> The FEZ normally extends above the coordinating altitude to the upper limit of either the assigned DCA or primary threat aircraft operating envelope.

<u>2.</u> Where a MEZ and FEZ overlap horizontally, they may be separated vertically.

<u>3.</u> Fighters are normally given a larger WEZ to perform an area defense mission and to accommodate their longer-ranged weapons system capabilities.

(h) **Establish a Crossover Zone.** To facilitate mutual support, defense in depth, and overlapping fires, MAGTF AD assets employ a crossover zone that overlaps a MEZ and FEZ. This allows C2, DCA aircraft, and ground-based AD weapons systems to coordinate engagement in this area by the most appropriate weapons system, while maintaining a MEZ/FEZ construct.

(i) **Position Airborne C2 Stations**

<u>1.</u> Station assets within ranges to perform their C2 function but where threats are minimal and assets cannot be easily engaged and destroyed.

<u>2.</u> Plan to dedicate fighter escort or CAP protection.

(j) **Determine Airborne C2 Coverage and Fire Control.** When planning coverage and fire control, consider the following:

1. DCA fighter aircraft are normally under positive control of a C2 element. Fighters may conduct intercepts autonomously when authorized.

2. With a lack of C2 aircraft or if the distance of operations precludes positive TACON, C2 agencies may provide broadcast information of target data.

3. US fighter aircraft usually operate with enhanced fire control radar and BVR weapons that allow simultaneous engagements of multiple targets.

4. Fighters normally are in communication with a C2 element that points out targets, provides CID when available, and may vector them toward airborne targets. The C2 element also provides a communications link between the JAOC combat operations division and the airborne fighters. This communication link provides a flexible and reactive C2 arrangement.

5. Dependent upon the situation and ROE, airborne C2 elements may have the capability to retask fighters to meet protection requirements.

(k) **Establish a JEZ.** The JEZ only is appropriate or possible when the JFC/JFACC/AADC has a high level of confidence in the CTP and positive control and separation that will prevent SAMs from targeting friendly fighters before and after launch. Dependent upon the operational situation and ROE, a JEZ may be employed when one or more of the following factors exist:

1. The enemy's employment of low altitude CMs dictates the need to ensure the ability to engage with all available forces throughout the zone, accepting risk to friendly aircraft.

2. There are significantly more assets that require defense than there are forces to defend them.

3. The operational characteristics of friendly aircraft and surface-based missile systems and the nature of the operation do not lend themselves to establishing a separate MEZ/FEZ.

4. The AADC and subordinate commanders (e.g., RADC/SADC) are confident that there is sufficient situational awareness and established CID procedures to reduce the possibility of fratricide.

(l) **Weapons Readiness States.** Determine the required degree of readiness of AD weapons which can become airborne or be launched to carry out an assigned task. Weapons readiness states are normally expressed in numbers of weapons and numbers of minutes. Examples of weapons readiness states are as follows:

1. 2 minutes—Sixteen PAC-3 missiles can be launched within 2 minutes.

2. 15 minutes—12 F-22 fighters can be launched within 15 minutes.

<u>3</u>. 3 hours—64 PAC-3 missiles can be launched within 3 hours.

<u>4</u>. Released—24 PAC-3 missiles are released from defense commitment for 6 hours.

8. Ballistic Missile Defense Planning

The best missile defense strategy is to destroy missiles prior to launch.

a. GCCs should locate, identify, and assess potential BM threats. To facilitate JFC planning, and specifically missile defense planning, those GCCs should produce target folders for potential missile threats. Target folders should be available for a subordinate JFC to complete and use when necessary, including for TSTs. For the joint force, the Commander, AAMDC (normally the DAADC) and CTF IAMD, and their staffs are acknowledged subject matter experts regarding the BM threat and missile defense. They can support OCA planners to help eliminate the threat and DCA planners to defend against it. For planning to counter the long-range missile threat across AOR boundaries, USSTRATCOM synchronizes planning efforts and coordinates support for BM defense operations with the affected GCCs. See Chapter II, "Command and Control," Paragraph 10, "Cross-Area of Responsibility Command Relationships Considerations."

b. **General BMD Planning Considerations.** BMD planning adds a unique aspect to the development of the AADP and to planning DCA operations. While plans for both air and BM defenses are integrated in the AADP, the BM threat normally is more difficult to counter. Generally, BMs do not require as much infrastructure and support as an air force; thus, they have a reduced footprint and signature. Mobility, dispersal, and concealment further complicate the offensive targeting process against enemy BMs so the primary tactic of destroying/negating the missile threats prior to their launch can be difficult. Once launched, some BMs often are difficult to detect and track for the purpose of engagement. The same 10 planning factors listed for AD planning should also be considered for missile defense planning (see paragraph 7a). Additionally, the following factors are considered in BMD planning and design:

(1) **Positioning of Assets.** Assets should be positioned to provide a shoot-look-shoot opportunity where possible. The judicious application of a shoot-look-shoot firing doctrine can reduce interceptor consumption and provide high levels of protection to those designated critical assets.

(2) **Salvo Sizes.** Salvo sizes can accommodate varying levels of protection for defended assets in accordance with the commander's guidance.

(3) **Launch Area Denied (LAD).** Assigning units to affect LAD by analyzing BM operating areas for assigning assets may be one method of consideration in formulating the defense design.

(4) **Interceptor Inventories.** Commander's guidance should establish interceptor inventory threshold levels at which operators may need to modify firing procedures to prevent premature inventory exhaustion.

(5) **Firing Doctrine.** Guidance should also be provided for inventory management to include threshold levels and modified procedures once those threshold levels are crossed. Factors include:

(a) Determining the single shot P_k for own force interceptors against threat missile types in the enemy missile order of battle.

(b) Formulating the number of upper-and-lower tier interceptors required to achieve the designated levels of protection.

(c) Equating threat BM impact point prediction with the designated level of protection for the threatened asset.

(d) Establishing a firing policy (e.g., first interceptor to be able to intercept the threat MB being the first interceptor battery to engage and the next system being designated to cover the engagement should the initial system miss).

(e) Firing lower-tier missiles in the last engagement window and factoring in their cumulative P_k in determining the number of upper-tier interceptors to fire in the final salvo.

c. **Active Missile Defense Design.** Based on an expected air and BM threat, the challenge for the AADC will be to balance competing air (including CMs) and BM (including short, -medium, -and long-range) defense demands. This could result in an economy of force issue: use land-and sea-based SAMs that are capable of both active BM and AD only for missile defense, while using purely AD assets for defending against the enemy air threat. For example, against a formidable BM threat that could not be eliminated by OCA operations, the AADC may use SAMs only against BMs, not against air threats, and increase reliance on fighter escorts and CAPs in a layered defense against air threats. A significant missile threat will have great impact on the AADP (i.e., the DAL, placement of WEZs, and types of defensive coverages). Flexibility will be required as there may not be enough resources to defend all assets.

SECTION B. DEFENSIVE COUNTERAIR OPERATIONS

9. General

The AADC develops the AADP in coordination with the joint force components, integrating DCA operations throughout the theater/JOA (see Figure V-1). The AADP reflects the JFC's objectives, priorities, and the specific need for air superiority and protection, and the appropriate component commanders provide the surface-, air-, and sea-based forces/capabilities for those DCA operations required to execute that plan.

Defensive Counterair Operations

Passive Air and Missile Defense	Active Air and Missile Defense

• Detection and warning systems	• Air Defense Targets
	  ○ Fixed- and rotary-wing aircraft
	  ○ Unmanned aerial vehicles
	  ○ Missiles (air-breathing)

• Camouflage and concealment	
• Deception	• Missile Defense Targets ○ Ballistic missiles
• Hardening	

• Reconstitution	• Active Air Defense
	  ○ Operations
	  ○ Area defense
	  ○ Point defense
	  ○ Self-defense
	  ○ High value airborne asset protection

• Chemical, biological, radiological, and nuclear defense equipment and facilities	
• Redundancy	
• Dispersal	

Figure V-1. Defensive Counterair Operations

10. Passive Air and Missile Defense

a. No defensive scheme is perfect. Focused attacks by adversary air and missile threats may overwhelm defense designs. Therefore, passive AMD techniques should be employed at every location, including those protected by active AMD assets. Commanders at all levels are responsible for planning and executing appropriate passive AMD measures.

b. Passive AMD provides individual and collective protection for friendly forces and critical assets and is the responsibility of every commander in the joint force. It includes measures, other than active AMD, taken to minimize, mitigate, or recover from the consequences of attack aircraft and missiles. Passive defense is generally similar for air and missile threats, with the exception of detection and warning timelines.

(1) The AADC is responsible for timely warning of air and missile attacks, which initiates some of the passive AD measures. Warnings may be either general or specific. General warnings indicate that attacks are imminent or have occurred, while specific warnings signify that only certain units or areas are in danger of attack. The timeliness and accuracy of AMD warnings may have a significant impact on the effectiveness of passive AD measures.

(2) Passive measures do not involve the employment of weapons, but they do improve survivability. Depending on the situation and time available, a variety of measures may be taken to improve the defensive posture of friendly forces and assets. Some measures should be planned and practiced during peacetime. **Those assets not assigned adequate AMD defense assets rely more heavily on passive AD measures for protection.**

(3) The likelihood and timing of an attack may be estimated by analyzing the expected enemy COA, targeting process, and offensive air and missile capabilities (including munitions characteristics and quantities).

c. **Considerations and Measures.** When planning passive AD, the following are four principal considerations and the passive AD measures they incorporate.

(1) **Detection and Warning Systems and Procedures.** Timely detection and warning of air and missile threats provide reaction time for friendly forces to seek shelter or take appropriate action. Reliable and redundant connectivity for communications and sensor systems is vital for accurate and timely warning. A combination of air-, space-, and surface-based detection and communication assets should be established to maximize detection and warning. **Warning methods and procedures must be established, disseminated, and rehearsed down to the unit level to be effective.** "All clear" procedures should also be established to notify forces when a warning is false or the threat no longer exists.

(a) Within the theater/JOA, the detection of enemy air-breathing threats and warning/cueing for AD measures are normally provided by the JFC's DCA, theater ISR, or national ISR assets. The JFC/AADC controls the surface- and air-based radars/sensors that detect and track the enemy air threats and the C2 systems that disseminate those warnings.

(b) National assets, under the control of CDRUSSTRATCOM, normally detect the launches of threat BMs, predict the impact points, and communicate warnings to the applicable JFC in the theater/JOA. When tasked, and upon the initial missile warning provided by national assets, theater-based radar may help track a threat missile. The JFC, in turn, is responsible for dissemination of the tactical warnings throughout the theater/JOA.

(2) **Reduction of Enemy Targeting Effectiveness.** Certain measures may be taken to reduce the effectiveness of enemy targeting and attacks, to include mobility, deception, and OPSEC.

(a) **Mobility.** Mobility reduces vulnerability and increases survivability by complicating enemy surveillance and reconnaissance efforts to pinpoint locations of targets. Mobility may be coupled with concealment to "hide" assets.

(b) **Deception.** Deception misleads adversaries by manipulating, distorting, or falsifying friendly actions. Deception may be used to cause an enemy to waste munitions on false targets, deceive their combat assessment process, and falsely influence their decision makers by feeding their intelligence collectors what appears to be credible information. Deception may deny the enemy the ability to gain correct tactical, operational, and strategic information when using their reconnaissance and surveillance systems.

(c) **OPSEC**

1. **Emission Control/Communications Security.** Communications security and an emission control program for infrared, electromagnetic, and acoustic signature reduction can deny the enemy sensor and reconnaissance assets timely acquisition and ID of friendly target systems (e.g., C2 nodes).

<u>2</u>. **Unit Security/Counter-Surveillance.** Local unit security is an important element in denying accurate targeting data to enemy SOF or other enemy agents. Patrolling and ground forces support is important to keep enemy threat forces of Level I (agents, saboteurs, and terrorists) and Level II (small tactical units) from conducting harassment or interdiction attacks against DCA assets.

<u>3</u>. **Nighttime Support Operations.** Consider nighttime for conducting time-consuming resupply or other operations that could highlight units' visibility and increase their vulnerability.

<u>4</u>. **Camouflage and Concealment.** Practice visual signature reduction measures that can "hide" or deny accuracy in locating friendly targets/target systems. These measures may be conducted continuously or in response to specific warnings. Timely intelligence concerning the overflight by enemy satellite and aircraft collection systems is important to the effort. Those measures also may be coupled with deception measures to further complicate chances of effective enemy attacks. The employment of obscurants can negate the effectiveness and accuracy of attack threats during DCA operations.

Refer to JP 3-13.3, Operations Security, *for additional discussion regarding OPSEC.*

Refer to JP 3-13.4, Military Deception, *for more details regarding deception operations.*

(3) **Reducing Vulnerability.** There are four measures that may enable friendly assets to survive enemy attacks by reducing their vulnerability.

(a) **Hardening.** Valuable assets and their shelters are hardened to protect against physical attack, electromagnetic pulse (EMP), and transient radiation. Hardening measures should be accomplished during peacetime whenever possible. Hardening reduces the effect of attack on systems and facilities (i.e., aircraft, missiles, air base support equipment and facilities, nuclear delivery systems, nuclear storage areas, C2 facilities, communications nodes, and logistic facilities). When EMP hardening is not feasible, an EMP vulnerability assessment should be made to identify suitable preparatory and defensive measures.

(b) **Redundancy.** A principal means of preserving combat power is duplication of critical nodes, capabilities, and systems that are particularly vulnerable to air and missile attack and for which other passive measures may be less appropriate. Redundancy includes dual, contingency, or backup capabilities that can assume primary mission functions (in whole or in part) upon failure or degradation of the primary system. Of primary concern are "soft" targets such as C2 nodes and sensors (antenne) and fixed sites such as airfields and ground stations for airborne sensors.

(c) **Dispersal.** Dispersal reduces target vulnerability by decreasing concentration and making a target system less lucrative. Combined with mobility and deception, dispersal increases enemy uncertainty as to whether a particular location is occupied and, if so, whether it will be occupied when the attack is executed.

(d) **Chemical, Biological, Radiological, and Nuclear (CBRN) Defense Equipment and Facilities.** CBRN defensive equipment and facilities protect against the effects of CBRN hazards by providing contamination detection, shelter, and decontamination. Individual protective equipment allows vital functions to continue in the CBRN environment and to minimize effects of WMD attacks.

See JP 3-11, Operations in Chemical, Biological, Radiological, and Nuclear (CBRN) Environments, *for further details regarding protection and operations in a CBRN environment.*

(4) **Recovery and Reconstitution.** Following an air or missile attack, units should be restored to a desired level of combat effectiveness commensurate with mission requirements and available resources. Resources should be made available to restore capabilities in accordance with JFC established priorities. Recovery and reconstitution after a WMD attack will require special planning considerations, as improper handling of CBRN casualties and contaminated material and equipment may impact other activities.

d. **Resources for Passive AD.** The components of the joint force bring unique capabilities to the different aspects of passive AMD. Engineers, CBRN defense and decontamination experts, explosive ordnance disposal personnel, and medical units may contribute significantly to passive AD efforts. A threat-based risk analysis, distributing area responsibilities, and establishing support tasks are factors that impact AMD. Some MNF members may specialize in passive AD capabilities. HN support and civilian infrastructure may augment or enhance joint force recovery efforts, either through government coordinated action or contracted support. It is essential that these capabilities, when available, are planned and integrated into the total passive AMD capability.

e. **Execution of Passive Air Defenses**

(1) **Responsibilities.** The AADC and chain of command are responsible for timely warning of attacks. Component commanders and their forces have delegated responsibilities to ensure passive AD measures are planned and executed in a timely manner down to the unit level.

(a) As a minimum, the AADC must be able to pass warnings directly to the joint force Service and functional component commands, and if applicable, establish procedures to pass warnings to and from HN authorities. BM warnings generally will originate from the theater event system. Airborne threat warnings generally are issued through the C2 system (e.g., RADC/SADC). Local commanders may declare local ADW based on the local threat.

(b) Component commanders establish and maintain communications links down to the lowest unit level.

(c) Cross-component support is a unit and component commanders' responsibility. Cross-component support may establish connectivity to geographically isolated units of other Services or MNF units that are unable to link within their parent organizations.

(2) **Defense Clustering.** To facilitate the span of control for local commanders, support activities may be grouped into clusters. Grouping defended assets with active DCA units or locating critical force elements near declared assets enables economy of force for protection and may enhance localized defense in depth. Clustering also may enhance the availability and contributions of HN assets. In the early stages of force projection, grouping allows any one location to draw upon the resources of the group.

11. Active Air and Missile Defense

a. **Active AD Operations.** Under the counterair framework, active missile defense is integrated with active AD as a DCA operation. Generally, the same capabilities used for missile defense are capable of AD. **The important factors are the enemy missile threat and the conservation of missile defense assets to prevent that unique capability from being exhausted against aircraft when an alternative AD strategy and tactics could be used against air-breathing threats.** For example, in some situations, a battle manager may require a missile defense-capable SAM to defeat the air-breathing threat to a high priority asset on the DAL.

b. **Active BMD Operations.** Active BMD involves direct defensive action taken to destroy in flight BM threats. Active BMD uses sensors, interceptors, and platforms that are both unique to BMD (e.g., sea-based X-band radar, AN/TPY-2, THAAD, and Aegis SM-3 [Standard Missile 3]), and those capable of the traditional AD (e.g., AN/TPS-59, Patriot, and Aegis SM-2 [Standard Missile 2]). The active BMD mission includes use of forward-based missile defense assets in the defense of the territory of the US as an augmentation to the Ground-Based Midcourse Defense (GMD) System.

(1) BMD assets and resources are under the control of the GCC/JFC to whom they are assigned or attached. Due to the short timelines involved in missile defense, tasking and engagement authority should be delegated to the lowest practical level. The process and means of ordering engagements will be clearly stated in AADPs, SPINS, or other orders. Engagement authority must be identified for proper coordination and synchronization of global and theater BMD assets. Engagement coordination requires the ability to optimize BMD resources considering the operational environment, decision timelines, and the ability to detect, identify, track, and engage multiple, simultaneous missile threats.

(2) A GCC under BM attack is the supported commander for BMD in their respective AOR. This means with multiple threat missiles in flight, the GCC may simultaneously be supported and supporting commander for BMD. The processes linking sensors to decision makers to fire control nodes that cross AOR boundaries will require coordination between neighboring GCCs to enable multiple engagement opportunities.

c. Active missile defense systems are primarily SAM systems and their supporting infrastructure. Although BM launches are detected and warnings are sent to the JFC with the predicted impact point, engagements are only possible once organic missile defense radars detect them. Other missiles such as CMs and ASMs present the same problem—they must be detected to be engaged and many use low-observable techniques or low altitude ingress to avoid detection. To conserve missile defense SAMs and improve the probability of raid annihilation, AD aircraft should be used to counter the enemy aircraft that normally carry CMs and ASMs before they are in threatening range.

d. Execution of DCA operations requires continuous surveillance of the theater/JOA. Integration and connectivity of sensors should provide a complete, reliable, and timely CTP for decision making. The track production (including ID) follows a sequential process with dissemination of track data as rapidly as possible. That detailed track data permits C2 nodes to evaluate tracks and determine their significance. Tactical warnings trigger some passive AD measures and cue active AD assets for action. Active AD forces then engage hostile tracks or allow passage of friendly tracks. Through effective battle management the positively identified threats are engaged by the optimum system available.

e. The AADC controls the battle using approved authorities (e.g., ID, commitment, and engagement) and the flexibility of the IADS. To decentralize execution, the AADC normally will delegate some or all AADC authorities down to the RADC/SADC level (if established). The AADC must specify the conditions and limits within which engagement authority is decentralized. **Based upon the threat level and the complexity of engagements, a control node should retain engagement authority if it can adequately perform battle management.** For air battle management, the AADC or a RADC/SADC uses three tools for which the authorities may be delegated further down to the tactical level: ADW, WCS, and fire control orders.

(1) **Air Defense Warning Conditions (ADWCs).** An AD warning, which includes missile attacks, is issued as an ADWC. The ADWC is a degree of air attack probability based on the threat assessment. The AADC establishes the baseline ADWCs for the joint force. ADWCs may be different for air-breathing threats than for BMs. Subordinate ADCs may issue higher but not lower ADWCs for their areas. ADWCs are disseminated though joint and components C2 channels to all AMD elements and fire units.

(a) ADWC White—An attack by hostile aircraft or missile is improbable.

(b) ADWC Yellow—An attack by hostile aircraft or missile is probable.

(c) ADWC Red—An attack by hostile aircraft or missile is imminent or in progress.

(2) **WCS.** WCS is a control measure designed to establish the freedom for fighters and surface AD weapons (including small arms weapons) to engage threats. The AADC establishes WCS for the joint force. The **WCS may be different for air-breathing threats than for BMs.** WCS authority originates with the AADC and can be delegated to subordinate commanders. **Different WCSs may be applied simultaneously to different weapons systems and in different airspace areas.** US forces use three standard WCSs that may be declared for a particular area and time. US forces do not disseminate these WCS orders via TDL. The WCSs are "free, tight, and hold."

(a) Weapons Free—The least restrictive status; when any target not positively identified as friendly in accordance with current ROE may be engaged. Weapons free zones may be established around key government infrastructure when other areas are designated weapons tight or weapons hold.

(b) Weapons Tight—The normal status. Units may only fire on targets identified as hostile in accordance with current ROE.

Note: Weapons free and weapons tight control orders impose a status or condition applicable to weapons systems within a defined volume of airspace, and normally, any unit directly threatened by a missile of any type, friend or foe, may engage it.

(c) Weapons Hold—The most restrictive status. Units may only fire in self-defense or when ordered by proper higher authority.

(3) **Fire Control Orders.** Fire control orders, which include both air and missile threats, are established to standardize tactical firing instructions issued during the conduct of an air battle. **They are given to direct or inhibit firing by surface-to-air weapons units based on the ROE and rapidly changing tactical situations.** Based on the ROE, the JFC-approved AADP should establish how fire control orders will be communicated. There are three primary fire control orders.

(a) **"Engage"** directs or authorizes units and weapon systems to fire on a designated target.

(b) **"Cease engagement"** or **"cease fire"** directs units to stop the firing sequence against a designated target; however, units may continue to track and missiles already in flight are permitted to continue to intercept.

(c) **"Hold fire"** is an emergency order used to stop firing. If technically possible, missiles already in flight must be prevented from intercepting.

f. **Weapon Systems Employment.** Although DCA operations are defensive in nature, they should be conducted as far from friendly areas as feasible. Advanced warning of hostile air and missile actions is vital for a layered defense. Intercepts as early as possible facilitate potential for multiple engagements. For effective attrition of enemy air and missile threats, the engagement process should continue throughout the approach, entry, and departure from the friendly operational area. Once CMs or BMs are detected, ROE normally should allow for their immediate engagement based on their unique target profiles, their potential warheads and threat to friendly assets, and the quick reaction necessary for success. **The strength of an IADS is the synchronization of the integrated surface-to-air and air-to-air systems in mutual support of defensive coverage for the operational area.**

(1) **Surface-to-Air Weapon Systems.** These weapons include SAMs and AAA and are employed in both area and point defenses—often in self-defense. Their effectiveness requires reliable ID/CID processes, C2 connectivity, and interfaces with airborne systems to preclude engagement of friendly aircraft and unnecessary expenditure of weapons against enemy threats. Surface weapon systems have optimal capabilities against targets at different ranges and altitudes as reflected in their WEZs. In extremely dynamic AD situations with a

multitude of targets, some systems are capable of automatic detection and engagement. **Surface-to-air systems operate under fire control orders based on the ROE and WCS.**

(2) **Air-to-Air Fighter Interception.** Fighter aircraft performing DCA or OCA missions may be tasked to respond to the detection of hostile, potentially hostile, or unknown airborne targets. Aircraft normally operate under positive control of a C2 element but may initiate and conduct intercepts autonomously when authorized (e.g., self-defense or depth of the operation precludes positive control). When close or positive control is not possible, the controlling element may provide general broadcast information on targets to all affected fighters. Air-to-air fighters operating with enhanced fire control radars can engage multiple targets with BVR weapons to defend against hostile targets before they are within threatening range of friendly assets. However, the ROE must allow use of BVR weapons.

(a) AD fighter aircraft normally perform CAPs, DCA fighter escort, or respond to airborne threats from ground alert locations. Fighters normally will be under positive control for vectors toward their airborne targets. CAPs include barrier CAPs for area defense and CAPs for base defense or local asset defense. Some CAPs also may have additional missions such as using barrier CAPs to inspect or "sanitize" returning strike packages to ensure enemy aircraft do not shadow "friendlies" back to base. Additionally, DCA fighters may be dedicated to protect HVAAs from airborne threats.

(b) C2 elements also provide a link between the JAOC combat operations division and the fighters. This communication link provides a flexible and reactive C2 arrangement for retasking flights to meet dynamic DCA operational requirements or to support OCA operations.

(c) NAVFOR CAPs defending carrier or amphibious groups may be positioned over land during littoral operations and can provide collateral defense of the land AO.

g. **Other Employment Considerations**

(1) **Movement and Mobility.** US surface-based AMD forces are normally moveable or mobile. When operations require ground AMD units to change location, displacement times must be considered. Dependent upon the weapon system and situation, these surface unit displacements may take hours or days. Extensive coordination may be required for convoy plans, permissions, protection, realignment of logistics, travel time, and shifting of backfill forces may be necessary. Maritime forces afloat are capable of full operations while repositioning.

(2) **Cross-Boundary Operations.** Boundaries between sectors and between forces and units are areas of risk. Procedures for distribution and control of fires between sectors and units should be addressed during planning. To minimize the risk of fratricide and prevent excessive weapons employment while providing a seamless defense, coordination must be rehearsed, not just planned. When engagements cross a unit boundary or are in a buffer zone, priority of fires normally will be given to the threatened unit.

(3) **Alert Posture.** Levels of readiness should be tailored to the level of threat and warning. Crews and systems cannot be maintained at high levels of alert status indefinitely.

Unless forces are actively conducting engagements or redeploying, some portion should be engaged in crew rest and/or maintenance. "All clear" procedures should be established when a threat no longer exists.

(4) **Transfer of Authority and Transitions in DCA Operations**

(a) Transfers of C2 functions such as airspace control, battle management authorities, etc., from one level of command or controlling element to another, should be accomplished smoothly, with the succeeding element not assuming C2 functions until the appropriate level of capability is actually in place—and rehearsed, if possible. Prior to hostilities, if possible, redundant or secondary C2 nodes should rehearse primary C2 functions.

(b) Temporary transfers of authority (e.g., ID or engagement authority) must be acknowledged by establishing and receiving elements and acknowledged by their subordinates. For example, if an AWACS is given a SADC function from a CRC, their subordinate air and surface fire control units, as well as the AWACS, must acknowledge the transfer. When the CRC regains that function, the AWACS and subordinates must again acknowledge the transfer. In all cases the next higher C2 node also must be notified and acknowledge the changes.

(c) Detection of enemy offensive preparations may be an indication or warning of an impending hostile act and signal a decision for transition from peace to combat operations. Detection of these preparations allows for the transmission of tactical warnings that alert commanders, automated weapon systems, sensors, fusion centers, C2 nodes, and, in some cases civil authorities, to anticipate the attack.

Intentionally Blank

APPENDIX A
COMBAT IDENTIFICATION

1. General

CID is the process of attaining an accurate characterization of detected objects in the operational environment sufficient to support an engagement decision. In counterair operations, CID should be accomplished with NRT or better exchange of information between airspace control/AD units and airspace users to meet the time and accuracy demands of combat operations. CID is essential to prevent fratricide in dynamic counterair operations and to ensure economy of force. Effective CID enhances joint force capabilities by providing confidence in the accuracy of counterair engagement decisions throughout the force. While CID is a process for all joint forces in both defensive and offensive operations, the focus in this appendix is on application of CID in counterair.

2. Objective

The objective of CID for AMD is to maximize effectiveness by providing high confidence IFF of a potential target so an engagement decision can be made in accordance with the ROE. The CID process complements the ID process, which is used for AD tracking and airspace control.

3. Considerations for Conducting Combat Identification

a. CID provides a process that allows an engagement decision based on the JFC's chosen balance between the confidence level of ID and the risk of fratricide or mistaking an enemy as friendly, all framed within the operational situation and supported by the ROE.

b. While the CID process uses some of the same systems and information used for the basic ID process, there are ID systems specifically designed for the higher confidence, positive ID that is more suitable for the purpose of CID. Some ID systems have an autonomous ID capability, with data links and digital information exchanges (including real-time imagery of targets/target areas) that greatly enhance their ability to perform more effective CID (e.g., blue force tracker).

c. ID information may be obtained from onboard or external surface-, air-, and space-based systems (e.g., radars, IFF systems, and selective ID features) and through established processes and procedures approved by the JFC. An effective C2 system (including reliable voice and data networks) is required to gather, assimilate, assess, and distribute this information from a myriad of sources and nodes.

d. Planning and executing the CID process requires thorough knowledge of the joint force scheme of maneuver, OPLANs, and ACMs documented in the ACP, AADP, and ACO. To avoid a single point of failure, normally no one C2 node acts as an exclusive end user of all CID information. Optimally, all CID information is disseminated to all C2 nodes applicable to their operational area.

e. Electronic methods provide the earliest and most reliable means of positive ID. Positive visual ID may be required by the ROE in some scenarios, but may not be practical in others due to time and distances or consideration of an enemy's BVR weapons capabilities. For example, due to their unique flight profiles, ROE normally allow BMs and CMs, with high-confidence ID, to be engaged immediately—the approved ROE being the controlling factor. It is important that ROE allow for the most advantageous means of ID. While airspace control can function with an effective combination of different methods of ID, AD engagements (with few exceptions) require positive ID (e.g., visual observation or electronic ID). For example, for SEAD operations, correct ID of all friendly electromagnetic signal emitters is important to prevent erroneous suppression (destruction or disruption) of friendly force electronic systems. Experience has shown that some friendly forces' electronic emitters are not properly identified to the SEAD forces. Those spurious emitters may be read as "unknown" or "hostile" by a SEAD aircrew, and dependent upon the ROE and intensity of the situation, that emitter may be engaged, perhaps in self-defense, unless positive ID is accomplished. If that friendly force with a spurious emitter could be positively identified by secure electronic means (i.e., CID), it would probably not be engaged in that context.

f. In the absence of positive ID, procedural ID may be used based on ROE and the commander's decision to accept the potential increased risks of fratricide or misidentification of enemy as friend. For example, when a surface AD unit becomes autonomous and procedurally reverts to a self-defense mode, the threat of fratricide may increase because that unit would be more likely to engage friendly aircraft that fly toward the unit. Procedural ID methods using airspeed, altitude, and planned flight corridors as parameters may mitigate the perceived threat to the AMD unit.

g. ROE are critical to both the ID and CID processes. ROE directly supports the CID process and should allow for the most advantageous means of identifying a detected object: the CID process identifies friend or foe and ROE determines response. A good example is the ID criteria for missiles, which normally should be different than that for aircraft. Because BMs have a distinct flight profile, with little warning, and a very short opportunity for intercept, the ROE should allow for advantageous ID and immediate engagement. Experience has shown the ROE for incoming enemy CMs, once detected and classified as a CM using high confidence means, also should allow immediate engagement because they are difficult to continuously track.

4. Identification Matrix

The AADC should develop an ID matrix to complement the ID process normally used for tracking and to facilitate engagement decisions. Often, track ID on the TDL may be from procedural methods that will not support the ROE criteria for engagement. The TDL will carry that track ID classification (e.g., a hostile ID track), but the engagement authority may require either positive ID, a determination of hostile act/intent, or violation of a procedural ID restriction before an engagement decision is made. To that end, CID criteria contained in the matrix and in all plans must be coordinated to ensure no conflicts arise during execution of counterair operations.

a. **ID Matrix Use Versus Implementation of TDL Track ID/Classification.** Track ID/classification data shared over a TDL may not support the CID process. Planners must consider how the IDs are determined and entered into the track ID/classification system (e.g., a TDL) that portrays a particular track throughout the C2 systems. The JICO cell planners should provide a list of ID classifications (e.g., unknown, friendly, hostile, neutral) to be used on the TDL.

(1) The ID matrix must take into consideration the limitations inherent in the employed systems that will implement the ID procedures. Once the set of track symbols is determined, the use of terminology for these symbols must be aligned. Each JFC should have ID criteria that include brevity code terms. For example, pay particular attention to the "bandit" codeword versus the system track symbol for "hostile." An enemy aircraft with a TDL tracking symbol for hostile could be called a "bandit" (ID as enemy not authorized to engage) or called a "hostile" (ID as enemy with authority to engage). The AADC should ensure only those specific voice brevity terms approved by the JFC for authority to engage are used throughout the CID process.

(2) Build the ID matrix to the lowest common denominator, that is, what everyone can classify/transmit/receive/forward to support the shooter. This will reduce the risk of missed targets and fratricide.

b. **ID Criteria.** ID criteria are used for application of ROE. The ROE supports CID criteria for an engagement decision dependent upon weapon systems capabilities. The AADC is responsible for recommending DCA ROE and developing ID and engagement criteria for JFC approval in the AADP, with specific instructions in the ATO and/or SPINS.

c. **Positive ID Methods**

(1) IFF Modes (1-5 per the ATO/SPINS).

(2) PPLI.

(3) A radar contact correlated with an authenticated/secure voice (position) report from an air or ground control agency.

(4) External/onboard CID systems (e.g., blue force tracker or noncooperative target recognition).

(5) Visual ID.

d. **Positive ID Considerations**

(1) Positive ID is an ID derived from visual observation and/or electronic systems, possibly combined with other factors (e.g., point of origin), with a higher confidence of accuracy than a simple lack of friend or lack of enemy. Positive ID criteria, as established by the commander's ROE, are a basis for CID for engagement (shoot/no-shoot) decisions, so it is useable for ID for airspace control and AD tracking. When available, positive ID is used because it provides the most rapid, reliable, and transferable means of ID. Most enemy

positive hostile IDs are derived from technology-based ID systems that exploit the physical or electronic characteristics of a target (e.g., noncooperative target recognition, signals intelligence, or electronic support measures).

(2) Not all CID participants may see the same ID-related information. This is dependent primarily on system implementation, J-series versus M-series message standards, and operator display capabilities. Because of the different implementation of TDL messages, planners should consider limiting the number of track classification symbols to reduce confusion and the potential for fratricide.

e. Figure A-1 provides a sample ID matrix for tracks.

For a detailed discussion of CID in an IADS, refer to FM 3-01.15/MCRP 3-25E/NTTP 3-01.8/AFTTP(I) 3-2.31, Multi-Service Tactics, Techniques, and Procedures for an Integrated Air Defense System.

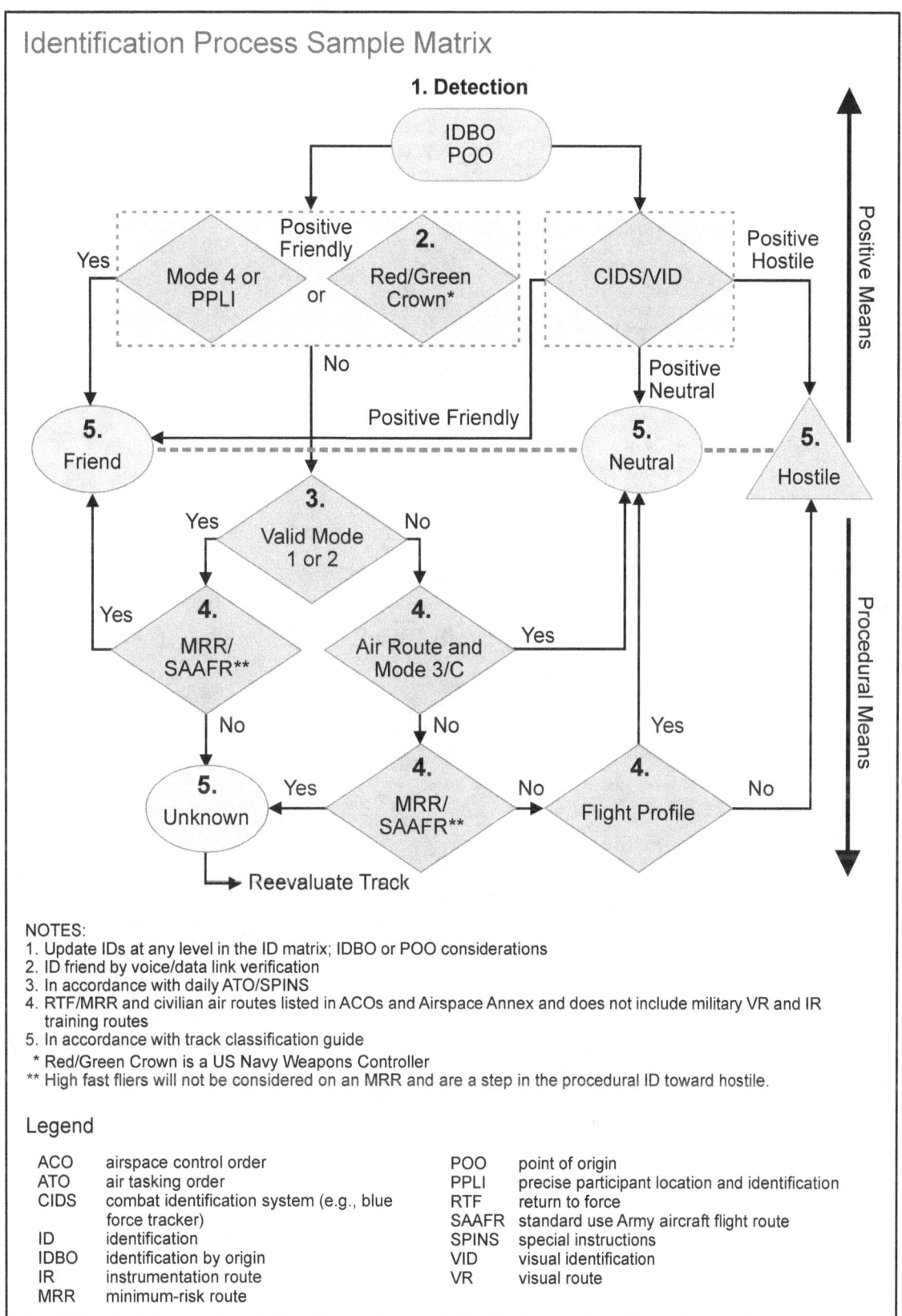

Identification Process Sample Matrix

1. Detection

IDBO
POO

Positive Friendly

2. Red/Green Crown*

Mode 4 or PPLI — or

Yes — No

CIDS/VID — Positive Hostile

Positive Means

5. Friend

Positive Friendly

Positive Neutral

5. Neutral

5. Hostile

3. Valid Mode 1 or 2

Yes — No

Yes — **4.** MRR/SAAFR** — No

4. Air Route and Mode 3/C — Yes — No

Yes — **5.** Unknown — Yes — **4.** MRR/SAAFR** — No — **4.** Flight Profile — No

Yes

Procedural Means

→ Reevaluate Track

NOTES:
1. Update IDs at any level in the ID matrix; IDBO or POO considerations
2. ID friend by voice/data link verification
3. In accordance with daily ATO/SPINS
4. RTF/MRR and civilian air routes listed in ACOs and Airspace Annex and does not include military VR and IR training routes
5. In accordance with track classification guide
* Red/Green Crown is a US Navy Weapons Controller
** High fast fliers will not be considered on an MRR and are a step in the procedural ID toward hostile.

Legend

ACO	airspace control order	POO	point of origin
ATO	air tasking order	PPLI	precise participant location and identification
CIDS	combat identification system (e.g., blue force tracker)	RTF	return to force
		SAAFR	standard use Army aircraft flight route
ID	identification	SPINS	special instructions
IDBO	identification by origin	VID	visual identification
IR	instrumentation route	VR	visual route
MRR	minimum-risk route		

Figure A-1. Identification Process Sample Matrix

Intentionally Blank

APPENDIX B
AREA AIR DEFENSE PLAN FORMAT

Copy No.

Issuing Headquarters

Place of Issue

Date/Time Group of Signature

AREA AIR DEFENSE PLAN: Operation/Exercise NUMBER OR CODE NAME

References: Maps, charts, and other relevant documents.

TABLE OF CONTENTS

1. Situation

Briefly describe the situation the plan addresses. The related OPLAN or concept plan, as well as any other applicable OPLAN/AADP that may apply, should be identified as appropriate. Include a description of the conditions under which the guidance and procedures in the AADP are applicable (e.g., the exercise, OPLAN, operation order, military operation, coordination between air and ground defense forces).

a. Guidance. Provide a summary of directives, letters of instructions, memorandums, treaties, and strategic plans, including any campaign/OPLANs received from higher authority, that apply to the plan.

b. Enemy Order of Battle. Provide a reference to the intelligence annex of the governing plan and/or a top-level summary of pertinent intelligence data, including information on the following:

(1) Composition, location, disposition, movements, and strengths of major enemy forces that can influence action in the operational area.

(2) Definition of threat axes, DCA operations, known WMD, and estimated enemy COAs.

(3) Known IPB for the operational area.

(4) Enemy vulnerabilities, COGs, and decisive points.

c. Friendly Order of Battle. State information on friendly forces assigned.

(1) Describe friendly AD forces, including C2, aircraft (including counterair, reconnaissance, surveillance, and support), location of SAM units, and support forces.

(2) Describe missile defense forces, including those with both AMD capabilities.

(3) Describe BM defense system capabilities if any are located within the JOA or can support the JFC.

d. Non-Allied Forces

(1) Describe neutral forces and AD capabilities in or near the theater that could impact operations. Include general statement and any specific information about COAs and WMD capabilities. Include air and sea routes, shipping lanes, location of SAM units, and ATC information.

(2) Describe noncombatants in or near the theater that could impact operations. Include information on shipping lanes and international air traffic, if known.

2. Mission

State the joint AD tasks and the purposes and relationships to achieving the AADC's objectives.

3. Air and Missile Defense Operations

a. Intent

b. CONOPS. Describe the CONOPS, including the mission assumptions, maintenance policies, and JOA within which the AADP applies.

(1) AD organization—AD area, regions, and sectors identified, including boundaries. Air and surface sensors, shooters, and C2.

(2) Provide or reference the list of critical assets to be defended (with asset criticality) with respect to campaign phase and timing within the campaign phase.

(3) Designation of prioritized defended assets with their associated levels of protection as approved by the JFC. May include specific responsibilities of defending commander and allocation of forces.

(4) AMD forces deployed locations overview.

(5) Phases of air defensive operations in relation to the plan.

(6) Timing and duration of phases.

c. Coordinating Instructions

(1) Describe the integrating policy, including the philosophy of the weapons control plan and interfaces between commanders at various levels. Include plans and procedures for employing air control units and missile control units. Also include a list of vital areas and target priorities policy and guidance, as well as return to ship/base procedures. Generally describe the passive AMD warning responsibilities, including MNF and HN notifications, with reference to Appendixes 1 and 3, in Annex C (Operations) of the AADP.

(2) Describe Weapons Coordination Policy and Code Words. Describe preplanned responses to tactical situations, including lost communications, approach of hostile aircraft or low/slow fliers, antiship CM/land attack CM launch/detection, transporter/erector/launcher detection or BM launch, reconnaissance aircraft detection, adverse weather, and detection of TSTs.

(3) ROE

(a) Include ID and CID procedures and requirements and deconfliction procedures.

(b) Describe the ROE's impact and constraints on joint AMD operations.

(4) Describe reporting requirements, including the ATO, SPINS, ACO, tactical operational data (TACOPDAT), daily intentions messages, OPTASKLINK, and status reports.

(5) Describe/discuss interaction between AMD operations and procedures and the ACP.

4. Logistics

Give references to where this information is maintained.

5. Command, Control, and Communications

a. Command Relationships. State the planned C2 structure for the entire joint AMD operation. Indicate any transfer of forces contemplated during the AMD operations, including the time of expected transfer. Give locations of all pertinent C2 agency locations and command posts for various commanders.

b. Communications. State where to find the communications plan(s).

c. Command Designators. If certain terms or code words are an integral part of a Service's DCA lexicon, be sure to define or explain them; for example, the Navy uses "Red Crown" for its airspace control center.

6. Area Air Defense Plan Guidance

The AADP is developed in collaboration with the JFC, component commanders, and MNF partners. Although the AADP is designed to be the AADC's plan of action, it is a "living" document. RADC/SADC may wish to provide supplements to the plan to reflect additional guidance or intentions. While the AADP includes topics for discussion, it may be written to reflect greater or lesser detail and may serve as a reference document to point users to other more detailed messages like the TACOPDAT, OPTASKLINK, SPINS, ATO/ACO, etc.

(Signed) (Commander—AADC)

ANNEXES: (List of notional AADP annexes, appendices, and tabs.)

Annex A: Air Defense Task Organization

Annex B: Intelligence

Annex C: Operations

Appendix 1: Launch Warning Reports

Tab A: Theater Voice Warning Report Format

Tab B: JFACC Tier II Voice Early Warning

Tab C: JFLCC Tier II Voice Early Warning

Tab D: JFMCC Tier II Voice Early Warning

Appendix 2: Combat Air Patrol Management and Control

Appendix 3: Air Defense Warning Conditions

Appendix 4: Critical Asset List/Defended Asset List

Tab A: Critical Asset List

Tab B: Phase I Defended Asset List

Tab C: Phase II Defended Asset List

Tab D: Phase III Defended Asset List

Tab E: Phase IV Defended Asset List

Appendix 5: Air Defense Procedures

Tab A: Low Missile Procedures

Tab B: Fire Control Orders

Tab C: SAM SHORAD Tactical Order Format

Tab D: Alert States

Tab E: Weapons Control Status

Tab F: Air Breathing Threat Engagement Reports

Tab G: BM Engagement Reports

Tab H: SAM Status Report Format

Tab I: Self-Defense Criteria

Tab J: Theater Air and Missile Defense Airspace Control Order Form

Appendix 6: Flush Procedures

Appendix 7: Kill Box Grid System

Appendix 8: Commander's Critical Information Requirements

Appendix 9: OPTASKLINK

Appendix 10: RADC/SADC/Operations Centers Reports

Appendix 11: OPSEC

Annex D through Annex I: Not used

Annex J: Air Defense Command Relationships

Appendix 1: Air Defense Area, Region, and Sector Boundaries

Annex K: Command, Control, Communications, and Computer Systems

Appendix 1: JRE and C2 Voice Connectivity

Appendix 2: TDL Network

Appendix 3: JICO Cell Communications

Appendix 4: Sensor Network

Appendix 5: ADA Brigade Network 1

Appendix 6: ADA Brigade Network 2

Appendix 7: ADA Battalion Network

Appendix 8: Link 16 Network

Annex L: Coalition Forces

Appendix 1: Ballistic Missile Shared Early Warning to Coalition Forces

Annex M through Annex Y: Not used

Annex Z: Distribution

Enclosure 1: References

Enclosure 2: Terms and Definitions

Enclosure 3: Acronyms

SECURITY CLASSIFICATION

APPENDIX C
DEFENSIVE COUNTERAIR ESTIMATE FORMAT

DCA ESTIMATE OF THE SITUATION

(Classification)

Headquarters
Place
Date, time, and zone
Message reference number

DCA ESTIMATE NUMBER ____

References: Maps, charts, or other documents.

Time Zone Used Through the Estimate:

1. Mission

Clearly state the task given to the AADC by the JFC and the purpose for the task. The task should describe what friendly DCA forces will do to the enemy. The purpose describes the reason for the task and should remain effective even after the task becomes outdated due to a change in the situation.

2. Situation and Considerations

This paragraph describes the conditions under which the unit will perform its mission and the possible COAs of the supported force.

a. Characteristics of the operational area. For this paragraph, determine those factors that influence friendly and enemy actions and that may influence the choice of a COA. In the absence of facts, use logical assumptions that might directly affect the mission. Include an analysis of the effects of conducting DCA operations.

(1) Weather. Put the analysis of data from predicted weather, atmospheric conditions, and solar/lunar data for the period in this paragraph. Climatological data also should be investigated when completing this paragraph. Assess how the weather influences friendly and enemy operations. For enemy operations include an evaluation of how current and forecast weather and solar/lunar data impacts enemy use of UASs; missiles; aircraft (fixed- and rotary-wing); and airborne or air assault operations. Try to determine or predict when the enemy is most likely to use those assets due to the weather.

(2) Terrain. Analyze the effects of terrain, including effects on observation and fire; cover and concealment; movement (surface and air); employment of friendly and enemy WMD; communications, EW, and combat surveillance; unconventional warfare; military information support operations; and other aspects of military operations. Determine key

terrain and air avenues of approach. Also discuss terrain features that limit air vehicle detection or target acquisition and terrain that might canalize or force air targets to fly a particular profile. Try to determine where the enemy will most probably use air assets.

(3) Other pertinent factors. List analysis of political, economic, sociological, psychological, and other factors (such as hydrographics, environment, communications, science, technology, materiel, transportation, safety and accident prevention, and manpower). Include deduction about their effects on friendly and enemy operations.

b. Enemy Air and Missile Forces

(1) Disposition. List locations of enemy air and missile forces that could participate in operations. Determine combinations of air platforms that the enemy may use when conducting a particular type of operation.

(2) Composition. How the enemy organizes for combat. Includes identity of units, types of air platforms and missiles, and armament. Also address the expected number of sorties and missiles flown per day and possible composition of those sorties.

(3) Strength. Numbers and sizes of committed and reinforcing units. Consider the enemy's location, doctrine, and mission. Identify air and missile assets and air support units that could or may affect the operations. When, where, and how many air platforms will the enemy fly during this operation?

(4) Other considerations. Enemy forces not discussed above.

(5) Recent and present significant activities. Summarize recent enemy activities that were both successful and unsuccessful. Highlight any enemy air activity, to include number, type of air platforms, and locations.

(6) Peculiarities and weaknesses. Indicate enemy peculiarities and weaknesses that might influence combat effectiveness, including vulnerability to deception.

(7) Courses of Action. Identify available information from which to determine possible enemy COAs and their relation to the enemy's joint COA.

c. Friendly Forces. Identify disposition, composition, and strength. Highlight the vulnerability of the joint force to enemy air and missile attacks and surveillance.

(1) Friendly COAs. State the JFC's COA. Include any guidance that affects DCA operations. Include description of any phasing of operations in the COA and the impact of those operations on support relationships or requirements.

(2) Current status of resources within theater/JOA. Identify the status of personnel and logistics in the unit. Identify civil-military operations requirements. Identify limitations that affect or may affect the conduct of DCA operations. Can the mission be accomplished?

(3) Current status of other DCA resources that affect theater/JOA.

(4) Comparison of DCA requirements versus capabilities and recommended solutions.

(5) Key considerations (evaluation criteria) for COA supportability.

d. Assumptions. State the assumptions relevant to the situation, mission, forces, capabilities, threat, etc., that will affect the commanders' decisions.

3. Analysis

Analyze each COA using evaluation criteria. Identify those aspects in the JFC's plan that create difficulty in providing DCA coverage and affect the ability of the force to accomplish its mission.

4. Comparison

a. Compare COAs using evaluation criteria. Rank order COAs for each key consideration. A decision matrix should visually support comparison. Present a DCA COA for each JFC COA.

b. Each COA should include the following aspects:

(1) DCA mission.

(2) DCA priorities.

(3) DCA fires.

(4) DCA scheme of maneuver.

(5) Task organization.

(6) Command and support relationships.

(7) Key passive AD measures.

5. Recommendations and Conclusions

a. Recommended COA based on the comparison.

(1) Indicate which joint COA(s) DCA can best support (using the elements of who, what, where, when, how, and why).

(2) Recommend list of DCA priorities.

(3) State the recommended DCA organization for combat and employment of other active DCA assets.

(4) Possible OCA targets.

        (5) Passive and active DCA measures that will be most effective.

        (6) Issues, deficiencies, and risks with recommendations to reduce their impacts.

    b. Conclusions.

ANNEXES: (as required)

APPENDIX D
THREAT MISSILE SYSTEMS

1. Background

a. Threat missiles include BMs, CMs, and ASMs (not including short-range, nonnuclear, direct fire missiles, bombs, or rockets such as Maverick or wire-guided missiles). Their targets are within a given theater of operations. Threat missiles have unique capabilities that must be considered when planning countermeasures. For example, no other target system can put a warhead into the theater JSA or threaten friendly population centers and neutral countries in a matter of minutes. Other target systems do not create public panic and a political situation each time a launch is broadcasted on television worldwide by reporters wearing gas masks. Effectively countering this threat, coupled with the somewhat elusive nature of some threat missile systems, requires the dedicated attention of determined, knowledgeable professionals.

b. Modern threat missiles can have very long ranges, deliver a variety of warheads, including high explosives and WMD, and can be difficult to counter. Because they are relatively cost-effective weapons, BMs are weapons of choice for many developing nations. Such weapons provide an offensive capability and, when mated with a WMD, may give a nation the ability to deter a potential adversary by holding population centers and/or military forces at risk. Rogue nations believe missiles provide them with a counter to sophisticated land, air, and naval forces. As a result, nations around the world are actively pursuing missile capabilities.

c. Threat missiles may be used alone or in conjunction with other weapon systems. Their targets can vary from political to military, such as population centers, ports, airfields, headquarters, AD sites, C2 elements, communications nodes, and logistics centers. They can quickly put key civilian facilities at risk, such as power and water stations, petroleum pumping and storage sites, and industrial complexes. BMs and CMs also present a serious threat to merchant shipping, critical sea-lanes, and maritime operations in the littorals. ASMs also have proven to be effective weapons against point targets, and they are difficult to defend against.

2. Generic Architecture

Although there are many variables between the different types of threat missiles, they generally share a common architecture. Missile programs may have one or more of the following aspects:

a. **Research and Development.** If a country is developing its own missile system or adapting a system purchased from another country, there will be a center, institution, and personnel responsible for the research and development (R&D) effort. However, if a country purchases the complete missile system, there may be no R&D effort unless they attempt to improve the design. R&D efforts should provide some signatures for intelligence sources.

b. **Manufacturing.** Countries that develop their own systems or adapt those produced by other nations require dedicated manufacturing and testing facilities. They also may have to develop or refine the fuel for the missile systems. Although the fuels are of a specific type, they are commonly available on the international market from several sources. The manufacturing process should produce signatures and products (the missiles) that intelligence sources should recognize.

c. **Purchase and Import.** Countries that purchase systems from other nations will have prepared sites for receipt of missile system components and fuels. These ports of entry may be air-, land- (road or rail), or sea-based. These locations may have receipt, inspection, and storage capabilities. If the equipment requires assembly, there may be facilities created nearby to support these activities.

d. **Transportation.** Missile components move from their manufacturing or importing site by rail, road, air, and/or sea to permanent storage sites. In some cases, the missiles may be carried by their transporter-erector-launcher (TEL) unit. The combination of purchasing and transportation should provide signatures or some trail or recognition for intelligence sources.

e. **Missile Storage.** Missile storage locations are required at the point of manufacture, at the point of receipt, in missile unit base locations, and at training installations. Missile storage sites are likely to be constructed and developed within projected operational areas as well. If not mounted on a TEL, storage may include innocuous containers or special canisters that house the missiles until they are launched.

f. **Warhead Storage.** Warhead storage sites are usually located in ammunition areas and may not be easily discernible from bunkers holding other munitions. However, WMD warheads require specialized storage, handling, and, most notably, higher security. WMD generally have telltale signs for not only storage but for movement as well.

g. **Basing.** Missile units are usually located at military bases for OPSEC and safety purposes. Most training and equipment maintenance occurs at these locations. Land-based units likely will move from their garrisons to conduct combat operations. Air units with CMs and ASMs conduct training and wartime operations directly from their home air bases or from dispersal fields. BM units are likely to utilize passive AD measures such as mobility, dispersal, and concealment to complicate their being targeted. Naval units generally have their missiles aboard ships for added mobility and movement to potential firing locations. Normally, intelligence sources should be able to identify adversaries with missile-capable aircraft and ships.

h. **Assembly Areas.** In cases where BMs and warheads are shipped and stored separately, one of the final stages of preparing the weapon for operations is mating the warhead to the missile body. This may be a training event so it can be efficiently done for combat operations. For aircraft, the loading process could be an indication and warning for intelligence sources, as would the assembly of BMs.

i. **Launch Areas.** Missile attacks normally take place from planned launch areas. The characteristics of the launch areas are dependent on missile type. Historically, BMs usually start from a hide position then move to the launch point. ASMs must be flown to a launch point within range of the target.

j. **Launch Preparation.** After arrival at a launch area, most BMs require some prelaunch preparation. These activities may involve fueling and testing the missile and warhead components along with some assembly operations. Launch preparations for liquid-fueled missiles generally require longer setup/checkout time than do solid fuel missiles. For CMs and ASMs, these activities likely will occur at an airfield or port and may involve simply moving the missile from a storage area to the delivery platform (aircraft or ship).

k. **C2.** Planning missile operations is normally a highly centralized process with tight control over the employment and selection of targets. Execution of missile operations may be either centralized or decentralized. The degree of centralization is generally determined by the degree of control desired by senior civilian or military leaders, the capability for secure communications, the ability of the opposing forces to detect or locate transmitters, and the tactics employed. WMD-armed missiles will be tightly controlled because of their political sensitivity and the possibility of retaliation. Thus, WMD-associated missile units normally will require robust communication links or constant communication with national leadership for launch authorization.

l. **Support Units.** Most missile systems require a support system. Support units provide a variety of functions to include maintenance, rearming and refueling, personnel replacement, etc. They also deliver replacement warheads and missiles and conduct all the electronic testing and repair. During peacetime, these units probably will be colocated with the missile firing units in garrison. For employment, they may move to FOBs or dispersal/staging airfields. For naval units the support is likely organic to the ship.

3. **Ballistic Missiles**

a. BMs (or SSMs) are characterized by their trajectory, having one or more boosters and an initial steering vector.

b. **Threat Employment Concepts**

(1) Prime targets for BMs are large, soft, or heavily defended facilities, critical to a nation's warfighting ability, that are normally located in rear areas. Examples include airfields, AD sites, transportation centers (ports and airfields), logistic hubs, and major C2 nodes. Additionally, key population centers are prime targets whose attack might create panic and foster a political crisis. BMs also may be used in a tactical sense to affect battlefield logistics and operations, although this is less likely given the strategic importance of such weapons to smaller or less developed nations.

(2) TBMs normally are carried on a TEL so mobility enhances BM survivability and, conversely, complicates their being targeted. Their long range affords the enemy increased options in selecting operating areas and determining potential targets. For example, BMs have been exported by many nations and can be set up and fired in less than

45 minutes and relocated within minutes. Missiles often present multiple tracks, either from staging or from their tendency to break up during terminal phase descent, thereby further complicating defensive efforts.

(3) SAM systems have been modified into SSMs in some countries, and this trend likely will spread to other nations. As missile systems and missile technology proliferate, nations will acquire or be able to produce missile systems using solid fuels. This will significantly reduce the dwell time required for system checks and fueling during launch preparation. This reduced dwell time will significantly reduce the missile's signature and the time available for attack operations.

c. **Threat Employment Operations.** TBM operations generally are broken down into five major phases. These include readiness, deployment, employment, sustainment, and reconstitution.

(1) **Readiness Phase.** The readiness phase encompasses normal day-to-day peacetime operations. During this phase, BM forces train on wartime tasks and practice doctrinal employment in the local training areas or in garrison. This normally entails TEL operation, missile erection, site preparation, and missile maintenance. Support units will perform maintenance on firing units and conduct resupply operations.

(2) **Deployment Phase.** The deployment phase may include initial movement from the garrison location(s) to the initial war fighting positions to support subsequent launch operations. BM force deployment will depend on the range to the target, missile capability, terrain, and survivability considerations. Firing units will move to either hide positions or directly into launch positions. Support units likely will move to a forward base and conduct support to include reloading operations. Deployments may or may not convey hostile intent, depending upon the circumstances.

(3) **Employment Phase.** The employment phase encompasses initial combat operations. During this phase, TELs move missiles to their initial firing positions from a hide site and then, after launch, move to another hide site or directly to reload operations. The support unit will establish that location based upon doctrine, terrain, the BM force commander's firing schedule, and the threat.

(4) **Sustainment Phase.** During the sustainment phase, support units likely will use a forward base/location to conduct the necessary repair/replacement operations to sustain the BM force. Sustainment operations require support units to use lines of communications from garrison locations, field storage areas, and/or the manufacturing infrastructure/import facilities to the forward bases and onward.

(5) **Reconstitution Phase.** The reconstitution phase encompasses continuous operations between firing units, support units, and higher echelon logistic locations to regenerate BM forces.

d. **Threat Employment—Tactics, Techniques, and Procedures**

(1) **TEL Operations.** TELs can serve as the transporter and launch platform for missiles. TELs present a small, extremely mobile target with very short dwell time. TELs generally travel only short distances between hide sites, launch sites, and transload sites, unless required to return to a forward base for additional maintenance. A TEL will be in launch configuration for a very short period of time and can displace to a new hide site in a matter of minutes.

(2) **Transload Site.** The transload site is where fueled, ready missiles are loaded onto TELs. Support unit personnel, vehicles, and equipment from the forward base or location will rendezvous at this site with firing unit TELs. At this site there generally are a number of vehicles: missile resupply vehicles (with one to three missiles), a crane (possibly attached to the resupply vehicle), and other ground support equipment as required by the missile type. The transload site usually is an open area large enough to allow the crane to lift/pivot the missile onto the TEL, approximately 50 by 50 meters. This operation can occur in large buildings or underground facilities with sufficient height, approximately 20 meters. When detected, this site will remain vulnerable throughout its established dwell time.

(3) **FOL.** The FOL is typically where warheads and missiles are mated, missiles are fueled, and missiles are loaded onto the resupply vehicle. The FOL remains in place from half-a day to 3 days. The FOL usually contains warheads and missile airframes, transporters, cranes, checkout vehicles, fuel trucks (vehicle and missile fuel), and resupply and other support vehicles. FOLs can be located in rural or urban settings and may be hidden in a building complex or underground facility. The FOL has a larger footprint than TEL or transload operations, but is still difficult to locate. Some countries may not employ FOLs, preferring to conduct these operations out of the FOB.

(4) **FOB.** The FOB is the main missile unit supply and storage activity and will be spread out over a large geographic area for survivability. The number of FOBs will depend on the size of the missile force (targets selected and acceptable travel distances for support units). In situations where a country's geographic area is small, it is possible that operations typically associated with the FOB could be conducted from garrison.

(a) A typical FOB contains warhead, missile, and propellant storage sites; transporters and cranes; checkout vehicles; fuel trucks (vehicle and missile fuel); and resupply and other support vehicles. An FOB can be established in an urban environment hidden in large buildings, in underground facilities, or in the field. The FOB normally will deploy support equipment to FOLs and/or transload sites as needed to sustain launch operations. FOBs require robust lines of communications (primarily roads and rail lines) to support continuous operations.

(b) The FOB cannot be easily hidden but may be difficult to distinguish from other logistic facilities. Once established, the FOB probably will not be moved in total, but certain components may be moved to complicate detection, create a deception, or facilitate launch operations.

4. Cruise Missiles

a. A CM is a guided missile, the major portion of whose flight path to its target is conducted at approximately constant velocity and depends on the dynamic reaction of air for lift and upon propulsion forces to balance drag. CMs are unmanned, self-propelled vehicles that sustain flight through the use of aerodynamic lift over most of their flight. CMs usually navigate autonomously to targets and, depending on their sophistication, can position themselves through a number of update methods along extended flight routes. CMs are capable of delivering the full complement of warheads from conventional to WMD.

b. **Threat CMs**

(1) Very few nations currently possess sophisticated CMs such as the Navy TLAM or the Air Force conventional air launched cruise missile (ALCM). Employment by developed nations has been limited. The majority of CMs in potential threat nations are short-range anti-ship/coastal defense CMs with ranges in excess of 100 nautical miles. Some countries are modifying anti-ship CMs for a land attack role.

(2) Future CM technology will build on existing low observable, sensor defeating designs using radar absorbing materials and composite materials such as Kevlar or carbon fiber to further reduce their radar cross-sections and render them more difficult to detect. CMs generally possess some of the following features:

(a) Radar cross-section under 1 square meter (-10 decibel and lower).

(b) Low infrared signature (varies by type of CM).

(c) Acoustic signature (varies by type of CM).

(d) Cruise altitude of 100 feet to 2000 feet above ground level or 50,000 feet above mean sea level.

(e) Range of 100 to 1000 nautical miles.

(f) Payload of 200 to 1000 pounds.

(g) Speed range of high subsonic (low altitude) or supersonic (high altitude).

(h) Air-, land-, or sea-launched.

c. **Threat CM Employment**

(1) CMs put stress on AD systems because they are difficult for theater sensors and weapons systems to detect, identify, track, acquire, and destroy. CMs are more difficult to detect than the larger BMs because they do not give off as large a heat signature at launch, fly at very low altitudes during their attack legs, and normally have a smaller radar cross-section. Ground-based surveillance radars have a difficult time detecting CMs when in low level flight (following terrain contours) because of line-of-sight restrictions created by radar

horizon and terrain masking. Similarly, airborne radar systems may have a difficult time isolating CMs from ground clutter. These traits, when combined with radar evasion techniques and low observable construction methods, cause delays in detection and engagement decisions by engagement authorities and shooters per the ROE. However, once detected in flight, CMs can be engaged by fighters, AAA, and SAMs. The best tactic is to shoot down the aircraft carrying the CMs.

(2) SLCMs and ground-launched cruise missiles (GLCMs) present opportunities for detection as well as challenges for surveillance systems. Surface launch systems normally must be boosted to "cruise" altitude. The boost phase often uses a rocket motor that will produce an infrared signature that could potentially be exploited by space-based or properly positioned theater assets. ALCMs do not have a boost plume since aircraft or UASs deliver them above the cruise altitude. Although the ALCM has a small radar cross-section, it is vulnerable to radar detection during descent to its low-level altitude. Once near the surface and in a terrain following mode, sensors have to filter radar ground clutter to extract a radar signature from these low-altitude profile missiles.

(3) High-altitude, high-mach profiles rely on altitude and speed to overcome defenses. Because the CM is high, ground-based radars will not be obstructed by the curvature of the earth, and airborne radars can discriminate them from ground clutter. As a result, when using the high-altitude profile, CMs are more likely to be detected earlier in flight than when using a low-level profile.

(4) CMs provide a significant standoff range for the aircraft or launch platform and remove the "manned" component of the weapons system from the immediate target area. The release range of CMs from aircraft and other platforms can easily be beyond a defender's radar and sensor range. The long distance release or launch of CMs and their smaller radar signature increase the possibility that surveillance assets will not detect them. Battle managers require cues to focus their search in detecting CMs in any surveillance area. Combining hostile aircraft attacks with CM and ASM attacks may allow "leakers" to get through. Indeed, CMs may resemble and be misidentified as manned aircraft.

(5) Rapid CID is critical for CM defense. CM defense is complicated by the use of low observable technology and the potential of SOF or other friendly aircraft without IFF transponders operating in the same airspace, thus requiring ID verification prior to engagement. CMs make surveillance and detection difficult because their flight profiles are specifically designed to defeat or confuse radar tracking. As with BMs, the objective is to eliminate as many CMs as possible before launch. CMs in flight may be part of TST target sets designated by the JFC. The challenge for defending against CMs is to find them early, before launch if possible, and engage them before they can navigate to their targets.

(6) Training patterns or identifiable launch sequence events for GLCMs are rarely observed or practiced in an overt environment. Consequently, the probability is small for conclusively identifying a GLCM TEL using current sensor data. Attacking a CM TEL requires the earliest possible detection of the target and the ability of sensors to discriminate between TELs and other targets. Successfully targeting CMs before launch will depend in great part on pre-hostility JIPOE/IPB efforts. Targeteers will require information on

infrastructure, logistic support patterns, movement discipline, and signatures of typical storage and assembly facilities. Identification by signature is key to finding CMs before launch, since detecting the launch itself or tracing the flight path back to the launch site may be extremely difficult when they are launched from maximum range.

d. **CM Target Development**

(1) Procedures for finding and targeting CMs on the ground are no different than for finding other targets using a variety of theater and national sensors. Space-based and theater reconnaissance, surveillance, and target acquisition assets normally will collect intelligence data on these targets prior to armed conflict as part of IPB. Sensors on JSTARS and UASs and SOF pass CM target information to analysts and battle managers by data link or voice. Data collected and fused from multiple sensors will provide the necessary confirmation of the target. Immediate threat data will be broadcast over intelligence processing and transmissions systems such as tactical related applications and tactical data dissemination systems.

(2) When conflict begins, sensors must be used to validate known target information. With proper ISR, aircraft and naval launch platforms for ALCMs and SLCMs provide identifiable signatures and will yield opportunities to detect, ID, track, and attack those platforms. GLCMs will present a more difficult target set. The following is a discussion of targeting methods against each category:

(a) **ALCM.** Destroying ALCM-capable aircraft on the ground or neutralizing their supporting airstrips/bases is the best means to prevent ALCM employment. In this context, missions against this target system do not differ from other OCA missions in terms of tactics or weapons. The IPB process must focus on providing the intelligence that targeteers need to determine which aircraft and air bases support ALCM activity and task missions against them accordingly.

(b) **SLCM.** Destroying the launch platform in port is the best means to prevent SLCM launch. The IPB process will provide the naval order of battle information to identify specific SLCM carriers and support bases for targeteers and battle managers to task missions against them. Signatures of naval vessels and their substantial support base infrastructure will facilitate finding SLCM targets by satellite, UAS, and other surveillance platforms.

(c) **GLCM.** GLCM platforms normally are an adaptation of any available vehicle chassis capable of supporting one to two tons. Any medium-to-large size truck or tracked vehicle could be developed into a CM TEL. These TELs likely will be considerably smaller and less distinct than heavier BM TELs; however, a robust IPB effort can catalog such known and suspected vehicles for exploitation by surveillance sensors. GLCM deployment and training in suspect nations must be collected against and studied for behavioral cues to detection. Long-range GLCM permit the enemy to establish a large number of well-dispersed, fixed-launch locations (both actual and decoys) deep within their own territory. The enemy can be expected to employ camouflage, concealment, and deception for fixed and mobile TELs to reduce probability of detection. Detecting and targeting mobile GLCM platforms or newly built fixed launch sites will depend on a robust IPB, dynamic management of ISR assets, dedicated and trained analysts aided by technology improvements such as automatic target recognition systems, and a responsive C2 architecture.

5. Air-to-Surface Missiles

ASMs employment can be expected on all battlefields. Like BMs and CMs, ASMs are capable of delivering a complete range of warheads and can be carried by a variety of rotary- and fixed-wing platforms. Flight profiles, short flight times, and reduced radar cross-section make these missiles difficult to detect, track, and engage. Additionally, their speed and relatively short flight times leave a small window for interception. ASMs increase the survivability of the delivery platform through standoff capability, usually beyond the range of some point defenses. Many of the North Atlantic Treaty Organization and former Warsaw Pact nations are equipped with US and Russian manufactured systems and have exported them throughout the world. The best method for countering ASMs is to target the delivery platforms and related bases and facilities.

6. Conclusion

While each missile system is unique, each category (BM, CM, and ASM) exhibits similar characteristics and functional operations. This appendix provides the essential

---

THE LURE OF THE UNEXPECTED

Deception is a key part of any combat operations. The examples below illustrate what happens when analysts stop analyzing events and begin to believe what they think they are seeing.

World War II

Prior to the beginning of the V-1 attacks against London on June 12, 1944, the Allied attack operations concentrated on an elaborate system of "sites" which were believed to be Nazi V-1 launch locations. The locations were dubbed "ski sites" because of the shape of several long, curved buildings that were characteristic in the aerial photographs of each location. These sites were targeted and heavily bombed from December 1943 through May 1944. Although the "ski sites" were largely destroyed, not one of the real V-1 sites was attacked during this period. Once Hitler unleashed his missile force on England in June, the volume of V-1 launches provided incontrovertible evidence that a second set of launch sites was actually being used. Not until then did the weight of the Allied bombing effort finally begin to shift to the correct targets. Even so, the real sites were so hard to find due to Nazi camouflage and concealment measures that attacks were still being made on nearby decoy "ski sites" until the end of June.

SOURCE: Based on Operation CROSSBOW
Volume of the US Strategic Bombing Survey

Gulf War

The initial hope of the planners in Riyadh that heavy attacks on the fixed Scud sites during the opening hours of the air campaign would largely eliminate Iraq's capability to launch tactical ballistic missiles against Israel or regional members of the US-led Coalition proved to be illusory. On the night of 16-17 January 1991, the fixed Scud launchers in western Iraq functioned as "decoys" that diverted attention away from the mobile launchers that had already deployed to their wartime "hide" sites, and the first of Iraq's extended-range Scuds were fired at Israel the following night. Once Scuds started falling, first on Israel and then on Saudi Arabia two days later, the next best military option would have been to locate and attack mobile launchers before they had time to fire. Soviet exercise patterns in central Europe with Scud-B's and Iraqi practice during the Iran-Iraq War, indicated that if the Iraqis followed prior practices, there might be enough pre-launch signatures and time to give patrolling aircraft some chance of attacking mobile launchers before they fired. However, the Iraqis dramatically cut their pre-launch set-up times, avoided any pre-launch electromagnetic emissions that might give away their locations before launch, and seeded the launch areas with decoys (some of which were very high in fidelity)...most (and possibly all) of the roughly 100 mobile launchers reported destroyed by Coalition aircraft and special operation forces now appear to have been either decoys, other vehicles such as tanker trucks, or other objects unfortunate enough to provide "Scud-like" signatures.

SOURCE: Gulf War Air Power Survey, 1993

framework for each in a generic fashion and serves as a foundation for an initial understanding of how missiles are employed. Specific analysis is required to apply this information to a particular missile system and country. The following vignette is a reminder that some "facts" should be verified, not simply accepted.

APPENDIX E
GLOBAL BALLISTIC MISSILE DEFENSE SYNCHRONIZATION

1. General

GBMD is the overarching characterization of the cumulative (worldwide) planning, synchronization, integration, coordination, and asset management of defensive capabilities designed to destroy, neutralize, or reduce the effectiveness of enemy BM attacks within or across any GCC's AOR boundaries.

a. **Global BM Threats.** The BM threat continues to increase both quantitatively and qualitatively. Worldwide trends indicate BM systems are becoming more flexible, mobile, survivable, reliable, and accurate. A number of states are favoring longer-range BMs and increasing their ability to penetrate missile defenses. Several states are also developing nuclear, chemical, and/or biological warheads for their missiles. Such capabilities could significantly increase their utility both during conflict as well as in times of relative peace, when adversaries may use them to coerce states into actions contrary to US interests. The potential for proliferation to state and non-state actors may have significant impacts to regional and global stability. Certain regional actors continue to develop long-range missiles that threaten the US and its friends, and allies. Uncertainty exists about when and how this type of intercontinental ballistic missile threat will mature. Additionally, SRBMs/MRBMs continue to increase as threats. The advance in threats and evolution of technical solutions necessitate strategic solutions to the deployment of low-density, high-demand missile defense assets at the theater level. BMD deployments must be tailored to the unique deterrence and defense requirements of each theater, which may vary considerably by geography, the character of the threat, and the military-to-military relationships on which to build partnerships and cooperation for missile defense. BMs, whether employed in standard, lofted, or depressed trajectories, present unique problems, including high velocities and short reaction times for the defender. Accordingly, the proliferation of missile technology and WMD requires BMD capabilities for defending the homeland and deployed forces, as well as protecting allies and partners overseas.

b. **BMD Systems.** To accomplish BMD globally, USSTRATCOM, working with the GCCs, integrates and synchronizes a wide range of sensors, interceptors, and C2 elements. Systems collectively employed include sensors (air, land, sea, and space), weapons (ground, air, and sea based), C2, manning, and logistics. These include GMD, THAAD, Aegis-BMD, Patriot, Upgraded Early Warning Radars (UEWRs), the COBRA DANE radar, the Sea-Based X-band radar, AN/TPY-2 Forward Based Mode radars, space-based Infrared System/Defense Support Program satellites, Command and Control, Battle Management, and Communications system, and applicable partner nation BMD capabilities.

c. GBMD is supported by communications, comprised of the infrastructure which physically connects strategic and regional missile defense assets in support of operational and/or research, development, test, and evaluation activities. The main communications network used by GMD is the BMD COMNET. This network may be comprised of numerous distinct communications systems including, but not limited to, military and commercial satellite communications and Defense Information System Agency provisioned terrestrial services. The BMD COMNET includes the GMD Communications Network and Command, Control, Battle Management and Communications BMD Communication Network.

2. Global Ballistic Missile Defense Roles and Responsibilities

a. The UCP tasks each CCDR with, "Detecting, deterring, and preventing attacks against the United States, its territories and bases, and employing appropriate force to defend the nation should deterrence fail." CCDRs will coordinate the employment of active and passive missile defense measures and strike forces to defeat BM attacks in all phases of flight, or prior to their launch. Each GCC is the "supported" commander for all operations conducted to defeat BM threats in their respective AOR. A missile launch that crosses AOR boundaries complicates C2 of defensive assets and requires coordination among multiple GCCs. For theater BMD, a GCC may control all elements involved; however, as the range of threat missiles increases, and depending on the location of their launchers, so does the potential for cross-AOR BM attacks. This will test the speed and reliability of C2 which ties sensors and interceptors to decision makers across traditional command boundaries. The need to close gaps and seams across AOR boundaries led to the UCP direction for CDRUSSTRATCOM to be responsible for synchronizing the planning for global missile defense. All GCCs and subordinate JFCs coordinate their BMD planning and support with USSTRATCOM JFCC-IMD.

b. Many organizations have a role in BMD. By its very nature, BMD is inherently joint and may be executed in multiple AORs simultaneously by the affected GCCs. Because there are no overarching GBMD C2 structures, GCCs use existing theater AMD C2 organizations (e.g., AADCs, AAMDCs, RADCs, and SADCs) to conduct BMD, and they must coordinate across AOR boundaries.

3. General Ballistic Missile Defense Characteristics

a. BMD consists of passive AD, active AD, attack operations, and battle management. It aligns with DCA required for BM threats when a JFC conducts counterair operations (see counterair framework diagram in Chapter I, "Introduction," Figure I-1).

b. GBMD includes capabilities to detect, deter, defend against, and defeat adversary BM threats. GBMD must synchronize and integrate defensive capabilities to destroy or disrupt adversary missiles prior to launch, or to defeat inbound missiles in all phases of flight. Effective and efficient GBMD requires a balanced use of resources among the GCCs. To achieve unity of effort, GBMD will need to fully synchronize defensive actions and supporting systems to engage a target with multiple weapons systems throughout its trajectory.

c. Effective GBMD battle management requires shared situational awareness, effective management of high-demand–low-density resources, directing and controlling the correct actions in a timely manner, and monitoring and assessing the execution. GBMD utilizes a wide range of integrated BMD battle-management and planning systems to mitigate complexities associated with multiple theater BMD events.

4. Global Ballistic Missile Defense Planning

a. GBMD requires a collaborative process that provides GCCs with the ability to coordinate cross-AOR BMD in multiple theaters while preserving functions performed at the GCC level and below. While such a planning process is designed to mitigate risks associated with BM threats, it also enhances a GCC's ability to employ forces and capabilities within their AOR in support of another GCC. Planners balance competing requirements for low-density and high-demand strategic resources.

b. To ensure that GBMD planning supports a CCDR's overall campaign planning and facilitates integration of missile defense force requirements with Global Force Management processes, the collaborative planning process must be conducted in accordance with established DOD deliberate planning activities.

c. Planning activities identify potential areas of risk to GCC and JFC operations. Any consideration of missile defense resources and shared airspace should account for the fact that BMD resources are integral to the theater counterair mission when the JFC desires air superiority to accomplish an assigned mission. Some BMD resources, specifically Aegis BMD ships, are multi-mission platforms that may also be required for strike and anti-surface or antisubmarine warfare tasking in support of the JFC's CONOPS. In addition to producing planning products, planning activities serve to identify capability shortfalls and explore materiel and non-materiel solutions to mitigate vulnerabilities in the protection of the homeland, deployed US forces, allies, and friends.

d. Planning for BMD should include coordination of launch warnings, offensive operations that support a missile defense strategy, plan assessment metrics, Global Force Management, and C2 of missile defense operations. Gaps and seams between AOR boundaries and between forces in different AORs can be areas of risk. Procedures for distribution and control of fires between AORs should be addressed during planning. Collaborative planning efforts should produce recommendations to mitigate operational gaps and vulnerabilities associated with BM threats.

e. In preparation for deployment of BMD forces in support of a GCC, the principal players will participate in joint collaborative planning. This is done using the supported GCC's priorities and CALs/DALs, and results in development of the theater AADP, finalization of the ROE and engagement criteria, refinement of existing defense plans, coordination of cross-AOR engagement requirements, and force allocation. Multinational BMD forces should be included in all phases of planning, and training of those forces must be considered.

5. Global Synchronization of Ballistic Missile Defense Planning

a. GCCs are responsible for planning and executing BMD within their geographic AORs and other areas as directed. SecDef designates supported and supporting commanders. As a general rule, a GCC under missile attack will be the supported commander. CDRUSNORTHCOM is the supported commander for homeland BMD and may be the supporting commander for BMD in other theaters. As either a supported or supporting commander, balancing regional missile defense priorities with homeland missile defense priorities is critical, especially in situations where multiple GCCs are under attack simultaneously. CDRUSSTRATCOM, as the global synchronizer for global missile defense planning, leads the GBMD collaborative planning process and is responsible for maintaining global situational awareness, performing globally focused cross-AOR analysis and developing inputs, recommendations, and assessments. CDRUSSTRATCOM facilitates the alignment of GCC plans in an effort to balance risk, standardize procedures, and mitigate operational seams to meet established priorities. CDRUSSTRATCOM is responsible for synchronizing planning for global missile defense and coordinating global missile defense operations support. For unanticipated situations, a collaborative planning process will facilitate adaptations or refinements to existing plans. For cross-AOR operations, execution will be based on the supported GCC's plans. During execution, CCDRs will retain execution authority over assigned and attached forces. Command relationships are established through plans or orders based on real threats. Increasing range, location of launchers, and other technological advances in BMs may necessitate missile defense forces in one AOR providing support to an adjacent CCDR. The supported GCC's plan establishes the overarching framework used by subordinate component commanders and supporting CCDRs to develop supporting plans.

b. CDRUSSTRATCOM has established the Missile Defense Global Synchronization Board as a general/flag officer resolution body to resolve issues related to GBMD plans, operational planning guidance or policy, plans assessments, and force management. Chaired by Deputy CDRUSSTRATCOM, this body includes general/flag officers from the combatant commands' operations and plans directorates, the Joint Staff, the Services, Missile Defense Agency (MDA), Joint Integrated Air and Missile Defense Organization, JFCC-IMD, and, as needed, Office of the Secretary of Defense. In all cases, CCDRs retain the prerogative to elevate irreconcilable issues to SecDef.

c. BMD Global Force Management. BMD resources are low-density, high-demand, and expensive. SecDef will assign or allocate forces to respective GCCs as required for BMD.

(1) Missile Defense Global Force Management Allocation Plan (GFMAP). SecDef allocates missile defense forces annually through the GFMAP. Modifications to the GFMAP can be made through a request for forces (RFF). CCDRs submit RFFs to support emerging or crisis-based operational requirements to SecDef via the CJCS.

(2) Missile Defense Joint Functional Manager. USSTRATCOM serves that function, including identifying, developing, and recommending globally optimized sourcing solutions for DOD missile defense capabilities in coordination with DOD joint force providers, Services, other CCDRs, MDA, and other DOD agencies. USSTRATCOM, through JFCC-IMD, is responsible for identifying and recommending missile defense assets in response to the requirements of the GCCs.

d. GBMD Planning Principles and Considerations. Successful GBMD planning is based on the principles of unity of effort, unity of command, centralized planning and direction, and when engagement authority has been delegated to subordinate commanders, decentralized execution.

(1) Unity of Command. GCCs are supported commanders for all BMD in their respective AORs. Due to speed, range, and the potential for cross-AOR missile threats, GCCs may simultaneously be supported and supporting for BMD. Changes in command relationships do not affect unity of command. For example, forces assigned to Commander, United States Central Command (CDRUSCENTCOM), supporting BMD operations in United States European Command's AOR, normally would remain under the command of CDRUSCENTCOM.

(2) Unity of Effort. BMD can be conducted simultaneously at theater, regional, AOR, and cross-AOR levels and require intratheater and intertheater integration and coordination of capabilities to optimize engagement opportunities. Integrating a full array of offensive options with active and passive missile defense measures is essential to establishing and sustaining a deterrence and defense against BM attack of the homeland, forward deployed troops, allies, and friends. Integration of multinational BMD capabilities into GBMD requires coordination of effort to support both passive air and active ADs. While, at times, a GCC may control all elements in an engagement, the processes linking sensors to decision makers to fire control nodes may cross AOR boundaries and will require coordination between neighboring GCCs to enable multiple engagement opportunities. A GCC must coordinate BMD with other combatant commands and multinational partners to ensure unity of effort.

(3) Centralized Planning. GCCs are responsible for planning all assigned missions within their AOR, including regional BMD, and support to HD. In addition, GCCs are responsible for coordinating and integrating cross-AOR activities with adjacent and other supporting CCDRs. Planning will reflect the differences in how BMD operations will be conducted based on threats of various missile classes, launch points, impact points, and projected numbers. Because BMs can rapidly cross AOR boundaries, the joint force must integrate layered BMD forces and resources across multiple commands to establish an effective defense in depth. Global collaborative planning enables the coordination and integration of all BMD capabilities. USSTRATCOM will lead collaborative centralized GBMD planning efforts to ensure gaps and vulnerabilities are mitigated in cross-AOR planning. Support relationships must be well-defined during planning to ensure clarity during mission execution and minimize operational gaps. Planning for BMD will factor in the multi-mission capabilities of BMD resources, cross-AOR attack operations, and the ability to have supporting fires and coordinated engagements among BMD forces. Planned responses and pre-coordinated engagement criteria between GCCs support the prompt, decisive engagement of BM threats. While it is the goal to provide warfighters the planning tools to conduct planning in the forward AORs at the strategic, operational, and tactical levels, certain threat prototype systems and other circumstances may require higher fidelity reachback planning from Service sponsors or acquisition authorities. Service specific reachback planning shall be coordinated through the applicable AOR Service component.

(4) Decentralized Execution. BMD forces and resources are under the control of the JFC to whom they are assigned or attached. Tasking and engagement authority will be

delegated to the lowest practical level consistent with the ROE, the DAL, the AADP, and the authority of the JFC. The process and means of ordering engagements will be clearly stated in AADPs, ACOs, and SPINS, or other orders. Engagement coordination requires the ability to plan GBMD resources to optimize the operational environment and decision timelines; identify and track multiple, simultaneous missile threats; and direct engagement against multiple BM threats. To optimize decentralized execution of BMD engagement opportunities, it is essential to have clear policy guidance, shared situational awareness, minimal system latency, and the capability to synchronize efforts across AORs. The one exception to decentralized execution of BMD is for homeland BMD, using the ground based mid-course defense system, which requires positive direction from the weapons release authority (WRA). WRA is the authority delegated from the President to use certain weapons against BM threats (e.g., ground-based interceptors).

(5) Support Relationships. Directives that establish a support relationship for GBMD must include the forces and resources allocated to the supporting effort; the time, place, level, and duration of the supporting effort; the relative priority of the supporting effort; the authority, if any, of the supporting commander to modify the supporting effort in the event of an exceptional opportunity or an emergency; and the degree of authority granted to the supported commander over the supporting effort. Unless limited by the establishing directive, the supported commander will have the authority to exercise general direction of the supporting effort. General direction includes the designation and prioritization of targets or objectives, timing and duration of the supporting action, and other instructions necessary for coordination and efficiency. The supporting commander determines the forces, tactics, methods, procedures, and communications to be employed in providing this support. The supporting commander will advise and coordinate with the supported commander on matters concerning the employment and limitations of such support, assist in planning for the integration of such support into the supported commander's effort as a whole, and ensure that support requirements are appropriately communicated with the supporting commander's organization. The supporting commander has the responsibility to ascertain the BMD needs of the supported commander and take action to fulfill them within existing capabilities, consistent with priorities and requirements of other assigned tasks.

(6) Offensive Operations. The GCC in whose AOR the threat resides is responsible to plan offensive options that support homeland BMD and cross-AOR BMD. Because of the relative scarcity of defensive assets when compared to the threat, GCCs and functional CCDRs should have well-developed plans and agreements with appropriate operating procedures in place for suitable offensive actions to counter BM threats. If offensive operations are directed by the President, other GCCs may be tasked to support a neighboring GCC by conducting offensive strikes against imminent missile threats (pre-launch) or BMD support after the launch and identification of a BM as hostile. CDRUSSTRATCOM may provide global strike in coordination with a supported/supporting GCC, as directed by the President. BMD planners should coordinate their efforts with combating WMD planners to optimize use of offensive actions/operations.

For additional information regarding combating WMD, see JP 3-40, Combating Weapons of Mass Destruction.

(7) ROE. ROE are the means to provide military commanders guidance for weapons employment consistent with law and policy. Due to short engagement timelines and the vulnerability of communications relating to GBMD, robust, prior political agreements will need to be reached, planning synchronized, and operations thoroughly trained and exercised. A set of general standing ROE is essential for all BMD and GBMD. ROE must comply with the requirements of any alliance, treaty, coalition, bilateral, or multilateral agreements to which the United States is a party. Agreements between coalition and/or allied nations should be reached to permit interceptor and sensor operations in territorial airspace.

(8) International Law. Due to the short engagement timelines and the vulnerability of communications between nations, tasking and engagement authorities for multinational forces and resources conducting GBMD must be planned and take into account individual national interpretations of international law and constitutional limitations. Planners must also recognize that each nation in a coalition or alliance may invoke separate, legal, and political obligations to third parties through treaties, alliances, and other such bilateral or multilateral agreements. DOD forces will adhere to the law of armed conflict during all military operations.

(9) Collateral Effects. Two key planning considerations are minimizing collateral effects of BMD offensive actions and defensive measures to minimize the effects of hostile BMD attacks. In principle, priority should be given to actions that maximize the probability of success of actions saving the most lives. Defense effectiveness should take primacy over debris mitigation when protecting a defended asset. Response actions to the collateral effects of BMD employment may include responding to personal injury, property loss, terrestrial or space debris cleanup resulting from BMD engagements or testing, high-altitude EMP, and CBRN. The coordination of information between organizations planning BMD and potential HN first responders is essential. Moreover, partner nations will require a system or systems to warn member nations and affected third parties on defensive actions and possible consequences.

For additional information regarding CBRN hazards, see JP 3-11, Operations in Chemical, Biological, Radiological, and Nuclear (CBRN) Environments, *and regarding CM, see JP 3-41,* Chemical, Biological, Radiological, and Nuclear Consequence Management.

    e. Contributing Capabilities

(1) Missile Warning. BMD is greatly enabled by persistent and reliable strategic indications and warnings. Space-based and ground-based systems are crucial for timely detection and communicating warning of nuclear detonations or adversary use of BMs against US forces and allies. Integrated tactical warning and attack assessment systems are essential for the execution of the US strategic missile warning for attacks on the US and Canada. Tactical warning is a notification to C2 centers that a specific threat event is occurring or has occurred. Attack assessment is an evaluation of information to determine the potential or actual nature and objectives of an attack for the purpose of providing information for timely decisions. The component elements that describe threat events include the country of origin, the event type and size, the country that is determined to be

under attack, and the time of the event. The two missile warning missions are strategic and theater; both use a mix of space-based and terrestrial sensors. Strategic missile warning is the notification to national leaders of a missile attack against North America or allied and partner nations. Theater missile warning is the NRT notification to operational command centers and the warfighter of a potential threat of a missile event-any event launched from, overflying, or projected to impact a designated AOR, JOA, and/or area of interest.

(a) Strategic Missile Warning. Space-based sensors, such as Defense Support Program and Space-Based Infrared System, usually provide the first level of immediate missile detection. The satellite sensors also accomplish nuclear detonation detection. Ground-based radars provide follow-on information on launches, attack assessment, and confirmation of strategic attack. Although the primary mission of the ground-based radars is conducting missile warning, a portion of the radar resource is allocated to conducting space surveillance; however, the radar is always scanning the horizon for incoming missiles. These ground-based radar systems include Ballistic Missile Early Warning System, PAVE PAWS [Perimeter Acquisition Vehicle Entry Phased Array Warning System], and Perimeter Acquisition Radar Attack Characterization System. UEWRs are multi-mission radars supporting the missile warning, space surveillance, and the missile defense missions, and are integrated into the BMDS to improve midcourse sensor coverage. There is no room for error in strategic missile warning; therefore, all information provided must be timely, reliable, accurate, and unambiguous.

(b) Theater Missile Warning. Because the reaction time for theater forces to respond to incoming missiles is very short (less than 5 minutes), GCCs have adopted a strategy known as "assured" warning, which weighs accepting potentially false reports against the time required to obtain unambiguous reports. Under this strategy, the GCCs have elected to receive quicker launch notifications, understanding the warning could be ambiguous or inaccurate.

(c) Shared Early Warning. The US exchanges missile detection and warning information with its allies and partner nations. Shared early warning (SEW) is the continuous exchange of missile early warning information derived from US missile early warning sensors and the sensors of the SEW partner, when available. Information on missile launches is provided on an NRT basis. This information can take the form of data, voice warning, or both. The objective of SEW is to enhance regional stability by providing theater BM warning to GCCs, sponsored partner nations, and North Atlantic Treaty Organization allies. GCCs will recommend/sponsor SEW partner nations. DOD policy is to provide continuous, NRT, BM early warning information on regional launches that is of the same high quality and timeliness as the launch warning that would be made available to US forces if operating in the same area at the same time. Currently, the SEW system provides both messages and voice warning to partner nations. The Shared Early Warning System includes both space-based warning and surface radar-based warning. Space-based warning provides BM warning information from space-based sensors. It is US policy to share with selected allies, with few exceptions, continuous, NRT, early warning information of BM launches of the same high quality and timeliness as made available to US forces. Missile warning data is provided to SEW partners subject to a country-by-country disclosure and arms control clearance. The release of BM data derived from surface-based radars to surface radar-based warning is authorized when this data is made available to US forces for BM early warning and to support active missile defense.

(2) Space Operations. The enabling capabilities that space operations bring to the joint force are significant for GBMD and are considered critical enabling activities for both global and regional BMD. Space-based systems provide BM launch warnings and attack assessments; launch locations; tracking data such as predicted headings and broad impact areas; global, theater-wide, or JOA-wide communications; current and forecast weather information; space-based ISR; global positioning system (and navigation and timing assets for accuracy of precision munitions); and theater- or JOA-wide CID systems support.

(3) Intelligence Operations. Intelligence on threat BMs is absolutely critical to GBMD success. A common assessment of the adversary BM capabilities and intent (shared among combatant commands, intelligence agencies, and partner nations) is imperative for unified action. Understanding the payloads of adversary missiles can aid decision makers in determining shot doctrine and interceptor and sensor allocations. Mobile missiles are especially challenging to defensive planners; detecting, tracking, and targeting mobile missiles are essential intelligence tasks that support GBMD. Understanding the strategic environment and providing indications and warnings of the entire situation, and not just the status of adversary BM readiness for launch, will assist national decision makers on the appropriate time to take action to mitigate BM threats. ISR platforms and their associated processing, exploitation, and dissemination capabilities must be tasked early to ensure they are involved before hostilities commence.

(4) Allied Capabilities. GBMD is both joint and combined; one nation's "region" may be another's "homeland." Integrating the capabilities of our allies into the theater BMD architectures is critical to implementing a global strategy to deter adversaries, mitigate operational gaps, and provide BMD protection to the homeland, forward deployed forces, allies, and friends. Building partner capability and integration of our allies into the planning process enhances the development of such a cohesive strategy. General BMD security cooperation objectives include encouraging friends and allies to develop their own BMD capabilities, or co-develop them with the US; gain agreements for HN use and support for US or partner nation BMD activities; political support for BMD capability deployments; integration of friends and allies into a defensive architecture; bilateral or multilateral BMD war games and exercises; and further the understanding and education of friends and allies on BMD systems, capabilities; and limitations. Efforts to integrate BMD with allies consider current requirements, policies, and restrictions regarding data sharing with each specific country, for each specific system, and the communications path under consideration.

6. **Global Ballistic Missile Defense Supporting Activities**

a. GBMD Asset Management. A key consideration of GBMD is collaborative asset management. Sensors, weapons and command, and control networks must be managed to ensure availability of the BMDS to national decision makers. CDRUSSTRATCOM supports day-to-day GBMD readiness via BMDS asset management, which ensures BMD systems globally are maintained at an appropriate state of readiness for the prevailing threat condition. Asset management allows the flexibility to conduct sustainment and research, development, testing, and evaluation to improve capabilities. The output from these collaborative planning efforts should be the ability to create effects recommended by the supported GCC for countering BM threats. GCCs operating assets within one AOR tasked to support BMD within another AOR have the responsibility to plan and coordinate with appropriate GCCs and USSTRATCOM. Multi-mission assets residing within a supported commander's area may be required to support another GCC's operations. MDA maintains control of R&D assets that are a potential source of additional BMD capability. When required, USSTRATCOM, in conjunction with applicable GCCs and MDA, will recommend to SecDef activating early delivery capability assets to support the missile defense mission. The BMDS Emergency Activation Plan governs activation of developmental BMD assets.

b. GBMD Logistics Support. The UCP assigns CDRUSSTRATCOM responsibility for coordinating global missile defense operations support. BMD logistics status reporting and assessment is a synchronized effort conducted with geographic and functional combatant commands and MDA. Logistics reporting is directly associated with operational capability reporting procedures, and a logistics situation report is initiated upon a change in the operational capability of a missile defense asset. USSTRATCOM and JFCC-IMD logistics directorates establish and verify BMDS logistics reporting and assessment procedures; they receive and consolidate reports from the GCCs, their components, and MDA, including assets in a developmental status identified to support operational missions.

c. GBMD Training and Exercises. To minimize the risk of fratricide while providing seamless defense, coordination must be rehearsed, not just planned. Demonstrating proficiency in the implementation of emerging BMD concepts requires training and exercises in cross-AOR BMD situations to refine and validate processes and procedures, highlight potential BMD gaps between AORs, and develop options to mitigate associated risk. USSTRATCOM, operational plans and interoperability directorate of a joint staff (J-7), and MDA tri-chair the BMD Training and Education Group, which identifies and resolves joint and multinational issues and establishes policies, procedures, and standards for BMD training and education as identified by the GCCs or Services. Additionally, the group assists combatant commands and Services in defining and coordinating enhanced, jointly integrated, standardized, and cost-effective BMD training and education for the warfighter.

d. GBMD Security and Force Protection. USSTRATCOM has oversight authority for determining security requirements for GBMD and designates security system levels for operational or operationally capable missile defense components and systems. USSTRATCOM provides basic standardized guidance on physical security requirements to protect missile defense mission systems and assets. GCCs have force protection authority and responsibility for missile defense sites or systems located in their AORs, and generally, that responsibility falls to the lead Service for the asset unless other agreements have been made.

e. GBMD System Certification. CDRUSSTRATCOM is responsible for the management and control of the integrity of systems responsible for strategic and space warning, theater warning, and missile defense. The certification process provides CDRUSSTRATCOM and GCCs with assurance that a new system or system change satisfies system integrity requirements and is capable of accomplishing its assigned mission.

USSTRATCOM will certify BMD assets as mission ready as they become available to the GCC.

f. GBMD Requirements Development and Advocacy. Due to the rapid development and fielding requirements to achieve an early initial operational capability, many aspects of BMDS development, acquisition, and sustainment take place outside of established DOD acquisition processes; nevertheless, compliance with required regulatory and policy oversight is maintained. The Missile Defense Executive Board, supported by five standing committees, provides senior policy and acquisition oversight over the BMDS. CDRUSSTRATCOM, as the Air and Missile Defense Integrating Authority, executes the Warfighter Involvement Process to collaboratively develop CCDR and Service AMD capability needs. BMD needs are forwarded to MDA via the BMDS Life Cycle Management Plan process, and AMD needs are forwarded to the Services via the Joint Requirements Oversight Council board structure.

Intentionally Blank

APPENDIX F
REFERENCES

The development of JP 3-01 is based upon the following primary references:

1. Strategic Guidance and Policy

Ballistic Missile Defense Review Report, February 2010.

2. Chairman of the Joint Chiefs of Staff Directives

a. CJCSI 3121.01B, *Standing Rules of Engagement/Standing Rules for the Use of Force for US Forces.*

b. CJCSI 3151.01B, *Global Command and Control System Common Operational Picture Reporting Requirements.*

c. CJCSI 5120.02B, *Joint Doctrine Development System.*

d. CJCSM 3115.01B, *Joint Data Network (JDN) Operations.*

e. CJCSM 6120.01D, *Joint Multi-Tactical Data Link Operating Procedures (JMTOP).*

3. Joint Publications

a. JP 1, *Doctrine for the Armed Forces of the United States.*

b. JP 1-02, *Department of Defense Dictionary of Military and Associated Terms.*

c. JP 2-0, *Joint Intelligence.*

d. JP 2-01, *Joint and National Intelligence Support to Military Operations.*

e. JP 2-01.3, *Joint Intelligence Preparation of the Operational Environment.*

f. JP 3-0, *Joint Operations.*

g. JP 3-10, *Joint Security Operations in Theater.*

h. JP 3-11, *Operations in Chemical, Biological, Radiological, and Nuclear Environments.*

i. JP 3-13, *Information Operations.*

j. JP 3-13.1, *Electronic Warfare.*

k. JP 3-14, *Space Operations.*

l. JP 3-16, *Multinational Operations.*

m. JP 3-27, *Homeland Defense.*

n. JP 3-30, *Command and Control for Joint Air Operations.*

o. JP 3-31, *Command and Control for Joint Land Operations.*

p. JP 3-33, *Joint Task Force Headquarters.*

q. JP 3-40, *Combating Weapons of Mass Destruction.*

r. JP 3-52, *Joint Airspace Control.*

s. JP 5-0, *Joint Operation Planning.*

t. JP 6-0, *Joint Communications System.*

4. Multi-Service Publications

a. FM 3-01.4/MCRP 3-22.2A/NTTP 3-01.42/AFTTP 3-2.28, *Multi-Service Tactics, Techniques, and Procedures for Suppression of Enemy Air Defenses.*

b. FM 3-01.15/MCRP 3-25E/NTTP 3-01.8/AFTTP(I) 3-2.31, *Multi-Service Tactics, Techniques, and Procedures for an Integrated Air Defense System (IADS) (with classified appendices).*

c. FM 3-27, *Army Global Ballistic Missile Defense (GBMD) Operations.*

d. FM 3-52.2/NTTP 3- 56.2/AFTTP(I) 3-2.17, *Multi-Service Tactics, Techniques, and Procedures for the Theater Air-Ground System (TAGS).*

e. Military Standard 6016D, *Tactical Digital Information Link (TADIL) J Message Standard.*

5. Service Publications

a. Air Force Doctrine Document 3-01, *Counterair Operations.*

b. Air Force Doctrine Document 3-52, *Airspace Control in the Combat Zone.*

c. FM 3-01.94, *Army Air and Missile Defense Command Operations.*

d. FM 3-01, *US Army Air and Missile Defense Operations.*

e. MCWP 3-22, *Antiair Warfare.*

f. MCWP 3-25, *Control of Aircraft and Missiles.*

g. Navy Warfare Publication 3-01.01, *Fleet Air Defense.*

h. Navy Warfare Publication 3-56, *Composite Warfare Doctrine.*

APPENDIX G
ADMINISTRATIVE INSTRUCTIONS

1. User Comments

Users in the field are highly encouraged to submit comments on this publication to: Joint Staff J-7, Deputy Director, Joint and Coalition Warfighting, Joint and Coalition Warfighting Center, ATTN: Joint Doctrine Support Division, 116 Lake View Parkway, Suffolk, VA 23435-2697. These comments should address content (accuracy, usefulness, consistency, and organization), writing, and appearance.

2. Authorship

The lead agent for this publication is the Director for Joint Force Development, J-7/JEDD. The Joint Staff doctrine sponsor for this publication is the Director for Operations (J-3).

3. Supersession

This publication supersedes JP 3-01, *Countering Air and Missile Threats,* 5 February 2007.

4. Change Recommendations

a. Recommendations for urgent changes to this publication should be submitted:

    TO: JOINT STAFF WASHINGTON DC//J-7-JEDD//
    JOINT STAFF WASHINGTON DC//J-5-JOWPD//

b. Routine changes should be submitted electronically to the Deputy Director, Joint and Coalition Warfighting, Joint and Coalition Warfighting Center, Joint Doctrine Support Division, and info the lead agent and the Director for Joint Force Development, J-7/JEDD.

c. When a Joint Staff directorate submits a proposal to the CJCS that would change source document information reflected in this publication, that directorate will include a proposed change to this publication as an enclosure to its proposal. The Services and other organizations are requested to notify the Joint Staff J-7 when changes to source documents reflected in this publication are initiated.

5. Distribution of Publications

Local reproduction is authorized, and access to unclassified publications is unrestricted. However, access to and reproduction authorization for classified joint publications must be in accordance with DOD 5200.1-R, *Information Security Program.*

6. Distribution of Electronic Publications

a. Joint Staff J-7 will not print copies of JPs for distribution. Electronic versions are available on JDEIS at https://jdeis.js.mil (NIPRNET), and http://jdeis.js.smil.mil (SIPRNET), and on the JEL at http://www.dtic.mil/doctrine (NIPRNET).

b. Only approved JPs and joint test publications are releasable outside the combatant commands, Services, and Joint Staff. Release of any classified JP to foreign governments or foreign nationals must be requested through the local embassy (Defense Attaché Office) to DIA, Defense Foreign Liaison/IE-3, 200 MacDill Blvd., Joint Base Anacostia-Bolling, Washington, DC 20340-5100.

c. JEL CD-ROM. Upon request of a joint doctrine development community member, the Joint Staff J-7 will produce and deliver one CD-ROM with current JPs. This JEL CD-ROM will be updated not less than semi-annually and when received can be locally reproduced for use within the combatant commands and Services.

GLOSSARY
PART I—ABBREVIATIONS AND ACRONYMS

AAA	antiaircraft artillery
AADC	area air defense commander
AADP	area air defense plan
AAGS	Army air-ground system
AAMDC	US Army Air and Missile Defense Command
ACA	airspace control authority
ACE	aviation combat element (USMC)
ACM	airspace coordinating measure
ACO	airspace control order
ACP	airspace control plan
ACS	airspace control system
AD	air defense
ADA	air defense artillery
ADAFCO	air defense artillery fire control officer
ADC	air defense commander
ADW	air defense warnings
ADWC	air defense warning condition
AFFOR	Air Force forces
AFTTP(I)	Air Force tactics, techniques, and procedures (instruction)
ALCM	air launched cruise missile
AMD	air and missile defense
AMDC	air and missile defense commander
AO	area of operations
AOR	area of responsibility
AR	air refueling
ARFOR	Army forces
ARM	antiradiation missile
ASM	air-to-surface missile
ASOC	air support operations center
ASR	air support request
ATC	air traffic control
ATO	air tasking order
AWACS	Airborne Warning and Control System
BCA	border crossing authority
BCD	battlefield coordination detachment
BDE	brigade
BM	ballistic missile
BMD	ballistic missile defense
BMDS	Ballistic Missile Defense System
BVR	beyond visual range

C2	command and control
CAL	critical asset list
CAP	combat air patrol
CAS	close air support
CBRN	chemical, biological, radiological, and nuclear
CCDR	combatant commander
CDRJSOTF	commander, joint special operations task force
CDRNORAD	Commander, North American Aerospace Defense Command
CDRUSCENTCOM	Commander, United States Central Command
CDRUSNORTHCOM	Commander, United States Northern Command
CDRUSPACOM	Commander, United States Pacific Command
CDRUSSTRATCOM	Commander, United States Strategic Command
CID	combat identification
CJCS	Chairman of the Joint Chiefs of Staff
CJCSI	Chairman of the Joint Chiefs of Staff instruction
CJCSM	Chairman of the Joint Chiefs of Staff manual
CJE	component joint data networks operations officer equivalent
CM	cruise missile
COA	course of action
COG	center of gravity
COMAFFOR	commander, Air Force forces
COMMARFOR	commander, Marine Corps forces
COMNET	communications network
CONOPS	concept of operations
COP	common operational picture
CRC	control and reporting center
CTF IAMD	commander, task force integrated air and missile defense
CTP	common tactical picture
CVT	criticality-vulnerability-threat
CWC	composite warfare commander
DAADC	deputy area air defense commander
DAL	defended asset list
DCA	defensive counterair
DOD	Department of Defense
EA	electronic attack
ECM	electronic countermeasures
EMP	electromagnetic pulse
EW	electronic warfare
EWCC	electronic warfare coordination cell
FEZ	fighter engagement zone
FM	field manual (Army)

FOB	forward operating base
FOL	forward operating location
FSCL	fire support coordination line
FSCM	fire support coordination measure
GBMD	global ballistic missile defense
GCC	geographic combatant commander
GCCS	Global Command and Control System
GCE	ground combat element (MGTF)
GCI	ground control intercept
GFMAP	Global Force Management Allocation Plan
GLCM	ground-launched cruise missile
GMD	ground-based midcourse defense
HD	homeland defense
HIMAD	high-to-medium-altitude air defense
HIMEZ	high-altitude missile engagement zone
HN	host nation
HVA	high-value asset
HVAA	high value airborne asset
IADS	integrated air defense system
IAMD	integrated air and missile defense
IBS-I	Integrated Broadcast Service-Interactive
IBS-S	Integrated Broadcast Service-Simplex
ID	identification
IFF	identification, friend or foe
IO	information operations
IPB	intelligence preparation of the battlespace
IRBM	intermediate-range ballistic missile
ISR	intelligence, surveillance, and reconnaissance
ITW/AA	integrated tactical warning and attack assessment
J-2	intelligence directorate of a joint staff
J-3	operations directorate of a joint staff
J-6	communications system directorate of a joint staff
J-7	operational plans and interoperability directorate of a joint staff
JACCE	joint air component coordination element
JAOC	joint air operations center
JAOP	joint air operations plan
JDAT	joint deployable analysis team
JDN	joint data network
JDNO	joint data network operations officer
JEZ	joint engagement zone
JFACC	joint force air component commander

JFC	joint force commander
JFCC-IMD	Joint Functional Component Command for Integrated Missile Defense
JFLCC	joint force land component commander
JFMCC	joint force maritime component commander
JFMO	joint frequency management office
JFSOCC	joint force special operations component commander
JICC	joint interface control cell
JICO	joint interface control officer
JIPOE	joint intelligence preparation of the operational environment
JOA	joint operations area
JP	joint publication
JRFL	joint restricted frequency list
JSA	joint security area
JSTARS	Joint Surveillance Target Attack Radar System
JTCB	joint targeting coordination board
JTF	joint task force
LAD	launch area denied
LOMEZ	low-altitude missile engagement zone
MAAP	master air attack plan
MACCS	Marine air command and control system
MAGTF	Marine air-ground task force
MANPADS	man-portable air defense system
MARFOR	Marine Corps forces
MARLE	Marine liaison element
MCRP	Marine Corps reference publication
MDA	Missile Defense Agency
MEZ	missile engagement zone
MNF	multinational force
MNFC	multinational force commander
MOC	maritime operations center
MRBM	medium-range ballistic missile
MRR	minimum-risk route
MTN	multi-tactical data link network
NALE	naval and amphibious liaison element
NAVFOR	Navy forces
NCC	Navy component commander
NFC	numbered fleet commander
NORAD	North American Aerospace Defense Command
NRT	near real time
NTACS	Navy tactical air control system

NTTP	Navy tactics, techniques, and procedures
NWP	Navy warfare publication
OCA	offensive counterair
OPCON	operational control
OPLAN	operation plan
OPSEC	operations security
OPTASKLINK	operations task link
OTC	officer in tactical command
PK	probability of kill
PPLI	precise participant location and identification
R&D	research and development
RADC	regional air defense commander
RFF	request for forces
RICO	regional interface control officer
ROE	rules of engagement
SADC	sector air defense commander
SADO	senior air defense officer
SAM	surface-to-air missile
SCA	space coordinating authority
SEAD	suppression of enemy air defenses
SecDef	Secretary of Defense
SEW	shared early warning
SHORAD	short-range air defense
SHORADEZ	short-range air defense engagement zone
SICO	sector interface control officer
SIPRNET	SECRET Internet Protocol Router Network
SJA	staff judge advocate
SLCM	sea-launched cruise missile
SOF	special operations forces
SOLE	special operations liaison element
SPINS	special instructions
SRBM	short-range ballistic missile
SROE	standing rules of engagement
SRUF	standing rules for the use of force
SSM	surface-to-surface missile
TAAMDCOORD	theater Army air and missile defense coordinator
TACC	tactical air command center (USMC); tactical air control center (USN)
TACON	tactical control
TACOPDAT	tactical operational data
TACP	tactical air control party

TACS	theater air control system
TAGS	theater air-ground system
TAOC	tactical air operations center (USMC)
TDL	tactical data link
TEL	transporter-erector-launcher
TGM	terminally guided munitions
THAAD	Terminal High Altitude Area Defense
TLAM	Tomahawk land attack missile
TST	time-sensitive target
UA	unmanned aircraft
UAS	unmanned aircraft system
UCP	Unified Command Plan
UEWR	upgraded early warning radar
USPACOM	United States Pacific Command
USSTRATCOM	United States Strategic Command
VID	visual identification
WCS	weapons control status
WEZ	weapon engagement zone
WMD	weapons of mass destruction
WRA	weapons release authority

PART II—TERMS AND DEFINITIONS

abort. None. (Approved for removal from JP 1-02.)

action information center. None. (Approved for removal from JP 1-02.)

active air defense. Direct defensive action taken to destroy, nullify, or reduce the effectiveness of hostile air and missile threats against friendly forces and assets. (Approved for incorporation into JP 1-02.)

Aegis. A ship-based combat system that can detect, track, target, and engage air, surface, and subsurface threats, including ballistic missiles on some modified ships. (Approved for inclusion in JP 1-02.)

aerospace. None. (Approved for removal from JP 1-02.)

air alert. None. (Approved for removal from JP 1-02.)

air and missile defense. Direct [active and passive] defensive actions taken to destroy, nullify, or reduce the effectiveness of hostile air and ballistic missile threats against friendly forces and assets. Also called **AMD.** (Approved for inclusion included in JP 1-02.)

airborne alert. A state of aircraft readiness wherein combat-equipped aircraft are airborne and ready for immediate action to reduce reaction time and to increase survivability. (Approved for incorporation into JP 1-02.)

airborne early warning and control. None. (Approved for removal from JP 1-02.)

air-breathing missile. A missile with an engine requiring the intake of air for combustion of its fuel, as in a ramjet or turbojet. (Approved for incorporation into JP 1-02.)

air defense. Defensive measures designed to destroy attacking enemy aircraft or missiles in the atmosphere, or to nullify or reduce the effectiveness of such attack. Also called **AD.** (JP 1-02. SOURCE: JP 3-01)

air defense area. 1. overseas—A specifically defined airspace for which air defense must be planned and provided. 2. United States—Airspace of defined dimensions designated by the appropriate agency within which the ready control of airborne vehicles is required in the interest of national security during an air defense emergency. (JP 1-02. SOURCE: JP 3-01)

air defense artillery. Weapons and equipment for actively combating air targets from the ground. Also called **ADA.** (Approved for incorporation into JP 1-02 with JP 3-01 as the source JP.)

air defense control center. None. (Approved for removal from JP 1-02.)

air defense direction center. None. (Approved for removal from JP 1-02.)

air defense early warning. None. (Approved for removal from JP 1-02.)

air defense operations center. None. (Approved for removal from JP 1-02.)

air defense region. A geographical subdivision of an air defense area. (JP 1-02. SOURCE: JP 3-01)

air defense sector. A geographical subdivision of an air defense region. (JP 1-02. SOURCE: JP 3-01)

air defense warning condition. An air defense warning given in the form of a color code corresponding to the degree of air raid probability with yellow standing for when an attack by hostile aircraft or missiles is probable; red for when an attack by hostile aircraft or missiles is imminent or is in progress; and white for when an attack by hostile aircraft or missiles is improbable. Also called **ADWC.** (Approved for replacement of "air defense warning conditions" and its definition in JP 1-02.)

air facility. None. (Approved for removal from JP 1-02.)

air intercept control common. None. (Approved for removal from JP 1-02.)

air interception. None. (Approved for removal from JP 1-02.)

air-launched ballistic missile. None. (Approved for removal from JP 1-02.)

air request net. None. (Approved for removal from JP 1-02.)

airspace control area. Airspace that is laterally defined by the boundaries of the operational area, and may be subdivided into airspace control sectors. (JP 1-02. SOURCE: JP 3-01)

air strike. None. (Approved for removal from JP 1-02.)

air superiority. That degree of dominance in the air battle by one force that permits the conduct of its operations at a given time and place without prohibitive interference from air and missile threats. (Approved for incorporation into JP 1-02.)

air supremacy. That degree of air superiority wherein the opposing force is incapable of effective interference within the operational area using air and missile threats. (Approved for incorporation into JP 1-02.)

air surveillance. None. (Approved for removal from JP 1-02.)

air-to-air guided missile. None. (Approved for removal from JP 1-02.)

antiradiation missile. A missile which homes passively on a radiation source. Also called **ARM.** (Approved for incorporation into JP 1-02 with JP 3-01 as the source JP.)

apogee. None. (Approved for removal from JP 1-02.)

area air defense commander. The component commander with the preponderance of air defense capability and the required command, control, and communications capabilities who is assigned by the joint force commander to plan and execute integrated air defense operations. Also called **AADC.** (Approved for incorporation into JP 1-02.)

Army tactical data link 1. None. (Approved for removal from JP 1-02.)

ascent phase. That portion of the flight of a ballistic missile or space vehicle that begins after powered flight and ends just prior to apogee. (Approved for inclusion in JP 1-02.)

autonomous operation. In air defense, the mode of operation assumed by a unit after it has lost all communications with higher echelons forcing the unit commander to assume full responsibility for control of weapons and engagement of hostile targets. (Approved for incorporation into JP 1-02.)

ballistic missile. Any missile which does not rely upon aerodynamic surfaces to produce lift and consequently follows a ballistic trajectory when thrust is terminated. (JP 1-02. SOURCE: JP 3-01)

ballistic wind. None. (Approved for removal from JP 1-02.)

barrier combat air patrol. One or more divisions or elements of fighter aircraft employed between a force and an objective area as a barrier across the probable direction of enemy attack. (Approved for incorporation into JP 1-02.)

battle management. The management of activities within the operational environment based on the commands, direction, and guidance given by appropriate authority. Also called **BM.** (JP 1-02. SOURCE: JP 3-01)

boost phase. That portion of the flight of a ballistic missile or space vehicle during which the booster and sustainer engines operate. (JP 1-02. SOURCE: JP 3-01)

buffer zone. 1. A defined area controlled by a peace operations force from which disputing or belligerent forces have been excluded. Also called area of separation in some United Nations operations. Also called **BZ.** (JP 3-07.3) 2. A designated area used for safety in military operations. (JP 3-01) (Approved for incorporation into JP 1-02.)

burn-through range. None. (Approved for removal from JP 1-02.)

centralized control. 1. In air defense, the control mode whereby a higher echelon makes direct target assignments to fire units. (JP 3-01) 2. In joint air operations, placing within one commander the responsibility and authority for planning, directing, and coordinating a military operation or group/category of operations. (JP 3-30) (Approved for incorporation into JP 1-02 with JP 3-01 as the source JP for Definition #1.)

close-controlled air interception. None. (Approved for removal from JP 1-02.)

combat air patrol. An aircraft patrol provided over an objective area, the force protected, the critical area of a combat zone, or in an air defense area, for the purpose of intercepting and destroying hostile aircraft before they reach their targets. Also called **CAP.** (JP 1-02. SOURCE: JP 3-01)

combat surveillance. A continuous, all-weather, day-and-night, systematic watch over the battle area in order to provide timely information for tactical combat operations. (Approved for incorporation into JP 1-02 with JP 3-01 as the source JP.)

commit. The process of assigning one or more aircraft or surface-to-air missile units to prepare to engage an entity, prior to authorizing such engagement. (Approved for incorporation into JP 1-02.)

common tactical picture. An accurate and complete display of relevant tactical data that integrates tactical information from the multi-tactical data link network, ground network, intelligence network, and sensor networks. Also called **CTP.** (JP 1-02. SOURCE: JP 3-01)

counterair. A mission that integrates offensive and defensive operations to attain and maintain a desired degree of air superiority and protection by neutralizing or destroying enemy aircraft and missiles, both before and after launch. (Approved for incorporation into JP 1-02.)

critical asset list. A prioritized list of assets or areas, normally identified by phase of the operation and approved by the joint force commander, that should be defended against air and missile threats. Also called **CAL.** (Approved for incorporation into JP 1-02.)

cruise missile. Guided missile, the major portion of whose flight path to its target is conducted at approximately constant velocity; depends on the dynamic reaction of air for lift and upon propulsion forces to balance drag. (Approved for incorporation into JP 1-02 with JP 3-01 as the source JP.)

decentralized control. In air defense, the normal mode whereby a higher echelon monitors unit actions, making direct target assignments to units only when necessary to ensure proper fire distribution or to prevent engagement of friendly aircraft. (JP 1-02. SOURCE: JP 3-01)

deck alert. None. (Approved for removal from JP 1-02.)

defended asset list. A listing of those assets from the critical asset list prioritized by the joint force commander to be defended with the resources available. Also called **DAL.** (Approved for incorporation into JP 1-02.)

defensive counterair. All defensive measures designed to neutralize or destroy enemy forces attempting to penetrate or attack through friendly airspace. Also called **DCA.** (Approved for incorporation into JP 1-02.)

dispersal. Relocation of forces for the purpose of increasing survivability. (Approved for incorporation into JP 1-02 with JP 3-01 as the source JP.)

dispersal airfield. An airfield, military or civil, to which aircraft might move before H-hour on either a temporary duty or permanent change of station basis and be able to conduct operations. (Approved for incorporation into JP 1-02 with JP 3-01 as the source JP.)

dispersion. None. (Approved for removal from JP 1-02.)

dual (multi)-purpose weapons. None. (Approved for removal from JP 1-02.)

dual-purpose weapon. None. (Approved for removal from JP 1-02.)

early warning. Early notification of the launch or approach of unknown weapons or weapons carriers. Also called **EW.** (Approved for incorporation into JP 1-02 with JP 3-01 as the source JP.)

engage. 1. In air defense, a fire control order used to direct or authorize units and/or weapon systems to fire on a designated target. (JP 3-01) 2. To bring the enemy under fire. (JP 3-09.3) (Approved for incorporation into JP 1-02.)

engagement. 1. In air defense, an attack with guns or air-to-air missiles by an interceptor aircraft, or the launch of an air defense missile by air defense artillery and the missile's subsequent travel to intercept. (JP 3-01) 2. A tactical conflict, usually between opposing lower echelons maneuver forces. (JP 1-02. SOURCE: JP 3-0)

engagement authority. An authority vested with a joint force commander that may be delegated to a subordinate commander, that permits an engagement decision. (Approved for inclusion in JP 1-02.)

escort forces. None. (Approved for removal from JP 1-02.)

fighter engagement zone. In air defense, that airspace of defined dimensions within which the responsibility for engagement of air threats normally rests with fighter aircraft. Also called **FEZ.** (Approved for incorporation into JP 1-02 with JP 3-01 as the source JP.)

fighter escort. An offensive counterair operation providing dedicated protection sorties by air-to-air capable fighters in support of other offensive air and air support missions over enemy territory, or in a defensive counterair role to protect high value airborne assets. (Approved for incorporation into JP 1-02.)

fighter sweep. An offensive mission by fighter aircraft to seek out and destroy enemy aircraft or targets of opportunity in a designated area. (JP 1-02. SOURCE: JP 3-01)

flash message. None. (Approved for removal from JP 1-02.)

fleet ballistic missile submarine. None. (Approved for removal from JP 1-02.)

flight advisory. None. (Approved for removal from JP 1-02.)

flight following. None. (Approved for removal from JP 1-02.)

flight plan correlation. None. (Approved for removal from JP 1-02.)

flight profile. None. (Approved for removal from JP 1-02.)

friendly. A contact positively identified as friendly. (Approved for incorporation into JP 1-02 with JP 3-01 as the source JP.)

global ballistic missile defense. Defense against ballistic missile threats that cross one or more geographical combatant command boundaries and requires synchronization among the affected combatant commands. Also called **GBMD.** (Approved for inclusion in JP 1-02.)

ground alert. That status in which aircraft on the ground/deck are fully serviced and armed, with combat crews in readiness to take off within a specified period of time after receipt of a mission order. (Approved for incorporation into JP 1-02.)

ground-based interceptor. A fixed-based, surface-to-air missile for defense against long-range ballistic missiles using an exo-atmospheric hit-to-kill interception of the targeted reentry vehicle in the midcourse phase of flight. Also called **GBI.** (Approved for inclusion in JP 1-02.)

ground-based midcourse defense. A surface-to-air ballistic missile defense system for exo-atmospheric midcourse phase interception of long-range ballistic missiles using the ground-based interceptors. Also called **GMD.** (Approved for inclusion in JP 1-02.)

ground liaison officer. None. (Approved for removal from JP 1-02.)

guard. None. (Approved for removal from JP 1-02.)

guided missile. An unmanned vehicle moving above the surface of the Earth whose trajectory or flight path is capable of being altered by an external or internal mechanism. (Approved for incorporation into JP 1-02 with JP 3-01 as the source JP.)

harassment. None. (Approved for removal from JP 1-02.)

high-altitude missile engagement zone. In air defense, that airspace of defined dimensions within which the responsibility for engagement of air threats normally rests with high-altitude surface-to-air missiles. Also called **HIMEZ.** (Approved for incorporation into JP 1-02 with JP 3-01 as the source JP.)

high value airborne asset protection. A defensive counterair mission using fighter escorts that defend airborne national assets which are so important that the loss of even one could seriously impact United States warfighting capabilities or provide the enemy with significant propaganda value. Also called **HVAA** protection. (Approved for incorporation into JP 1-02.)

homing guidance. None. (Approved for removal from JP 1-02.)

hostile intent. The threat of imminent use of force against the United States, United States forces, or other designated persons or property. (Approved for incorporation into JP 1-02.)

identification. 1. The process of determining the friendly or hostile character of an unknown detected contact. 2. In arms control, the process of determining which nation is responsible for the detected violations of any arms control measure. 3. In ground combat operations, discrimination between recognizable objects as being friendly or enemy, or the name that belongs to the object as a member of a class. Also called **ID.** (Approved for incorporation into JP 1-02 with JP 3-01 as the source JP.)

indirect fire. Fire delivered on a target that is not itself used as a point of aim for the weapons or the director. (Approved for incorporation into JP 1-02 with JP 3-01 as the source JP.)

inflight report. None. (Approved for removal from JP 1-02.)

initial point. None. (Approved for removal from JP 1-02.)

integrated air and missile defense. The integration of capabilities and overlapping operations to defend the homeland and United States national interests, protect the joint force, and enable freedom of action by negating an adversary's ability to create adverse effects from their air and missile capabilities. Also called **IAMD.** (Approved for inclusion in JP 1-02.)

intercontinental ballistic missile. A land-based, long-range ballistic missile with a range capability greater than 3,000 nautical miles. Also called **ICBM.** (Approved for inclusion in JP 1-02.)

intermediate-range ballistic missile. A land-based ballistic missile with a range capability from 1,500 to 3,000 nautical miles. Also called **IRBM.** (Approved for inclusion in JP 1-02.)

intrusion. None. (Approved for removal from JP 1-02.)

joint data network operations officer. The joint task force operations directorate officer responsible to the commander for integrating data from supporting components into a common database used to generate the common tactical picture. Also called **JDNO.** (Approved for inclusion in JP 1-02.)

joint engagement zone. In air defense, that airspace of defined dimensions within which multiple air defense systems (surface-to-air missiles and aircraft) are simultaneously employed to engage air threats. Also called **JEZ.** (Approved for incorporation into JP 1-02 with JP 3-01 as the source JP.)

joint interface control officer. The senior interface control officer for multi-tactical data link networks in the joint force who is responsible for development and validation of the architecture, joint interoperability and management of the multi-tactical data link networks, and overseeing operations of a joint interface control cell. Also called **JICO.** (Approved for incorporation into JP 1-02.)

joint suppression of enemy air defenses. None. (Approved for removal from JP 1-02.)

launch time. None. (Approved for removal from JP 1-02.)

launch window. None. (Approved for removal from JP 1-02.)

lock on. None. (Approved for removal from JP 1-02.)

low-altitude missile engagement zone. In air defense, that airspace of defined dimensions within which the responsibility for engagement of air threats normally rests with low- to medium-altitude surface-to-air missiles. Also called **LOMEZ.** (Approved for incorporation into JP 1-02 with JP 3-01 as the source JP.)

medium-range ballistic missile. A ballistic missile with a range capability from about 600 to 1,500 nautical miles. Also called **MRBM.** (Approved for inclusion in JP 1-02.)

midcourse guidance. None. (Approved for removal from JP 1-02.)

midcourse phase. That portion of the flight of a ballistic missile between the boost phase and the terminal phase. (JP 1-02. SOURCE: JP 3-01)

missile defense. Defensive measures designed to destroy attacking enemy missiles, or to nullify or reduce the effectiveness of such attack. (JP 1-02. SOURCE: JP 3-01)

missile engagement zone. In air defense, that airspace of defined dimensions within which the responsibility for engagement of air threats normally rests with surface-to-air missile systems. Also called **MEZ.** (Approved for inclusion in JP 1-02.)

mode (identification, friend or foe). The number or letter referring to the specific pulse spacing of the signals transmitted by an interrogator or transponder used for radar identification of aircraft. (Approved for incorporation into JP 1-02.)

multiple warning phenomenology. None. (Approved for removal from JP 1-02.)

nickname. None. (Approved for removal from JP 1-02.)

notice to airmen. None. (Approved for removal from JP 1-02.)

offensive counterair. Offensive operations to destroy, disrupt, or neutralize enemy aircraft, missiles, launch platforms, and their supporting structures and systems both before and after launch, and as close to their source as possible. Also called **OCA.** (Approved for incorporation into JP 1-02.)

offensive counterair attack operations. Offensive action by any part of the joint force in support of the offensive counterair mission against surface targets which contribute to the enemy's air and missile capabilities. Also called **OCA attack operations.** (Approved for incorporation into JP 1-02.)

on-call. 1. A term used to signify that a prearranged concentration, air strike, or final protective fire may be called for. 2. Preplanned, identified force or materiel requirements without designated time-phase and destination information. (Approved for incorporation into JP 1-02.)

over-the-horizon radar. None. (Approved for removal from JP 1-02.)

pass. None. (Approved for removal from JP 1-02.)

passive air defense. All measures, other than active air defense, taken to minimize the effectiveness of hostile air and missile threats against friendly forces and assets. (Approved for incorporation into JP 1-02.)

Patriot. A point and limited area defense surface-to-air missile system capable of intercepting aircraft and theater missiles, including short-, medium-, and intermediate-range ballistic missiles in the terminal phase. (Approved for inclusion in JP 1-02.)

penetration aids. None. (Approved for removal from JP 1-02.)

positive identification. An identification derived from observation and analysis of target characteristics including visual recognition, electronic support systems, non-cooperative target recognition techniques, identification friend or foe systems, or other physics-based identification techniques. (Approved for inclusion in JP 1-02.)

positive identification and radar advisory zone. None. (Approved for removal from JP 1-02.)

preset guidance. None. (Approved for removal from JP 1-02.)

procedural identification. An identification based on observation and analysis of target behaviors including location and trajectory, as well as compliance with airspace control measures. (Approved for inclusion in JP 1-02.)

profile. None. (Approved for removal from JP 1-02.)

radar beacon. None. (Approved for removal from JP 1-02.)

radar coverage. None. (Approved for removal from JP 1-02.)

radar horizon. None. (Approved for removal from JP 1-02.)

radar netting unit. None. (Approved for removal from JP 1-02.)

recognition. 1. The determination by any means of the individuality of persons, or of objects such as aircraft, ships, or tanks, or of phenomena such as communications-electronics patterns. 2. In ground combat operations, the determination that an object is similar within a category of something already known. (Approved for incorporation into JP 1-02.)

regional air defense commander. Commander, subordinate to the area air defense commander, who is responsible for air and missile defenses in the assigned region and exercises authorities as delegated by the area air defense commander. Also called **RADC.** (Approved for incorporation into JP 1-02.)

return to base. An order to proceed to the point indicated by the displayed information or by verbal communication. Also called **RTB.** (Approved for incorporation into JP 1-02.)

satellite and missile surveillance. None. (Approved for removal from JP 1-02.)

sector air defense commander. Commander, subordinate to an area/regional air defense commander, who is responsible for air and missile defenses in the assigned sector, and exercises authorities delegated by the area/regional air defense commander. Also called **SADC.** (Approved for incorporation into JP 1-02.)

short-range air defense engagement zone. In air defense, that airspace of defined dimensions within which the responsibility for engagement of air threats normally rests with short-range air defense weapons, and may be established within a low- or high-altitude missile engagement zone. Also called **SHORADEZ.** (Approved for incorporation into JP 1-02.)

short-range ballistic missile. A land-based ballistic missile with a range capability up to about 600 nautical miles. Also called **SRBM.** (Approved for inclusion in JP 1-02.)

sighting. None. (Approved for removal from JP 1-02.)

simultaneous engagement. The concurrent engagement of hostile targets by combination of interceptor aircraft and surface-to-air missiles. (Approved for incorporation into JP 1-02 with JP 3-01 as the source JP.)

space-based infrared system. A consolidated system for infrared space, air, and terrestrial surveillance and reconnaissance along with associated communications links, designed to meet missile defense, missile warning and intelligence, surveillance, and reconnaissance mission requirements. Also called **SBIRS.** (Approved for inclusion in JP 1-02.)

supporting attack. None. (Approved for removal from JP 1-02.)

suppression. Temporary or transient degradation by an opposing force of the performance of a weapons system below the level needed to fulfill its mission objectives. (Approved for incorporation into JP 1-02 with JP 3-01 as the source JP.)

suppression of enemy air defenses. Activity that neutralizes, destroys, or temporarily degrades surface-based enemy air defenses by destructive and/or disruptive means. Also called **SEAD.** (JP 1-02. SOURCE: JP 3-01)

surface-to-air missile site. A plot of ground prepared in such a manner that it will readily accept the hardware used in surface-to-air missile system. (Approved for incorporation into JP 1-02 with JP 3-01 as the source JP.)

terminal phase. That portion of the flight of a ballistic missile that begins when the warhead or payload reenters the atmosphere and ends when the warhead or payload detonates, releases its submunitions, or impacts. (Approved for incorporation into JP 1-02.)

terrain following system. None. (Approved for removal from JP 1-02.)

theater missile. None. (Approved for removal from JP 1-02.)

track. 1. A series of related contacts displayed on a data display console or other display device. 2. To display or record the successive positions of a moving object. 3. To lock onto a point of radiation and obtain guidance therefrom. 4. To keep a gun properly aimed, or to point continuously a target-locating instrument at a moving target. 5. The actual path of an aircraft above or a ship on the surface of the Earth. 6. One of the two endless belts on which a full-track or half-track vehicle runs. 7. A metal part forming a path for a moving object such as the track around the inside of a vehicle for moving a mounted machine gun. (Approved for incorporation into JP 1-02.)

track correlation. Corrclating track information for identification purposes using all available data. (Approved for incorporation into JP 1-02 with JP 3-01 as the source JP.)

track management. Defined set of procedures whereby the commander ensures accurate friendly and enemy unit and/or platform locations, and a dissemination procedure for filtering, combining, and passing that information to higher, adjacent, and subordinate commanders. (Approved for incorporation into JP 1-02 with JP 3-01 as the source JP.)

track production area. None. (Approved for removal from JP 1-02.)

track telling. None. (Approved for removal from JP 1-02.)

traverse level. None. (Approved for removal from JP 1-02.)

unknown. 1. A code meaning "information not available." 2. An unidentified target. An aircraft or ship that has not been determined to be hostile, friendly, or neutral using identification friend or foe and other techniques, but that must be tracked by air defense or naval engagement systems. 3. An identity applied to an evaluated track that has not been identified. (Approved for incorporation into JP 1-02 with JP 3-01 as the source JP.)

vulnerability. 1. The susceptibility of a nation or military force to any action by any means through which its war potential or combat effectiveness may be reduced or its will to fight diminished. (JP 3-01) 2. The characteristics of a system that cause it to suffer a definite degradation (incapability to perform the designated mission) as a result of having been subjected to a certain level of effects in an unnatural (man-made) hostile environment. (JP 3-60) 3. In information operations, a weakness in information system security design, procedures, implementation, or internal controls that could be exploited to gain unauthorized access to information or an information system. (JP 3-13) (Approved for incorporation into JP 102.)

warning of attack. None. (Approved for removal from JP 1-02.)

warning red. None. (Approved for removal from JP 1-02.)

warning white. None. (Approved for removal from JP 1-02.)

warning yellow. None. (Approved for removal from JP 1-02.)

weapon engagement zone. In air defense, airspace of defined dimensions within which the responsibility for engagement of air threats normally rests with a particular weapon system. Also called **WEZ.** (Approved for incorporation into JP 1-02 with JP 3-01 as the source JP.)

weapons control status. An air defense control measure declared for a particular area and time by an area air defense commander, or delegated subordinate commander, based on the rules of engagement designed to establish the freedom for fighters and surface air defense weapons to engage threats. Also call **WCS.** (Approved for inclusion in JP 1-02.)

weapons free zone. An air defense zone established for the protection of key assets or facilities, other than air bases, where weapon systems may be fired at any target not positively recognized as friendly. (Approved for incorporation into JP 1-02 with JP 3-01 as the source JP.)

weapons readiness state. The degree of readiness of air defense weapons which can become airborne or be launched to carry out an assigned task, and normally expressed in numbers of weapons and numbers of minutes. (Approved for incorporation into JP 1-02.)

weapons release authority. The authority originating from the President to engage or direct engagement of ballistic missile threats using ground-based interceptors of the ground-based midcourse defense. Also call **WRA.** (Approved for inclusion in JP 1-02.)

wingman. None. (Approved for removal from JP 1-02.)

JOINT DOCTRINE PUBLICATIONS HIERARCHY

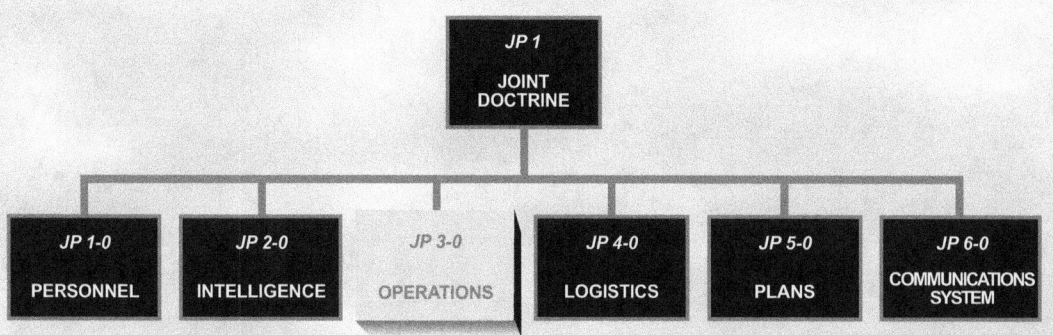

All joint publications are organized into a comprehensive hierarchy as shown in the chart above. **Joint Publication (JP) 3-01** is in the **Operations** series of joint doctrine publications. The diagram below illustrates an overview of the development process:

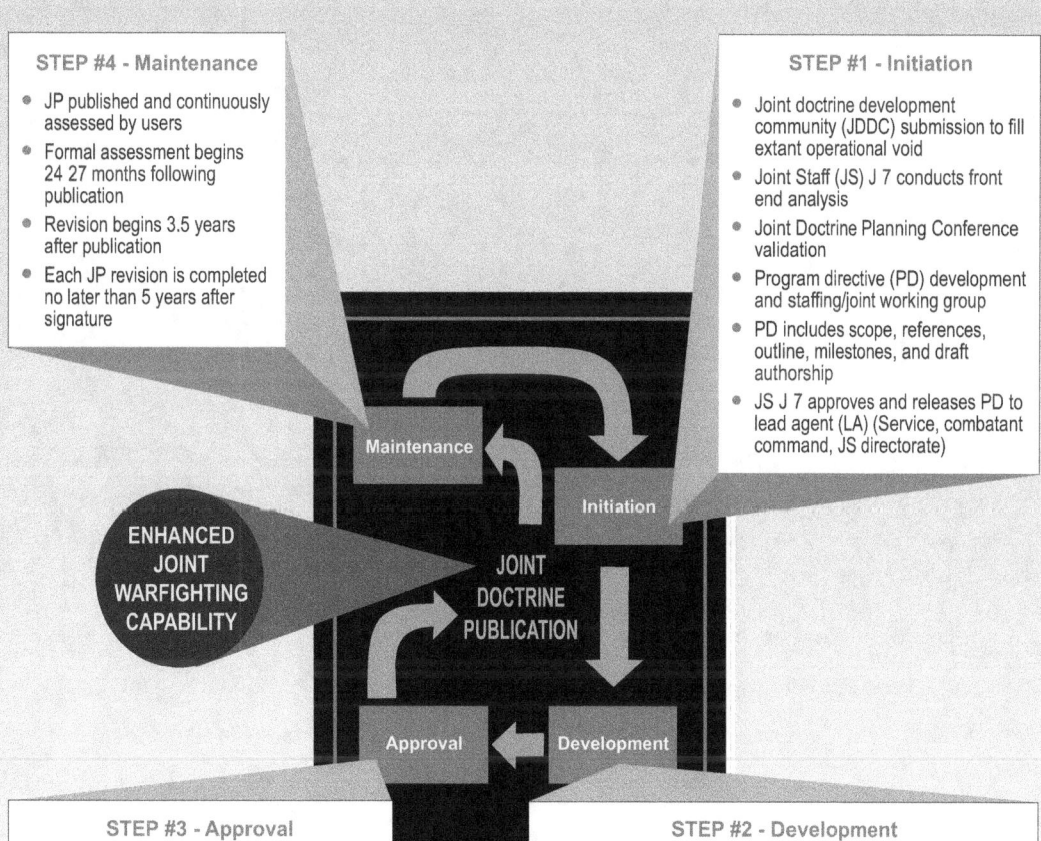

STEP #4 - Maintenance

- JP published and continuously assessed by users
- Formal assessment begins 24 27 months following publication
- Revision begins 3.5 years after publication
- Each JP revision is completed no later than 5 years after signature

STEP #1 - Initiation

- Joint doctrine development community (JDDC) submission to fill extant operational void
- Joint Staff (JS) J 7 conducts front end analysis
- Joint Doctrine Planning Conference validation
- Program directive (PD) development and staffing/joint working group
- PD includes scope, references, outline, milestones, and draft authorship
- JS J 7 approves and releases PD to lead agent (LA) (Service, combatant command, JS directorate)

STEP #3 - Approval

- JSDS delivers adjudicated matrix to JS J 7
- JS J 7 prepares publication for signature
- JSDS prepares JS staffing package
- JSDS staffs the publication via JSAP for signature

STEP #2 - Development

- LA selects primary review authority (PRA) to develop the first draft (FD)
- PRA develops FD for staffing with JDDC
- FD comment matrix adjudication
- JS J 7 produces the final coordination (FC) draft, staffs to JDDC and JS via Joint Staff Action Processing (JSAP) system
- Joint Staff doctrine sponsor (JSDS) adjudicates FC comment matrix
- FC joint working group